625
Y

WITHDRAWN

THE POLITICAL THOUGHT OF
LORD SALISBURY
1854–68

MICHAEL PINTO-DUSCHINSKY

The Political Thought of
Lord Salisbury
1854–68

ARCHON BOOKS
LONDON

Published by
Constable and Company Ltd.
10–12 Orange Street London WC2
© 1967 Michael Pinto-Duschinsky

First published 1967

JC
223
S 3P5

Printed in Great Britain by
The Garden City Press Limited
Letchworth, Hertfordshire

TO AUNTY
with love

ACKNOWLEDGEMENTS

I would especially like to thank Mr. Ronald Butt and Dr. Zbeniew Pelczynski for their kindness and help and also Professor Alan Altshuler, Dr. Brian Harrison, Professor Clinton Rossiter and Mr. Philip Williams, who all made many useful suggestions about the manuscript.

The Marquis of Salisbury kindly lent the photograph of his grandfather for the frontispiece.

M.P.-D.

Nuffield College
Oxford
December 1966

CONTENTS

INTRODUCTION

IN 1854, when he was twenty-three years old, Salisbury took his seat in the House of Commons in the Conservative interest and his fluent and extremely unyielding speeches quickly brought his talents to notice. In 1866, he was appointed Secretary of State for India in Derby's Third Ministry and had a place in the Cabinet. Nine months later he resigned from the Government when it introduced its Reform Bill, and the next year, upon the death of his father, he took his seat in the House of Lords. When the Conservatives returned to office in 1874, Disraeli generously offered him back the position of Secretary of State for India and four years later took him as his Foreign Secretary to the Congress of Berlin. After the Liberal victory of 1880 and Disraeli's death in 1881, Salisbury became leader of the Conservative Party in the House of Lords and in July 1885, following the resignation of Gladstone's Liberal Ministry, the Queen called on him to form a government. From 1885 to 1902, with two short interludes of Liberal rule, Salisbury continued as Prime Minister, and for all but two years of this period he was Foreign Secretary as well. Throughout this time there was no challenge to his leadership of the Party, and the Party itself enjoyed an ascendancy unmatched in any period following the Reform Act of 1832. When he finally resigned, the reason was not defeat but old age, and he was able to leave a victorious party in the hands of his nephew, Arthur Balfour. During the fourteen years that he was the undisputed ruler of England and her Empire, he must have been one of the most powerful men in the world.

The subject of this study is not Salisbury the statesman, but Salisbury the political thinker. There is an attempt in the concluding chapter to relate his thought to his political activity as an M.P. before the Second Reform Act, and his thought is seen throughout against the background of the issues of the time. But this piece of work has been carried out in the belief that it is worth examining the arguments of a politician like Salisbury on their merits, and as significant in themselves rather than as a mere key to his political actions. Consequently, Salisbury's views have not been examined issue by issue, or chronologically, but they have been presented in the form of an analysis starting with a consideration of his general assumptions about the foundations of knowledge and of politics and continuing with an examination of the central theme of his work—the maintenance of constitutional government at home and peace abroad. Accordingly, the first chapter is designed to highlight his intellectual background and his temperament rather than the details of his political career, and the concluding chapter is not 'biographical' in the plain sense of the term, but reviews his political activities as an expression of his political thought. The disadvantage of abandoning a chronological framework is that it becomes more difficult to account for the developments of a thinker's ideas over time. In the case of Salisbury this difficulty is at a minimum as the basis of his thinking had already matured by the time he entered the House of Commons and remained fundamentally the same thereafter. The general aim is to show that Salisbury's conservatism did not involve him in romantic, irrational thought, for he is a paradigm example of that curiously neglected strand of English Conservative thought—Empirical Conservatism.

Throughout his time as an M.P., his activity was conditioned by his desire to prevent the passage of a reform bill such as the one which was passed in 1867. After this, English politics, and especially Salisbury's part in them, passed into a distinctly new phase. By a coincidence, the next year saw the death of his father and Salisbury's elevation to the House of Lords, and it was also at this time that his literary output came to an almost complete stop. There is no reason to suppose that Salisbury's later thought was radically different; but the period from 1854 to 1868, when he was involved on the fringes of politics and still had time from week to week to expound his ideas in writing, forms a convenient and distinct period for study. The appendix includes the articles he wrote later, but these are only used when they illustrate views that he held before 1868. From his birth until 1865, his name was Lord Robert Cecil and from 1865 to 1868 he was Lord Cranborne, but he is referred to throughout by his final title, Lord Salisbury.

The sources chiefly used are Salisbury's speeches in the House of Commons and his articles in the *Quarterly Review* as well as his recently identified writings in other periodicals such as *The Saturday Review*; the files of *The Times, The Lincoln, Rutland and Stamford Mercury, The Morning Chronicle* and *The Standard*; the Salisbury Papers; the Minutes of the Oxford Union Society.

ABBREVIATIONS

B.Q.R.	*Bentley's Quarterly Review*
Cecil	Lady Gwendolen Cecil, *Life of Robert, Marquis of Salisbury*
Cecil, Memoir	Lady Gwendolen Cecil, *Biographical Studies of the Life and Political Character of Robert, Third Marquis of Salisbury* (Hodder and Stoughton, printed for private circulation)
H.C.	*Hansard*, Third Series
N.R.	*National Review*
Q.R.	*Quarterly Review*
S.R.	*Saturday Review*
(R)	review
(M)	middle
(L)	leader

The following system of numbering is used in the Appendices: 'Q.R. (7)' is the seventh article Salisbury wrote for *The Quarterly Review*; 'H.C. (125)' is the one hundred and twenty-fifth speech he made in the House of Commons, and so on.

References to articles and speeches in the notes give volume and page (or column) references followed by the numbering of the item in the Appendix: e.g. Q.R. Vol. 110, p. 544 (7), H.C. clxxxiv, 331 (125).

CHAPTER I

Salisbury as a Young Man

THE level of academic achievement reached by many Prime Ministers of the nineteenth century was remarkably high. Peel's virtuoso performance as an undergraduate at the Examination Schools is celebrated in Oxford history; Derby won University prizes for verse composition in Latin and, according to Gilbert Murray, was responsible for some of the finest translations of Homer of his time; and Gladstone's double first was the prelude to a lifetime of scholarly work. But, in all probability, the most intellectual of them all was Lord Salisbury. He was clever, studious, awkward in his movements, stooping, short-sighted, sickly, unsporting, unsocial, unromantic and a polar opposite to the archetypal conception of an aristocratic Conservative.

His childhood was lonely: his elder brother and two sisters were more than five years older than he was and his brother was four years younger. His mother died when he was nine years old.* When he was eleven, his schoolmasters reported that he wrote papers in theology 'in a very extraordinary manner for so young a boy'.[1] At twelve, he was already in the Fifth Form at Eton—a class in which the average age was fifteen. He learnt German in addition to the ordinary Classical curriculum, practised languages by writing letters to his family in French and continued his studies in the school holidays with a tutor.

* Except where otherwise noted, the biographical information in this and in following chapters is taken from Lady Gwendolen Cecil, *The Life of Robert, Marquis of Salisbury* (1921–32).

At Eton he was friendless and complained that he was bullied from morning till night:

> In later life he was once asked how he had acquired the curiously intimate acquaintance which he possessed with all the back by-ways, the passages, alleys and mews in the neighbourhood of his London home. He replied that it was while he was a boy at Eton. He had lived in such dread of meeting his school-fellows during the holidays, that he always tried to avoid the larger thoroughfares where he might be likely to come across them. It was a statement which expressed more vividly than pages of description the atmosphere of terror in which the boy lived. The very unreasonableness of the fear, the fact that no Eton enemy, however malevolently inclined, could really have injured him on the pavement of Piccadilly, was a measure of the suffering which had produced it. Bruises heal quickly, but this burden of prolonged mental oppression probably inflicted lasting mischief both upon the boy's physical nerves and, at the least, upon his superficial relations with his fellowmen in after life.[2]

When he was fifteen—and already in the top form—his father responded to Salisbury's continual grumbles and finally agreed to let him leave school and retire to the solitude of the family seat at Hatfield. A fellow of St. John's College, Oxford, was employed to tutor him and for two years he passed his time in the study of science, botany, German, ethics, theology, history and politics. The sense of deprivation which he felt so keenly during his motherless youth is reflected in a speech about education which he made when he was twenty-six years old. Education, in the fullest sense of the word,

> must be the result of the influences which breathe around the daily life in a well-ordered home; of a mother's affectionate care and tender vigilance; of holy lessons instilled and fostered under the genial warmth of that soft religious sympathy which speaks not in catechisms, but heart to heart; of that which teaches more than words can teach—the daily example of a parent's virtuous life ... But how should we look for such results from the exercise of the schoolmaster's craft?[3]

He went up to Oxford in January 1848, just before he was

eighteen. At first he seems to have been tempted to continue in his hermit's ways,[4] but he did emerge to take an active part in undergraduate life both in his College and in the Oxford Union Society. He joined the Union in May 1848 and gave his maiden speech three weeks later.* The memories of his contemporaries solicited later when he was already famous probably exaggerate the part he played in the debates. Only once did he move a motion, though he spoke frequently from the floor; and, though he was Secretary and Treasurer, he never contested the senior offices of Librarian and President, probably because he was not asked to stand and was reluctant to put his own name forward. He worked hard on his speeches and they quickly seem to have gained in fluency, though their character was marked, in the recollection of a contemporary, by a 'deadly earnestness'.[5] His interest in the business and the rules of the Union was very active and he frequently introduced procedural motions—most of which were turned down. He was specially concerned with the running of the library and with the books that the Society purchased for it. These purchases were the subject of discussions to which Salisbury was a keen contributor. He was opposed, for instance, to the acquisition of the *Dictionnaire de l'Académie*, the *Mémoires Completes et Authentiques de St. Simon*, and Leigh Hunt's *Imitations from the Italian Ports*, while he favoured the purchase of Newman's *Discourses* and Dugdale's *Monasticon Anglicanum*. Most but not all of the debates in which he spoke were political or religious. There are no signs of any youthful Radicalism in his views; he was already firmly Conservative, opposing any extension of the suffrage, the removal of Protection, the removal of Jewish Disabilities, the endowment of the Catholic Priesthood, or any change in the ecclesiastical policy of the Government.

He took no further part in the Union after February 1850 and his university career was to be cut short a few months later by ill health. 'His doctor forbade hard work and urged that he should secure his degree and leave Oxford as soon as

* Information in the following paragraph comes from the minutes of the Oxford Union Society.

possible.' He availed himself of a nobleman's privilege which then existed and took his degree after only two years' residence. Though this meant that he could only take a pass degree, he was awarded an 'honorary fourth'—a degree which was given to those who had taken the Pass School with special distinction.

Oxford did not cure Salisbury of his shyness, and his fits of extreme depression became more frequent. Soon after he went down, and while he was studying for the Bar, he had a complete nervous breakdown and was sent on a two-year trip of convalescence to South Africa, Australia and New Zealand. His recovery was fairly satisfactory, but

> he remained through life liable to attacks which he used to speak of as 'nerve storms'. They operated in that borderline between mind and body whose boundaries medical science has hitherto failed to delimit. Sometimes they seemed to have their origin in mental worry, sometimes in physical exhaustion; they would be accompanied by an overwhelming depression of spirits and also by great bodily lassitude and by a morbid acuteness of the senses of touch and hearing.[6]

There survives from this period the diary he kept during his visit to the Australian gold-fields[7] as well as a number of long letters. They show in their content that the views which he was to express in the years that followed had matured at this early age, and they demonstrate quite clearly the mind of the social thinker at work: Australia was the laboratory for his wider theories about society and politics. Observing that the lower classes at the gold diggings had had their heads turned by the El Dorado less than the insolent shop-keepers, he 'stored up the fact as a commentary on the enthusiasm which histories, reviews and newspapers lavish on "those bulwarks of our liberty" the middle classes'.[8] The absence of crime at the gold-fields made him reflect on the nature of law and order. A visit to a convict settlement was the occasion for a discussion of criminal reform and punishment, and the particular governmental scandals that crossed his path led him to generalised views on colonial government which were reflected directly in his later speeches and articles.

On his return to England in 1853, three years after he had
left Oxford, he went back again to compete, successfully, for
a fellowship at All Souls. It was the first time that a nobleman had gained this signal honour and, had Salisbury come
from a more modest family, he would probably have become
a don. But his social position opened other prospects. A few
weeks after his success at All Souls, his father managed (by a
stroke of good fortune) to find him a seat at the pocket
borough of Stamford which was under the patronage of the
Marquis of Exeter, the head of another branch of the Cecil
family. The by-election, which took place in August 1853,
was no more than a formality:[9]

> There was no excitement whatever on the occasion; and if it
> had not been for the ringing of the bells, and the distant
> sounds of a band of music just before the time fixed for the
> nomination, no one would have conjectured that a Parl-
> iamentary election was about to take place.[10]

A Member of Parliament at the age of twenty-three,
Salisbury was in a highly advantageous position. But it was
also precarious. He was a younger son of the Second Marquis
of Salisbury and it was not until 1865 (when he was thirty-
five years old) that the death of his elder brother made him
heir to his father's estates and titles. Until then he was in
considerable financial need and the situation was made much
more difficult by his marriage in 1857 to Miss Georgina
Alderson, the daughter of a judge. His father strongly disapproved of the match, largely because she did not have the
means he considered necessary to enable Salisbury to continue his career in the House of Commons. The result was an
estrangement between Salisbury and his family which lasted
for several years. The need to earn money was a major
inducement to journalism: here at least was an occupation he
could carry out discreetly and which was acceptable for a
gentleman. At the same time, it would be wrong to suggest,
as he seems to have maintained himself, that money was
Salisbury's only motive. There is evidence in the Salisbury
Papers that he was already the director of several companies
by the early 1860s and, though some of his ventures failed,

he must on balance have been earning a considerable income from his business activities. Yet, as he became more involved in business, his journalistic output did not lessen, but appears to have increased. In the late 1850s the financial motive may have been paramount; in the 1860s he probably wrote because he was unwilling to give up the influential position he derived from being a leading contributor to two such prominent journals as *The Quarterly Review* and *The Saturday Review*.

Throughout this period, though, he remained conscious of what was in his opinion an anomalous social position. In his articles in *The Saturday Review* there are continual references to the disabilities of 'younger sons' and Salisbury deals with the subject fully in an article published on 11 October 1862.[11] Its immediate pretext was a scandal concerning the catering arrangements for the International Exhibition of 1862 which had been held at Kensington. Cadogan, the younger son of a peer, had been appointed to help with the catering: it was unclear what his duties had been, but he had been paid £3,000 per annum, and the catering contractor who had been appointed by the Commissioners of the Exhibition was now bankrupt. Salisbury was quick to draw the conclusion that here was a case of jobbery at work. He also pointed out a moral:

> If the son of a peer does not make money out of his social position, what other wares has he to sell? So long as the Peers persist in the practice of bringing up their younger sons in a condition of well-dressed pauperism, they must expect an occasional scandal now and then...
>
> Unless a family living happens to be vacant, a younger son who has not the peculiar talents required for the Bar has none of the careers open to him by which, in these days, wealth is to be obtained. Men are growing rich in England every day as doctors, as bankers, as merchants, as manufacturers, and in many other ways besides; but from all the share in this harvest, this luckless section of the Commons of England have cut themselves off by a kind of traditional taboo. They condemn themselves to a limited circle of 'gentlemanly' vocations, which hold out nothing more solid than gentility as their reward. When a class superstition condemns the members of it to this

species of self-sacrifice, they generally submit to its require-
ments passively enough. But occasionally there will occur a
discontented spirit who claims to be restored to the ordinary
hopes and rights of other human beings; and then a scandal is
apt to rise. The Suttees went through the process of being
reduced to a cinder, for the most part without objection to it.
But sometimes a widow was profane enough to dislike the
ceremony; and then it was necessary to drown her cries with
gongs and drums lest the faithful should be offended. With
equal resignation the mass of the younger sons of peers, unless
they chance to marry heiresses, are content to struggle on
through life, hanging about the drawing-rooms of great men,
jobbing for small promotions, and never attaining to even a
hope of overtaking their tailor's bills.

The lack of money and status that went with his position
as a younger son was one of the reasons (or rationalisations)
that made the young Salisbury shun London society. In a
series of articles with titles like 'Marriage Settlements',[12]
'Match-Making Mammas',[13] 'Marriage Market and Belgravian Intelligence',[14] 'Practical Young Ladies'[15] and
'Heir Hunting' he complains that

> The arrangement is that the Mother is to choose really, and
> the daughter to choose apparently. The lacquer of romance is
> to cover the homely reality of bargain and sale.[16]

Girls and their mothers are interested only in rich eldest sons
with the result that 'the market is absolutely glutted with un-
saleable young ladies'. He suggests as a remedy that eldest
sons be allowed, nay forced, to be polygamous and that
younger sons be banished to Athos.[17] Life is as difficult for
eldest sons as for their younger brothers:

> If they are even genial to a girl, then her Mother will ask for
> his 'Intentions', if he does not marry the girl, the dowager will
> spread the gossip that 'he has behaved infamously' . . .
> He is evidently puzzling himself the whole time how to draw
> the narrow and imperceptible line which, in the case of eldest
> sons, separates rudeness from love-making.[18]

So Salisbury rarely went to balls and spent his time visiting churches, reading and writing.* In spite of his usual reticence in quoting from other authors, it is possible to build up a good idea of the extent of his reading from his articles. He was grounded in Latin and Greek. He made a special study of Church history and was proficient in the German language and very widely read in its history and literature. He was fully acquainted with the French language, history and literature and, to a lesser extent, with those of Italy. He was interested in the study of botany and carried his experiments in the natural sciences to the point where he was able to write articles in learned journals. The more speculative branches of philosophy did not concern him (although there are indications in the articles that his grasp of epistemology was more than adequate)—he gave more attention to ethics. He was also interested in the attempts being made at the time to promote the study of sociology; he laid great stress on the study of social statistics (he was a regular subscriber to the *Journal of the Statistical Society*), and he had a keen concern for economic and political thought. Among others, Locke, Milton, Bentham, Burke, Adam Smith, Disraeli, Mill, Sismondi, Montesquieu, Condorcet, Rousseau, Schelling, Hegel, Humboldt, Madison, Jefferson and Tocqueville are quoted or referred to by name in his writings. The list of historians is even wider: Ranke, von Sybel, Macaulay, Carlyle, Buckle, Froude, as well as many lesser names.

This wide list of reading departs significantly from the narrow study of the Classics that formed the normal academic curriculum in Salisbury's day. Most of the subjects in which he was interested fall into the category of 'social studies' and he attacked the classical curriculum in several of his articles. In 1861, he wrote a slashing review of a piece

---

* He appears to have been closely attached to Alexander Beresford-Hope the husband of his sister Mildred. Beresford-Hope was a very rich man who spent much of his money in the building of churches and was also the owner of *The Saturday Review*. It seems to have been through him that Salisbury was introduced to the Aldersons. cf. W. and I. Law, *The Book of the Beresford-Hopes* (1925).

written in defence of Eton by one of the assistant masters, which had appeared in *The Cornhill Magazine.*

> The discontent of the boys at the uselessness of the instruction which is offered them is a new thing in education, and is an ominous symptom which Eton will do well not to neglect. The signs of the times are multiplying which predict an early doom to the classical supremacy. Things are altered since the day when Lord Wellesley increased his fame as a versifier . . . Mr. Gladstone is the last of the long series of statesmen who for many generations have made Horace an habitual element in their House of Commons oratory, and is almost the only man there who can quote him now without being laughed at. The tags of Latin quotation which used to be a grace of composition are now carefully avoided by all writers of good taste. Everywhere new sciences, new arts, new literatures are pressing in and are claiming an equal share in the honours which up to this century were claimed for Latin and Greek alone. The 'traditions' to which (the writer of the article under review) pays such undoubting homage, however tenacious they may be, will not long keep back the in-coming flood.[19]

Salisbury's writings, especially those in *The Saturday Review*, combined with the sensitive accounts of his daughter Lady Gwendolen Cecil suggest that there are many surprising parallels between his mode of thought and that of another distinguished Victorian, John Stuart Mill.[20] Surprising, because the two were at opposite ends of the political spectrum. The interest of the comparison for present purposes is that it highlights a central contention of this study: that there is no one style of Conservative thought or of Liberal thought; and neither is there any one type of mind that can be called a 'Liberal Mind' nor any single mentality that can be described as 'The Conservative Mind'.[21]

In Mill as in Salisbury there is the same intellectual precocity in youth (more greatly marked in Mill, it is true); the same pattern of studies, starting in the Classics and going on to an interest in botany, science, languages, literature and culminating in an eclectic study of the subjects they both considered were of the most immediate relevance—the social sciences. Both had a lively style of writing which they combined with clarity of exposition and stringency of argument. Both aimed at coming to practical conclusions about society by a detailed study of social phenomena.

The comparison extends also to their personalities and temperaments.

As a child Mill was also brought up in isolation, his life filled with unending study and reading. His father carefully prevented him from spending his time with other boys of his own age and he grew up with few friends. In his early twenties, Mill had a nervous breakdown which he describes at length in his Autobiography.

> I was in a dull state of nerves, such as everybody is occasionally liable to; insusceptible to enjoyment or pleasurable excitement; one of those moods when what is pleasure at other times becomes insipid or indifferent; the state, I should think, in which converts to Methodism usually are when smitten by their first 'conviction of sin'.[22]

He ceased to perceive any purpose in life and

> for some months the cloud seemed to grow thicker and thicker . . . I became persuaded that my love of mankind, and of excellence for its own sake, had worn itself out. I sought no comfort by speaking to others of what I felt. If I had loved anyone sufficiently to make confiding my griefs a necessity, I should not have been in the condition I was. I felt too that mine was not an interesting, or in any way respectable distress. There was nothing in it to attract sympathy . . .

Though this depression was gradually to lift, Mill always remained isolated from society. He regretted that 'general society as now carried on in England, is so insipid an affair, even to the people who make it what it is, that it is kept up for any reason rather than the pleasure it affords', and wrote that he sought only the company of a very few close friends.[23]

Lady Gwendolen's descriptions of Salisbury's mental state have already been quoted. They closely mirror an article which Salisbury wrote in *The Saturday Review* in 1862. It is called 'Invalids'.

> Social miseries are not very acute in their nature, but, like the bites of midges, they make up for their minuteness by their

quantity . . . If a man's memory could reach back so accurately that he could count up all the minutes of mental pain he had endured in his life, he would probably find that a very small number of them comparatively were traceable to causes which could be dignified with the name of sorrow or misfortune; and by far the larger proportion would be due to sufferings so petty that he would be ashamed to put them into words . . .

Invalids are amongst the greatest sufferers in this category. Of course their physical condition sharpens every little sting they undergo, by giving a praeternatural sensitiveness to their power of suffering . . .

Men who are really ill are allowed for but 'delicate' men are not, nor are 'depressed' men.

There is no bigotry in existence so complacent, so absolutely self-satisfied, as the bigotry of robustness. It looks on the professing invalid either as a hypocrite of the basest kind, or else as the victim of a strange delusion.

The average of mankind, at least in England, are not naturally merry; and their tendency to that condition of mind is by no means increased when they find themselves under a kind of social conscription, and are impressed to join in a dance, round game, or *petit jeu*, whether they like it or no . . .[24]

At least twice in his writings he complains of the ease with which alleged madmen are incarcerated. There is a whole article on the subject in a *Saturday Review* 'middle' called 'Tear 'em Rehabilitated'. The article was occasioned by a speech in the House of Commons by Roebuck ('Tear 'em') who had complained that the Tories had fetched a lunatic member to vote in a debate and suggested that no M.P. be allowed to vote if he was certified by two doctors. The article starts with Salisbury in his most witty vein with anecdotes including the one about the Irish member 'who had been gained over by the Tories at the cost of a sumptuous dinner at which he got so drunk that he voted in the Whig lobby after all'. Then, becoming serious, he asserts that the M.P. who was the subject of Roebuck's attack was 'no more mad than Oliver Cromwell was, or any other man who is subject to fits of extreme depression . . . Nothing more cruel can be done to one whose nerves are depressed than to hold him up to the world as a man of doubtful sanity. It is one of those cases in which predictions are likely to fulfil themselves.'[25]

One of the results of Salisbury's continuing dislike of social occasions was a distaste for the appearances required by political life. His emotional fear of democracy was largely due to his obsessive dislike of appearing before the public and of making political small talk. Fortunately he was rarely forced to do this while he remained the Member of Parliament for Stamford. After the passing of the Second Reform Act he was not compelled to change his ways as the death of his father in 1868 took him to the House of Lords and effectively removed him from the need to appear in public.

A man who has to swallow a string of pledges dictated to him by an unreasoning and passionate herd of ignorant men must have first seared out of his mind, by the strong caustic of self-interest, all feelings of self-respect . . .

A public man who exists by the favour of the democracy must be thoroughly free from all acute susceptibilities or sensitive refinement; otherwise he will never be able to go through the humiliations which his exacting and rough-natured patrons are in the habit of requiring . . .

In the entire absence of all political feeling, the tendency to elect on purely parochial considerations is gaining more and more ground with the constituencies. Sir James Elphinstone has secured his seat at Portsmouth by taking a house at Southsea . . .

The ten-pounder cares little for politics but 'likes to have his hand shaken deferentially, and his vote asked in a tone of politeness almost supplicating, by those who on ordinary occasions, get rid of him with very curt and business-like contempt'. And the richer people expect his time to speak to their societies and to listen to their pet schemes.[26]

And, once elected, the M.P. is expected to 'stump' so that Salisbury compares the function of the M.P. in the recess to the functions of the Court Jesters of old.

From thus forth, all successful politicians are to be distinguished professors of Genialism. Much is not said about the intellectual qualities of the English statesmen of the future. These are comparatively immaterial and may be left to take care of themselves. The 'social element' is the one thing needful. Riding, shooting, fishing and cricket are henceforth to be the necessary qualities. And even a British Premier must seem to enjoy a whole day and half a night of intercourse with men with whom he can have no ideas in common, as much as if they were his chosen inmates.[27]

The falseness of it all is what offends Salisbury: 'It is right to like society and if you do not like it you must pretend that you do, in order to keep up with the social ways of our fore-fathers'.[28]

Salisbury's shyness remained throughout his life, and a result of the lack of social ease of which he was so morbidly conscious was a general cynicism about society and about life in general. His feelings are typically expressed in an article entitled 'Shy People'.

> The softest-hearted woman that ever existed never felt a pure unadulterated pity for a stiff neck. The pain is considerable; but the sufferer is so helplessly comic in his efforts to avoid it that sympathy is out of the question. Shyness is a mental affliction of the same order. Nobody pities the unfortunate victim to it, and he is fortunate if he escapes being soundly rated for it by all whom friendship or relationship may have invested with the privilege of saying disagreeable things. Most people who do not happen to be afflicted in that way look upon it as a deliberate offence against themselves, planned for their especial annoyance . . . When two people sit next to each other during two hours of mastication, and do not utter a word, the excuse generally made on their behalf by shocked spectators is that they are very shy. But nothing analogous to the feeling of fear has probably entered into the mind of either of them. They are very likely neither timid, nor diffident, nor awkward. The idea never seems to occur to anybody that they may have omitted to perform their onerous social *corvée* from pure inability to do so. The majority of mankind in England, and the whole of the rest of Christendom, happily for themselves, can talk. When their neighbour has done his sentence, some-thing suggests itself to them which they can say in return, and so keep the conversation going until the moment of release arrives. But there is a strong minority who cannot talk at will. Of course they can talk upon their own subjects with persons who take interest in the same class of ideas. But this is not sufficient for the requirements of society. They must be able to

interchange a regular flow of observations with persons whom
they have never seen before, and with whom they have no
ideas in common, upon subjects that are perfectly unfamiliar to
them.[29]

He repeatedly writes acid (but usually very funny)
articles about the artificiality of the social events which he
was forced to attend, such as public dinners, débutante
dances and teas. In a further article, he is cynical about
friendship in general and, in another, he refers to life as 'the
one great sham in which we all live'.[30]

CHAPTER II

Published Writings and Speeches

IDENTIFICATION OF SALISBURY'S WRITINGS

THROUGHOUT his life Salisbury seems only to have
published six articles under his own name. The fourth
and last volume of *Oxford Essays*, published in 1858,
includes a long essay by Salisbury on 'Theories of Parliamentary Reform'. In Volume XLV of *The Philosophical
Magazine* (1873), he wrote an article on 'Spectral Lines and
Low Temperatures'; it is a highly technical scientific piece
and does not come within the scope of the present study.
Another signed article appeared in *The National Review*
(Vol. II, November 1883) on the subject of 'Labourers' and
Artisans' Dwellings', and he subsequently wrote three more
signed articles for the same review. The election addresses he
gave to the electors of Stamford in 1853, 1857, 1859 and 1865
and some letters to *The Times* also appeared under his name
but the great bulk of his writing was published anony-
mously according to the practice of the day.

In January 1904, there was an article in *The Quarterly
Review* on 'Lord Salisbury and "The Quarterly Review"';
it described his contributions in some detail and revealed
that he had written thirty-three articles for the Review.
In 1905, six of them were published in a two volume edition.[1]
There was a further account of the articles in 'The Centenary of "The Quarterly Review" (II)', an article which
appeared in the issue of July 1909, and a list of his contributions was given in Algernon Cecil's article on his uncle
in the *Dictionary of National Biography*.[2]

Both Algernon Cecil and Lady Gwendolen Cecil considered that 'the most important part of his literary work was done for *The Quarterly Review*'.[3] They were therefore little interested in enquiring into the reports that he also wrote for other reviews and newspapers. Lady Gwendolen mentions his connection with *The Saturday Review*, but states in the first volume of her biography that 'no record remains as to the exact extent of Lord Robert's connection with the *Saturday*'.[4] In 1941, M. M. Bevington published a thesis on 'The Saturday Review, 1855–1868' in which about a dozen articles were attributed to Salisbury.[5]

There the matter stood until May 1961, when an article appeared in the Bulletin of the Institute of Historical Research on 'The Third Marquess of Salisbury and the *Saturday Review*'. In this, Dr. J. F. A. Mason, the Librarian of Christ Church, states:

> There survives in Salisbury's papers (now deposited at Christ Church, Oxford) a document entitled in Lady Gwendolen Cecil's handwriting 'List of the articles written by Lord Salisbury for *The Saturday Review*' and written throughout in her unmistakable hand. How it was that Lady Gwendolen was apparently only able to compile this list after the publication of her first volume in 1921 is not known; she may have obtained the information from the records in the hands of her Beresford-Hope kinsman, whose male line had ended in 1917, and whose papers were used by two members of the family who published *The Book of the Beresford-Hopes* in 1925.[6]

The list, which Mason reproduces in his article, is very long and identifies 607 articles as being the work of Lord Salisbury. The list also gives the amount that he earned for the earlier articles written from 1856 until 1860. By the side of some of her entries, Lady Gwendolen notes 'No payment recorded to any contributor'. This would suggest that she was copying from a book of records, and possibly from the original records of *The Saturday Review* which had been handed down to the Beresford-Hope family from its first owner A. J. Beresford-Hope, Salisbury's brother-in-law. W. I. and I. Law, in *The Book of the Beresford-Hopes*, also seem to be using these records.[7]

Thus there is no reason to doubt the authenticity of the list, which is also amply confirmed by the internal evidence of the articles themselves.

Dr. Mason, in the same article, identifies one further *Saturday Review* article as being the work of Salisbury. On 22 November 1868, William Scott, who was the main leader-writer of *The Saturday Review*, wrote a letter to Salisbury which is now in the Salisbury Papers at Christ Church requesting an article on 'the results of Dizzy's Toryism as shown in the Elections'. On 3 December he wrote again conveying the gratitude of the new editor, Harwood, for 'your excellent answer to my request', and also a cheque. This article (S.R. 608 in the Appendix) must have been the leader 'How the Old Tories Look at the Elections', which appeared in the issue of 28 November 1868. The article is very like the one he was to write in the following year for *The Quarterly Review*.

According to Dr. Mason, Salisbury wrote no other articles for the *Saturday*.

In April 1859, Richard Bentley the publisher attempted to launch a new quarterly review. The enterprise was not a financial success and only four issues appeared. The editor of the new review, which was called *Bentley's Quarterly Review*, was J. D. Cook who was also editor of *The Saturday Review*. In this way Salisbury became involved in the venture. Lady Gwendolen says the following about it:

> No record remains as to the authorship of the articles. They are anonymous, and, though two or three can with some confidence be attributed to Lord Robert on the ground both of their style and of their matter, there is only one—in the July number—as to which any certain external evidence of his authorship exists.[8]

The article in the July number is 'The Faction Fights' and the reason why Lady Gwendolen was able to identify it is that it contained an attack on Disraeli which was so violent that it brought letters of protest from Salisbury's father, and Salisbury's reply has survived among his papers.

But Lady Gwendolen's judgement is too cautious on this

33

matter. There is adequate evidence to show that he wrote at least four articles for the *Review*. In a letter to his wife dated 22 September 1859, Salisbury mentions an article which he was doing for *Bentley's Quarterly Review*, and writes that he was waiting to read it over to his 'colleagues'.[9] This would suggest that he was more than an ordinary contributor. In another letter, written two days later, he says: 'We have pretty well settled our next number, and shall settle it finally on Monday.'[10] This would also suggest that he was on the editorial board. There is confirmation of this in the article on Richard Bentley in the *Dictionary of National Biography* which states that Salisbury and Scott assisted Cook in editing the *Review*. The same is asserted in the obituary of Bentley in *The Bookseller* (3 October 1871).

It would seem likely that Salisbury was the political editor and wrote the political article which was at the start of each issue. There is further external evidence to support this supposition. As it has been stated above, there was a close connection between *Bentley's* and the *Saturday*. In July 1859, an article appeared in the *Saturday* which reviewed the second number of *Bentley's Quarterly Review*.[11] Its purpose was evidently to advertise the new periodical, but its interest for present purposes is that the writer must have been aware of the authorship of the articles in *Bentley's*. He says the following of 'The Faction Fights':

> The number opens as did its predecessor with the political article . . . There is a delicate and refined humour both in this article and its predecessor in No. I., 'English Politics and Parties', which places its writer in a very conspicuous literary eminence.[12]

Thus the author of 'The Faction Fights', who we already know was Salisbury, was also the author of 'English Politics and Parties'.

In the letter of 22 September 1859, which has already been quoted, Salisbury writes that he is doing another review for the October issue. In the letter of 24 September, in which he refers to the editorial meeting, there is no indication that his article was refused and it is reasonable to infer that one of

34

the articles in the third number is also by Salisbury. By a process of eliminating the most unlikely candidates— articles whose subject matter was probably unfamiliar to him and others which express opinions to which he was opposed—we are left with two possibilities: 'France and Europe', the political article at the beginning of the issue, and an article on 'The Court of Lewis XVI'. He may indeed have written both these articles, but it seems very likely that he at least wrote the former one. In its subject-matter, its opinions and its style it bears a striking resemblance to the article on 'English Politics and Parties' and also to some of the earlier Salisbury articles in *The Quarterly Review*. Its main theme is the danger of French aggression, a question which concerned him greatly at the time. There is a characteristic analysis of the internal factors which he sees as driving Louis Napoleon to war (this compares with a passage in Q.R. April 1860, 526(1), a condemnation of Russell's foreign policy and several minor 'signature-themes' of Salisbury.

The internal evidence for authorship of the political article at the beginning of the fourth issue, 'The Coming Political Campaign', is overwhelming. The article is an almost exact preview of the one he was to write three months later for *The Quarterly Review*. It also contains an outline of a scheme for the reform of the House of Lords which he was actually to introduce some ten years later.

The combined weight of the evidence of Salisbury's letters, the various pieces of external evidence, and the internal evidence makes it almost as certain as such indirect evidence can be that the articles formed a series of which Salisbury was the author. Excluding the scientific article in *The Philosophical Magazine*, 650 articles have been identified as Salisbury's. The question remains: did he write any others? It was widely rumoured during his lifetime that he wrote also for the daily press. Fox Bourne, in his standard work *English Newspapers*, published in 1877,[13] stated that in the 1860s Salisbury wrote leading articles for *The Standard*. He is supported in this assertion by another journalist T. H. S. Escott in a review article of Lady Gwendolen's biography which he wrote in February 1922 entitled 'Lord Salisbury and Journalism'.[14] In this article, Escott maintains that Salisbury contributed to *The Morning Chronicle* in the years before 1855, when Cook was the editor and Beresford-Hope a contributor. He also says that he was later associated with *The Standard*. His connection with *The Standard* derived, according to Escott, from the acquaintance at Oxford with Thomas Hamber whose father was friendly with the owner.

> Till 1859 he [Salisbury] called daily in Shoe Lane for his editor's instructions, and left behind him memories unforgotten while the paper itself survived.[15]

Escott is in a good position to make this assertion, for he was himself a leader-writer for *The Standard* from 1866 onwards, and most of Salisbury's colleagues on the newspaper must still have been there at that time. In an earlier book *Masters of English Journalism*, published in 1911, Escott is even more categorical:

> The present writer had it directly from the late Lord Salisbury himself that, while his regularly supplied articles for *The Standard* ceased during the early sixties, he had occasionally something to do with this newspaper's leaders after that date . . .[16]

But it is unlikely that Salisbury would have had time in the 1860s to fulfil any regular assignments other than those which are already known. He was writing some four thousand words a week for *The Saturday Review* and a long article almost every three months for *The Quarterly Review*. During the early 1860s his growing business commitments would also have meant that he had less time and reason to undertake any further journalistic work.

In the years before 1860, however, things were different. Lady Gwendolen's list shows that he made £92 8s. in 1857, £39 18s. in 1858, £60 18s. in 1859 and £113 8s. in 1860 from his writings for *The Saturday*.[17] This indicates that in the hardest years immediately following his marriage, Salisbury's earnings from *The Saturday Review* actually diminished from the level they reached in 1857. It seems all the more plausible, then, that he was contributing on a regular basis at this period to a newspaper—which squares also with Escott's statement that it was in the period until 1859 that Salisbury wrote regular leaders.

Against this evidence, and against the feeling that there must be some fire behind the smoke, there is Lady Gwendolen Cecil's categorical statement that 'The late Sir Charles Alderson, k.g.b., his brother-in-law, was convinced that *The Saturday Review* was the only newspaper to which Lord Robert ever contributed'.[18] Certainly the rumours about Salisbury's connections with the press had reached fairly wide proportions by the 1870s and the 1880s. They are perhaps illustrated by the anecdote told years later by a veteran journalist, George Saintsbury:

> I myself once wrote an article entitled 'Confessions of an English Leek-Eater', which made quite a sensation. Persons in the Upper Houses of Fleet Street asked seriously whether it was not the late Lord Salisbury's . . . and the interest in it almost survived the twenty-four hours—till a treacherous friend spoilt the fun by blurting out that it was mine.[19]

Even Lucy, writing in 1885, repeated the totally unrealistic conjecture that 'he was pretty regularly engaged as a leader writer on *The Times*'.[20] The Salisbury Papers contain very little correspondence dating from the 1850s and early 1860s and there is no evidence of his association with the daily press at this time. Nor does his later correspondence with journalists such as Escott, Hamber and Cook throw light on the matter either way.

The internal evidence of *The Standard* in the period 1858–59 suggests that Salisbury was not regularly writing political leaders at this time, since those appearing in its columns express opinions diametrically opposed to his own. For example, the leaders constantly support Disraeli's 'practical recognition of the wants of the day'[21] at a time when Salisbury was writing of Disraeli as an 'artless dodger' and 'the grain of dirt that clogs the whole machine'. The style and content of the leading articles in *The Morning Chronicle* up till 1855 do not exclude his authorship. But it does seem unlikely that he was already writing leaders at this early period. Besides, if Cook had been willing to trust Salisbury with leaders when he was editor of *The Morning Chronicle*, why, as editor of *The Saturday Review*, was he so reluctant to give him anything but reviews when he started to be a contributor in the late 1850s?[22]

It is not possible to come to a firm conclusion either way. It is unlikely that he contributed regularly to the daily press, but he may well have published pieces spasmodically. However, this remaining uncertainty in no way affects the substance of what is to follow. It is highly unlikely that there are any major themes in his thought which he did not develop in the 650 articles that have been examined in the preparation of this work.

A GENERAL SURVEY OF THE ARTICLES AND SPEECHES

Salisbury's writings divide themselves into two kinds. There are the long articles which he wrote for periodicals, and the short ones which were published in *The Saturday Review*.

The average length of the forty-two long articles is about 17,000 words. The Oxford Essay, the contributions to *Bentley's* and most of the *Quarterly Review* articles cover thirty to thirty-five closely printed journal pages. The *National Review* articles are shorter—from ten to fifteen pages. The longest pieces are his *Quarterly Review* articles on 'The Danish Duchies' and 'The Foreign Policy of England'. The latter, as A. L. Kennedy points out in his biography of Salisbury, 'runs to 23,000 words, the length of a small book'.[23]

The vast majority of *The Saturday Review* articles are a standard two columns long—that is, about 1,800 to 2,000 words, the length of a short essay. A few of the earlier 'middles' are little more than a single column, whereas the reviews of German Literature are generally three columns, and the special annual articles on 'The Session' and 'The Year' are five or six columns.

Each issue of *The Saturday Review* consisted of articles of three kinds. At the beginning, there was a series of leading articles similar to those in the daily papers, but, it was claimed, of superior quality owing to the fact that the writers had more time to compose them. The leaders were followed by 'middles': these were a speciality for which *The Saturday* was renowned. They were either background articles to the news (descriptions of debate scenes in the Commons, for example), or they were humorous essays on social topics, or, sometimes, they were little different in style and content from the leading articles in the preceding section. The final section contained book reviews.

At first, Salisbury contributed only reviews and occasional middles. Gradually, he began to concentrate on middles. He had been with *The Saturday Review* for nearly five years before his first leader appeared. After this, his leading articles became more and more frequent and in his last three years with *The Saturday* he wrote little else. Of the 259 leaders he wrote, only three were first leaders and twenty-five were second leaders.[24]

The following table, compiled by Dr. Mason, shows the year by year distribution of Salisbury's contributions.[25]

Year	Leaders	Middles	Reviews	Total
1856			1	1
1857		10	34	44
1858		3	16	19
1859		19	10	29
1860		18	17	35
1861	15	53	42	110
1862	48	36	22	106
1863	71	30	11	112
1864	79	12	3	94
1865	44	11		55
1866	1	1		2
1868	1			1
	259	193	156	608

Until the present, it has been upon the long articles that Salisbury's literary reputation has rested. The reason for this, as has been explained, is that most of these writings have been known for many years to have come from Salisbury's hand, whereas the short articles have only recently been brought to light.

The earliest of the periodical articles was the Oxford Essay on 'Theories of Parliamentary Reform' which was signed and dated 1 February 1858. Salisbury classes the Reformers under three heads:

1. The Educational Reformers
2. The Democratic Reformers
3. The Symmetrical Reformers.[26]

He examines their various arguments, rejecting each in turn. He recognises the existing anomalies in the English Constitution, but is of the view that any change will upset the precarious balance of institutions that have in practice worked so well. This leads him to the conclusion that 'We must either change enormously or not at all.'[27] The unbending resistance to democratic reforms expressed in this first article sets the key for almost all of the long articles that follow. The subject is directly dealt with in three of the *Bentley's Quarterly Reviews* and over half of the *Quarterly Reviews*. Four other articles are about Church matters[28] and three deal with the Civil War in the United States.[29] In fact, the real subject of all these articles is Reform: the Church because it was one of the main institutions under attack from the Radicals; and America because it was an example of the kind of democratic state that Britain would become if its Constitution were reformed.

Of the remaining *Quarterly Reviews*, two are about miscellaneous subjects: one expresses opposition to the Radical schemes for 'Competitive Examination',[30] the other is an article on 'Photography'[31] which, in Algernon Cecil's apt words, 'exhibits great power of lucid exposition and of practical foresight'.[32] The rest deal with foreign affairs or biography.

Two of the articles on foreign affairs, 'The Political Lessons of the War'[33] and 'The Commune and the Internationale'[34] turn out to be further cautionary tales about Reform. They are rather forced and garbled and are probably his least creditable pieces. The other articles on foreign affairs are relatively free of the Reform theme and consider foreign policy as a largely independent subject.

During 1861 and 1862 he wrote two articles on Stanhope's *Life of Pitt*[35] (Pitt the younger) and another on Sir Archibald Alison's biography of Lord Castlereagh.[36] Salisbury had unbounded admiration for both statesmen, and these reviews give him the opportunity for expressing his general principles of statesmanship in both domestic and foreign affairs. They are, perhaps, his most polished works and were republished after his death together with three articles on foreign affairs ('Poland',[37] 'The Danish Duchies'[38] and 'The Foreign Policy of England'[39]).

The articles he contributed to *The National Review* are somewhat different from the rest: they are signed contributions written by Salisbury when he was already an eminent politician. They are shorter, more specific in content and less ornate in style than most of his other productions. One is on 'Labourers' and Artisans' Dwellings',[40] and is the only detailed treatment of a social issue in all the periodical articles; another is concerned with the 1884 Reform Bill,[41] a much milder piece than those he had written about Reform proposals in the 1860s; the other two concern the powers of the House of Lords.[42]

It has sometimes been stated as a matter of complaint against the long articles that the question of Reform, like a Salisburian leitmotif, runs through almost all of them. No such complaint could be made against the shorter contributions to *The Saturday Review*. The Reform question is discussed in these articles—and treated very fully—but it is only one among an immense variety of topics.

A high proportion of his earliest contributions were reviews of pot-boiling novels such as *Freida the Jongleur*,[43] *Nightshade*,[44] *The Rival Suitors*,[45] *Cousin Harry*[46] and *Cousin Stella*.[47] On most of these he performed the efficient hatchet work of which he was very capable. His most frequent complaint was against novels which were sermons in disguise.[48] In these book reviews and in the reviews of architecture and of music (which occasionally occurred later on in the middles) he showed his tastes to be quite un-Victorian in his liking for

41

the simple and for the amusing in preference to the ornate
and the didactic.[49]

There were several early reviews of church histories.[50] He
regarded most of these as pedantic and over-scholarly and
did not take the serious interest in them that he would
undoubtedly have done if he had been reviewing the same
books a few years previously.

He was not bored with all these early reviews, however;
some of the books he dealt with were about social and
political issues such as the Poor Laws or Free Trade, others
were concerned with travel, history or the Colonies. The
most surprising of the early pieces are the reviews he wrote,
mostly in 1857, of books about America and slavery.[51] He
was violently opposed to what he called the 'curse of slavery';[52] he said that it was not only a crime but a blunder,[53]
and he strongly condemned Southern tactics in securing the
extension of slavery to Kansas.[54] These reviews are especially
significant in the light of the many later articles in both *The
Saturday* and *The Quarterly Review* in which he sides strongly
with the South. Throughout these articles, many of which
were written while the Civil War was being fought, he
maintains that the main issue at stake in the War is not
slavery but the tariff;[55] thus, he sees no inconsistency in
opposition to slavery combined with support of the Confederacy.

From 1859 to 1864, Salisbury wrote a series of reviews,
which usually appeared monthly, on German Literature. In
each article he dealt with an average of ten books and he
must have covered about five hundred in all. The books are
on all sorts of subjects ranging from children's books and
travel-guides to abstruse historical chronicles, treatises on
comparative linguistics,[56] 'mythography',[56] 'geological statistics',[57] 'social anthropology',[58] and grammar.[59] There are
two particular points of note in these articles. They show his
full awareness of the forces of the new German nationalism,[60]
and they also give him an opportunity to consider the
historical and philosophical movements in Germany at the
time. In the course of considering books such as von Sybel's
History of the French Revolution[61] and Ranke's *History of*

England[62] he takes the opportunity of analysing trends in historiography; and, in dealing with various commentaries on the works of philosophers such as Schopenhauer and von Humboldt[63] and also the German Biblical critics, he is able to give a full account of his own views on the nature of science and of political and religious knowledge. In the periodical writing he hardly mentions these subjects, and these *Saturday Review* articles are thus specially useful. He develops his views on these matters in further articles such as 'Lord Lindsay on Scepticism'.[64]

His articles of the early 1860s include fewer reviews than previously, but some of the books he reviewed are of great importance and merit, and the review of *The Life of the Duke of Wellington*[65] and *Supplementary Despatches of the Duke of Wellington*[66] are of the calibre of his article on Castlereagh in *The Quarterly Review*.

Many of the early middles were descriptions of scenes during debates in the House of Commons, and, occasionally, in the House of Lords.[67] Salisbury had a very happy capacity for vivid description, and these articles are among his best, even though they are not among the most important. Some of these descriptions were incorporated almost verbatim into the periodical articles. For example, the description of 'The House of Commons at the Dentist's'[68] (Disraeli's speech introducing the Conservative Reform Bill of 1859) appears in 'The Faction Fights',[69] and the account of Gladstone's budget speech of 1860[70] is repeated in 'The Budget and the Reform Bill'.[71]

All *The Saturday Review* articles were written in the decade preceding the Second Reform Bill. At that time, the multiplicity of party groups and the consequent weakness of the executive gave private Members of Parliament, Parliamentary committees and pressure groups more power than they had had previously and much more than they were to have subsequently. Salisbury has a series of articles on Committees,[72] Private Members' Bills,[73] party discipline,[74] Parliamentary questions[75] and pressure groups[76] both in Parliament and also outside it. There are further articles on the House of Lords,[77] the Civil Service[78] and the

Monarchy.[79] In other articles, such as the reviews of Lord Colchester's *Diaries*,[80] he examines the historical development of the powers of the House of Commons during the nineteenth century. Many of these articles are of great value to the student of political institutions, as Salisbury was in Parliament all this time and was therefore able to comment at first hand on the working of the constitution at one of its most complex periods.

The questions of Reform and Disestablishment are treated fully[81] and with great variety of argument, but they are by no means the only political issues with which he deals. He says a good amount about education, mostly in connection with his attack on Robert Lowe.[82] Many of these articles were written while he was making attacks on Lowe in the House. He touches on several occasions on the local government issues that were to occupy him during his Second Ministry,[83] and writes a large number of articles on the housing of the poor,[84] the Poor Laws,[85] prison discipline and penal reform.[86] These articles on social issues are of importance for they are almost his only writings in this field. It is said that he did not have the social conscience of other politicians such as Disraeli, and one of the main criticisms of his years as Premier was to be his neglect of social amelioration. The strength of feeling which is shown in these articles is thus surprising.

Discussions of foreign policy in *The Saturday Review* articles mirror those in *The Quarterly* in their opposition to Russell's policy of bluster.[87] He also considers the problems of the organisation of the Army in some detail and speculates with great foresight on the effects of scientific developments on the conduct of war.[88] Colonial problems are covered very fully[89] (they are hardly mentioned in the long articles); he is obviously very well-informed on Colonial matters and the articles are significant for the extreme anti-jingo views which are expressed in them. The Maori Wars that were being fought at the time in New Zealand receive special attention;[90] his interest probably stems largely from his visit there in 1852. Ireland is the subject of a large number of articles.[91] Salisbury expresses understanding and compassion for the historical injustices which the Irish people have suffered, but he combines this with the strongest condemnation of the lawlessness which he acknowledges to be the result. Religious questions figure prominently among his contributions to *The Saturday*.[92] They include a long series in which he criticises the Bishops and the Puseyites for their attacks on Bishop Colenso for his allegedly heretical views on the Creation and in which he deplores the heresy-hunt against Jowett for his contribution to *Essays and Reviews*.

Some of the most fascinating of all the articles are the middles on social and personal questions. Salisbury's humour is sometimes spoilt by his bitter cynicism, but most of them are eminently readable and some are brilliant. There is a succession of essays on the theme of marriage in smart society[93] and another series on the boredom and artificiality of public dinners.[94] There are further essays on gossip,[95] crinolines,[96] country doctors,[97] prostitutes[98] ('soiled doves'), compliments,[99] white lies,[100] drawing-room furniture,[101] bathing,[102] advertising,[103] travel,[104] invitation begging,[105] cosmetics,[106] etc.

One of the chief interests of such writings is their highly autobiographical nature. He always writes in general terms but, especially in such articles as 'Invalids',[107] 'Shy People'[108] and 'Friends',[109] he is in reality talking about himself. External evidence shows this in several cases and it is not unreasonable to make the inference that in other cases too he may be using the anonymous article as a form of personal diary. The almost complete absence of other material on the personality of Salisbury in his youth makes these articles particularly valuable.

Salisbury's speeches, in contrast to his articles in *The Saturday Review*, are limited in their scope. In part this is a reflection of the fact that the subject matter of Parliamentary debate, unlike that of the weeklies, is necessarily limited to the business at hand. It is also a consequence of Salisbury's lack of faith and interest in general Parliamentary legislation. The table overleaf shows the distribution of his speeches year by year.

Session	Number of Speeches	Session	Number of Speeches
1854	3	1862	14
1855	5	1863	17
1856	4	1864	25
1857	5	1865	8
1858	3	1866	17
1859	3	1867	18
1860	13	1868	5
1861	12		

He spoke very little in the period before the defeat of Derby's Ministry in 1859. It was in 1860 that he started speaking more frequently—about the same time as he started contributing to *The Quarterly Review* and writing much more intensively for *The Saturday*.

Of the 152 speeches (most of them are quite brief), twenty-one deal directly with the question of parliamentary reform, but the majority of others are concerned with the general issue of constitutional change, speeches about the Church, education, taxation and competitive examination. There are comparatively few speeches on foreign and colonial policy. India is the subject of nine speeches which he gave either while or immediately after he was Secretary of State for India. There are a dozen speeches on the Civil War in the United States and several on the colonial topics that concerned Salisbury in his articles, such as the Maori Wars in New Zealand. Finally there is a small miscellany of speeches about electoral corruption, committees of the House of Commons, Poor Relief, the Macdonald Case, the cattle plague, criminals, and one or two others.

The speeches deal with no subjects that are not also covered in the articles. In some cases articles and speeches share almost identically worded passages and though there is some difference (but surprisingly little) between the presentation of the speeches and that of the writings, the arguments he uses under the veil of anonymity bear a striking consistency to those he offered publicly. It is not, therefore, because the articles differ from his public views and express his 'real' opinions that they are specially valuable. Their usefulness consists rather in the great detail, intimacy and variety with which he is able to expand on the views outlined in the speeches in the crude terms demanded by debate. As Salisbury once wrote: 'the logical elucidation of a controversy is not the chief value of a Parliamentary debate. Spoken argument can never be so exhaustive or so close as written'.[110]

At this point, some readers might wish to raise an objection. In the case of Burke, admittedly, much of his political theory is taken from his speeches. But is it not quite artificial to 'extract' political theory in this way from Salisbury's journalistic writings? He was a practical politician, he was not a theorist and would probably not have wished to be treated as such.

As the objection is an important one, the final section of this Chapter is devoted to answering it.

THE EXTRACTION OF POLITICAL THEORY FROM JOURNALISTIC WRITINGS

The question will be considered on three different levels: in general terms; with reference to the nineteenth century; and in reference to Salisbury himself.

The objection of artificiality assumes that there is a neat division between theory and practice in politics. But does 'pure' political theory exist? Have the great political theorists of the past invented their models in the abstract, without regard to any possible application of their theory? Or have they been stimulated into their theorising by the existence of immediate political problems which demanded settlement?

It becomes evident from even a cursory examination of the standard texts of the political thinkers that most of them are trying to give answers in general terms to the fairly specific, pressing problems of their age. It is impossible, for example, to grasp Plato's *Republic* without an awareness of the difficulties that had faced the Athenian democracy at the end of the fifth century B.C. and of its disastrous war with the opposing system of Sparta. And without some understanding

47

of the Italian city states in the fifteenth and the beginning of the sixteenth centuries, the work of Machiavelli becomes little more than a set of general aphorisms. Karl Marx is perhaps one of the most systematic of all political thinkers— yet he is an eminent example of the way in which theory and practice are interwoven. For Marx, political activity and the formulation of general theory were two elements of one and the same vocation. A recent book on the political writings of Hegel—and it is difficult to find a political theorist more highly abstract or 'philosophical'—argues that it would be more fruitful to disregard the husk of philosophical jargon altogether and to concentrate on what Hegel had to say about the political problems and the political future of the Germany of his day.[111]

It is not necessary to go as far as this. One need not be forced to the extreme of saying that political theory is no more than political propaganda clothed in fancy verbiage. This position, however, is not as unreasonable as the other extreme which maintains that political theory is of the same status as, say, formal logic, pure mathematics or theoretical physics.

But even if political thought is never pure, it is, as has been suggested above, more than just a way of advocating specific political measures. Consequently, while it might be difficult to gain a true perspective on many theories of politics without an attempt at an understanding of the period in which they were formulated, it is equally necessary to examine political arguments in and of themselves. For a general theory may originally be devised as a solution to certain problems, but often it will survive those problems which gave it its birth and continue to lead a life of its own. We have seen in our own times, for example, that national-istic feelings originating in the existence of specific abuses and embodied in theories of national rights have lasted, pre-served by the force of theory, after those abuses have ended. Indeed, at any time, the most practical of politicians are likely to be influenced in their actions by theoretical con-siderations. They may be influenced in the choice of the goals which they think possible or right, in their evaluation of the best means to those goals, and in their advocation of those means and those goals to others.

We come to the conclusion that, if there is no such phenomenon as pure theory, it is also rare to find complete pragmatism. The difference between theory and practice is a matter of emphasis, and depends largely on the nature of the political problems of any given age. In some ages political questions involve theoretical considerations less than in others. In Britain today it is often argued that politics is a matter of personalities and of technical questions, for there are no points of deep disagreement between the two major parties. If this view is correct we should not expect the formulation of general answers to political problems. On the other hand, during the Civil War in England three centuries ago, the very issues were of a scope such as was likely to breed political discussion of a general nature.

Thus, it is impossible to make a clean division between theory and practice in politics. The theoretical and the pragmatic forms of political discussion appear not so much as two different activities but rather as two different styles of thought about political problems: two forms of the same activity, and forms, moreover, between which there is no precise line of demarcation.

A corollary of this is that it is also impossible to demarcate the systematically 'theoretical' from the 'practical' by the form in which it is expressed. If some thinkers are more systematic than others, the fact does not necessarily show itself in the medium which they use. Locke's 'treatises' look very systematic: the works are of a respectable length and are neatly divided into chapters and sections. The works of Marx are quite the opposite—they consist largely of political pamphlets, letters, newspaper articles, partisan accounts of contemporary history, notes and sundry polemics and very little that is organised in treatise or in book form. Yet, which is the more systematic? Locke's organised arrangement certainly does not suffice to guarantee the organisation and consistency of his thought, and the ragged form of Marx's writings certainly do not disqualify them from having these qualities.

Plato used dramatic dialogues and allegories as the form of

49

expounding his ideas on politics. Thucydides used history. Hobbes wrote a book, Rousseau employed the discourse and letters. Hume wrote essays. Disraeli wrote novels. Burke made speeches. All were great political thinkers.

There are therefore no general grounds for dismissing a politician's claims as a political thinker either because he was a political actor, or because he did not write treatises. Closer examination must be made of the nature of the political problems with which he dealt and of his manner of writing (or speaking) about them. The nineteenth century was an age of revolution, of unparalleled industrial development and of constitutional change in most of the Western countries. In England, some of the political questions during the century were admittedly 'technical', such as the detailed consideration of the results of a lowering of tariff walls. Other alternatives were personal—notably the choice between Gladstone and Disraeli. But, through them all ran deeper considerations. During most of the century, Constitutional Reform was the central question and had such wide ramifications that it was very difficult to exclude questions of rights, of ultimate effects and discussion of the form of the ideal polity. The century also witnessed the new phenomena of industrialisation—the great and increasing wealth, the trade cycles and the sufferings of the urban working classes. These were not isolated occurrences but were present repeatedly and concertedly; and these general phenomena called for general explanations. The nineteenth century was thus an age in which it was almost impossible to consider specific political questions without entering into deeper, general discussion.

Although it was an age which produced a great deal of thought, it did not produce many long political works. In this respect, it was not unlike other periods of English history. As Alan Bullock and F. W. Deakin point out in their General Preface to the series of volumes on 'The British Political Tradition',

> The riches of British political thought are to be found less in the philosophers' discussions of terms like 'The State', 'freedom' and 'obligation'—important though these are—than in the

writings and speeches on contemporary political issues of men like Lilburne, Locke, Bolingbroke, Burke, Tom Paine, Fox, the Mills, Cobden, Disraeli, Gladstone, and the Fabians. No other literature in the world is so rich in political pamphlets as English, and the pages of *Hansard* are a mine not only for the historian of political events but also for the historian of political ideas. It is in the discussions provoked by the major crises in British history—the Civil War, the Revolt of the American Colonies, the Reform Bills of the nineteenth century—that our political ideas have been hammered out.

In the nineteenth century, it was not pamphlets so much as periodicals which provided the vehicle for political expression.

At the beginning of the century, a review was founded by a group of Whigs in Edinburgh. Lord Brougham was one of the main contributors and it was in *The Edinburgh Review* that Macaulay's celebrated Essays were to appear. So influential was this review that John Murray, the Tory publisher, in co-operation with Canning and Sir Walter Scott (who had first supported the *Edinburgh*, but who had become dissatisfied with both its political and literary views) started *The Quarterly Review* in 1809.[112] Scott himself wrote about a dozen articles in the *Quarterly*. Other regular contributors were Southey, who contributed over thirty articles (many of them on political subjects), and Croker (the Tory politician and friend of Wellington) to whom at least 258 contributions can be traced, many of them on literary topics. Among other early contributors were Archbishop Whately, Malthus, Keble and Washington Irving. Periodical journalism gave these distinguished contributors an outlet for the systematic exposition of their literary and political views, while at the same time giving them a larger audience (and more certain profit) than they were likely to obtain by publishing their views in book or pamphlet form.

The Radicals, not to be outdone, started *The Westminster Review*. Its founder was Bentham himself and the Mills also played a central part. A full account of the founding of the Review is given by John Stuart Mill in Chapter IV of his *Autobiography*. Mill is typical of the Victorian thinkers in his use of periodicals and newspapers as vehicles of his thought. The essays on 'Liberty' and 'Representative Government' were published separately, but almost all of his other political works appeared either in *The Westminster Review* (these include the essays on Bentham and Coleridge), or other Reviews such as *Fraser's Magazine* (in which 'Utilitarianism' first appeared), or in newspapers such as *The Examiner, Morning Chronicle* or *The Daily News*. A list of his works which he had copied while he was preparing his *Autobiography* survives among his papers and reveals many hundreds of anonymous articles which he wrote for newspapers and periodicals.[113]

Among those who wrote for *The Quarterly Review* around the time that Salisbury was a contributor were Guizot, Ruskin, Shaftesbury, Whewell, Gladstone, Bulwer-Lytton, Lord Acton, Matthew Arnold, J. A. Froude, Sir Henry Maine and Lord John Manners. *The Saturday Review* also attracted a distinguished set of contributors including E. A. Freeman, J. A. Froude, Goldwin Smith, Charles Kingsley, Walter Bagehot, Sir Henry Maine, James Bryce, Sir William Harcourt and John Morley.[114]

Nor were the periodicals and papers that have been mentioned above the only distinguished ones. For example, Bagehot was editor of *The Economist* and brought out a series in *The Fortnightly* at the time that Salisbury was writing for *The Saturday* that is now known, in collected form, as his classic work on 'The English Constitution', Disraeli's associations with *The Times* are well known, and Peel and Palmerston had written in *The Courier*. The influence of these articles on the thought of their time was immense. But, alas, many of the articles are anonymous and this has prevented them from taking the prominent place in the study of British political thought that they must otherwise deserve.*

Salisbury was writing at the time when the issue of Reform drew together the activities of political theorising and of political activity. The titles of the articles themselves illus-

---

* The situation will undoubtedly be remedied, in part at least, by the completion of the *Wellesley Index of Victorian Periodicals*, the first volume of which appeared in 1966.

trate his concerns. When he considers the Civil War in
America, the question is not only the immediate problem
facing the British of how far they should recognise the
Confederacy,[115] there is the more general question of the
fate of the democratic system of government: thus he uses the
United States 'as an example'[116] and sees 'Democracy on its
Trial'.[117] In considering the affairs of the St. Marylebone
constituency, he is not prompted by any particular concern
or interest in the petty quarrels concerning St. John's Wood
or Regent's Park, 'Fiat Experimentum in Corpore Vili' is the
title of one of his articles on the subject.[118] It is the wider
implications in which he is interested. The folly of Russell's
Blairgowrie speech[119] and the rebuff from Russia which was
the result are treated not as matters of vital moment in
themselves but as case studies designed to show the disadvantages of certain diplomatic procedures in general.

The varied articles which Salisbury wrote are the expression of a unified system of thought. Both the custom of
the age and Salisbury's personal circumstances made the
quarterly and the newspaper a natural medium for the
expression of 'theoretical' views.

CHAPTER III

Foundations of Knowledge

TWO TYPES OF CONSERVATIVE THOUGHT

IRRATIONAL, religious, visionary, romantic—it is with these words—and more of the same kind that the 'British Conservative Tradition' is usually described. In his introduction to *The Conservative Mind*, Russell Kirk states, as the first canon of Conservative thought:

> Belief that a divine intent rules society as well as conscience, forging an eternal chain of right and duty which links great and obscure, living and dead. Political problems, at bottom, are religious and moral problems. A narrow rationality, what Coleridge calls the Understanding, cannot of itself satisfy human needs . . .[1]

And the second canon, he says, consists of:

> Affection for the proliferating variety and mystery of traditional life.[2]

R. J. White, in the Introduction to *The Conservative Tradition*, emphasises the Conservative subordination of politics to religion, 'to the attainment of the Beatific Vision'.[3] And he goes on to talk of the 'wondrous imagination'[4] of Disraeli, and the vision of the values of an older Europe 'seen through the mists of poppy and mandragora by S. T. Coleridge'.[5] Hearnshaw says that Disraeli's religious beliefs were 'something of an Asian mystery',[6] and he also states that his first political principle was 'The religious base of society'.[6] In similar vein, Clinton Rossiter, in a chapter on 'The Conservative Tradition', writes:

The Conservative reverence for God is matched by his respect for history, and thus for those traditions of his community that have stood the test of time. Out of the past—protean, mysterious, immemorial—have come the values and institutions that have lifted man far above his nature. History is the creator of all the Conservative holds dear, and in the logic of its glacial progress he detects the hand of God.[7]

All these writers emphasise Burke's pronouncements about the religious basis of politics and the limited range of human reason. Nowhere is this view of Conservatism expressed better than in Mill's essays on 'Bentham' and 'Coleridge'. These two great men were, says Mill, examples of the Progressive and the Conservative.[8] Bentham was an ardent empiricist. His strength and his novelty lay in the use of the 'method of detail',[9] a method derived from Bacon, Hobbes and Locke and described by Mill in the following manner:

> It is a sound maxim, and one which all close thinkers have felt, but no one before Bentham ever so consistently applied, that error lurks in generalities: that the human mind is not capable of embracing a complex whole, until it has surveyed and catalogued the parts of which that whole is made up; that abstractions are not realities *per se*, but an abridged mode of expressing facts, and that the only practical mode of dealing with them is to trace them back to the facts (whether of experience or of consciousness) of which they are the expression.[10]

Bentham's weakness was his 'deficiency of Imagination'.[11] With Coleridge it was the opposite. He had a full measure of the imagination that Bentham lacked, and he reacted violently against Benthamite empiricism in favour of the essentialist German philosophy:

> The Germano-Coleridgian doctrine . . . expresses the revolt of the human mind against the philosophy of the eighteenth century. It is ontological, because that was experimental; conservative, because that was innovative; religious, because so much of that was infidel . . .[12]

In emphasising its intuitive, anti-empirical nature, Mill

55

and the other writers that have been quoted are drawing attention to a strand of thought that has indeed been an important element in the British Conservative Tradition. However, if they think that they are describing the only strand or the 'essential' one, they are mistaken. There has been a second strand which has in many ways been just as prominent. In an article on 'Hume and Political Scepticism', in *The Philosophical Review* of July 1954, Marshall talks of 'Empirical Conservatism'. Sheldon Wolin[13] makes a similar distinction and talks of Conservatism with a small 'c' (i.e. empirical conservatism) as distinguished from big 'c' Conservatism (i.e. the intuitive variety that has already been described). The terms 'Empirical Conservative' and 'small "c" Conservative' apply to those thinkers whose 'liberal' empiricism in matters of philosophy fails to be accompanied in politics by 'radical' or 'progressive' views. The empiricist tradition has, of course, been fundamental to British thought in the past three or four hundred years and in practice it has been largely conservative; consequently, this second strand has occupied a significant place in the political thought of Britain.

Of the four great British empiricists Hobbes, Locke, Berkeley and Hume, three also wrote important political works. Hobbes' pessimistic view of human nature leads him to advocate a highly authoritarian form of government and to oppose seditious doctrines and rebellion in the strongest terms. He condemns those who, lacking 'political prudence' and 'animated by false doctrines, are perpetually meddling with the fundamental laws'. The greatest problem and evil facing Hobbesian man is the insecurity of his condition. The end of government, therefore, is 'the procuration of the *safety of the people*' and the permanently based security that is a necessary condition for the existence of any type of civilisation. Governments which are themselves unstable cannot provide lasting peace for their subjects, and the Leviathan is consequently designed to last as long as possible, free 'of those things that weaken, or tend to the dissolution of a Commonwealth'. Authoritarianism and opposition to constitutional change in the Hobbesian system is justified on utilitarian grounds, so that Hobbes's brand of conservatism contrasted in its own day with the Divine Right theories in much the same way as the later Empirical Conservative attitudes have differed from the big 'c' Conservative philosophies of later times.

At first glance, the political theory of Locke is very different from that of Hobbes. His view of human nature appears to be rosier, the need for unchanging authoritarian government seems less and he argues in favour of a right of rebellion. In his own lifetime he was involved in the Revolution of 1688 and he has often been considered as a father of Liberal thought. Yet this need not be the end of the matter. Recent scholars have emphasised the points of similarity rather than the differences that are to be found in the political writings of Hobbes and Locke. In his book on *Locke on Peace and War*, Cox draws attention to the group of passages in which Locke talks of the State of Nature almost in Hobbesian terms as a brutal and uncertain State of War. For Locke, as for Hobbes, the end of civil government is the preservation of the lives, liberties and estates of men. And it will only achieve this end if there is 'an established, settled known law', supported by a settled system of justice and of government to back it up. Thus government must be stable if it is to fulfil the purposes for which it was established.

If the essence of good government is stability, why then does Locke favour the citizens' right of rebellion? It is easy to overestimate the function of rebellion in Locke's framework. He is fully aware of the possible objection to admitting the right of rebellion, that 'no government will be able long to subsist if the people may set up a new legislature whenever they take offence at the old one'. But he denies strenuously that this will be the result. In the first place, rebellion will follow injustice whether there is a 'right of rebellion' or no; secondly, 'such revolutions happen not upon every little mismanagement in public affairs'; they only occur after 'a long train of abuses, prevarications and artifices'. Thirdly, 'this power in the people for providing for their safety anew by a new legislature when their legislators have acted contrary to their trust by invading their property, is the best

57

fence against rebellion, and the probablest means to hinder it'.

Rebellion is not a part of the normal process of relations between rulers and governed, it is kept in reserve as a warning and an ultimate sanction against gross misgovernment. The difference between Hobbes and Locke is that, in the terms to be introduced in Chapter IV, Hobbes regards change as 'explosive' whereas, in extreme circumstances, Locke sees the possibility of its stabilising and palliative effects. The important aspect for the present argument is that Locke opposes the view that governors are 'sons of Jupiter . . . sacred and divine, descended or authorised from heaven'. But on prudential grounds he favours governments that are in all but the most exceptional circumstances stable and secure.

Hume is easily identifiable as a Conservative. He was an empiricist and a utilitarian par excellence. Like Bentham, who must have been much influenced by his writings, he was a sceptic, but, unlike Bentham, he did not turn the force of his scepticism on to existing institutions; instead, he directed it against the perfectionist schemes for substituting other institutions in their place. Wolin, writing in the issue of *The American Political Science Review* of December 1954, emphasises Hume's respect for the existing Constitutional balance, a structure shaped not by speculative reason but by custom and expediency. Above all else, this relies on stability of government:

> An established government has an infinite advantage by that very circumstance of its being established; the bulk of mankind being governed by authority, not reason, and never attributing authority to anything that has not the recommendation of antiquity.

The position is argued in detail in his essay 'Of the Original Contract'. He does not even consider the possibility of a Divine Right of Kings and rejects the contractual theory of political obligation.

> If the reason be asked of that obedience to [government], I readily answer *Because society could not otherwise subsist;* and this

answer is clear and intelligible to all mankind . . . The general obligation, which binds us to government, is the interest and necessities of society; and this obligation is very strong. The determination of it to this or that particular prince, or form of government, is frequently more uncertain and dubious. Present possession has considerable authority in these cases, and greater than in private property; because of the disorders which attend all revolutions and changes of government.

Wolin contrasts this conservatism with that of Burke. Hume's conservatism had no recourse to 'divine tactic', it was constructed from the very materials of the Enlightenment and reflected not a period of revolution but the 'peace of the Augustans'.

An examination of the political essays written by Hume shows their striking similarity with those that Salisbury was to write a century later. There is the same empirical style of analysis which is applied to politics in the same way. They give similar accounts of the origins of property and both have the same view of the desirability of a balance of power in domestic as well as in international affairs. With regard to the politics of their respective times, they both think that a position of equilibrium has been reached and that it would be unwise to tamper with the Constitution in such a way as to upset the balance.

This is not meant to imply that Salisbury was a disciple of Hume. The similarity arises, rather, from the fact that Salisbury like Hume reflected the same basic tradition, that of an Empirical Conservatism.

EMPIRICISM

Salisbury was a follower of the English 'common sense' school of philosophy. He said that 'a gram of experience is worth a ton of theory'[14] and vigorously opposed what he called the German 'mania for barren metaphysics'.[15] He mocked the metaphysicians for their belief in the value of intuition and 'innate ideas'[16] and his manner of talking about the German philosophers was always highly contemptuous:

59

Locke has never commanded the influence in Germany which he exercised in England and, for a short time, France. His philosophy was too practical, too simple, too easily understood. Moreover it barred the way to many an elevated region of cloudy metaphysical speculations.[17]

He talks of Schopenhauer in a characteristically off-hand manner:

Schopenhauer was a metaphysician of more than usually abstruse leanings, who in many points exalted the office of intuition even more highly than Hegel or Schelling. His views never attracted very general attention . . .[18]

His review of the first volume of Schelling's *Die Weltalter* is more biting:

In form, it is a history of times past, times present, times to come, to each of which divisions a volume was to have been devoted. In substance, it is a philosophical rhapsody, which it requires not only a close study, but also a deep appreciation of German philosophy, rare in Englishmen to appreciate. It has all the fervour of imagination, all the boldness of speculation, as well as the utter absence of intelligible meaning, which distinguish Schelling's other works, which procured for him at one time such boundless popularity in Germany, and which absolutely debar him from an English reputation. What will strike an English reader most is the audacious length to which he pushes his confidence in the supposed faculty of intuition. Man consists, he says, of two principles—one, the logical—mean, ignorant and dark, but doing the menial work of interpreting its greater colleague to the outer world; the other, the intuitive—transcendental and super-mundane, knowing all things that are and that have been without learning them—even up to the history of the creation.[19]

The distrust of intuition and imagination which appears in the above passages is shown throughout his writings. In his view, the use of intuition is merely an illicit substitute for the process of gaining knowledge by a patient study of facts, and imagination is often, in practice, no more than fabrication. In answer to Lord Lindsay's praise of Imagination and condemnation of Reason (i.e. Scepticism) as 'a retrogressive

impulse in the march of human civilisation', Salisbury refers
with approval to the Radical historian Buckle:

> Mr. Buckle proves, with as much learning and elaboration as
> Lord Lindsay himself employs, that all the civilisation of
> modern Europe is due to the spirit of scepticism.[20]

He expands on his criticism of imagination in a series of
reviews of the didactic novels that were being turned
out at the time. 'Why', he complains, 'will not novelists
always remember the great canon of their art, that their
primary object is amusement, and leave instruction and
edification to others?'[21] He adds that 'the crime of binding
up a sermon as a three-volume novel is hardly less than that
of an Eton boy who brings into chapel a novel bound up as a
prayer-book'.[22] The motives that lead to the production of
didactic novels are easy to fathom:

> How to convey the discoveries of the learned to the ignorant
> mass has always been one of the most perplexing problems of
> controversial tactics. To refute an adversary is, at least in one's
> own estimation, a very easy matter. Learning, logic and a good
> cause will go a long way with those who read and think; but
> if a man were as profound as Aristotle himself, it would puzzle
> him to argue into conviction people who will not read his
> arguments. Various have been the devices to which prosely-
> tisers have had resort in order to overcome this difficulty.
> Erasmus undermined the Papacy by squibs. The detestable
> casuistry of the Jesuits fell before Pascal's playful letters . . .
> But it has been reserved for these days . . . to invent the
> religious novel.[23]

His main complaint is that it is possible to use this method to
'prove' almost anything. In a pro-Catholic novel, all the
nuns have sweet voices and gentle thoughts. In the anti-
Catholic novel, all the villains turn out to be Jesuits in
disguise. He is especially indignant about the use of the novel
as a weapon by both the Abolitionists and their opponents in
the United States. He dislikes the sentimentality of Harriet
Beecher Stowe and says that the main argument against
slavery is not to be found in the existence of an occasional
brutal Legree. Similarly, he opposes the novels which were
brought out in 'answer' to *Uncle Tom's Cabin* and which

showed the happy, contented lives of the slaves. Arguments on matters of this seriousness should consist of something more than competitions in story-telling:

> It is a mere question of statistics. Is marriage regarded or disregarded, are slaves taught or not taught, treated well or treated ill on the majority of slave estates?[24]

His early experiences as a reviewer of novels led him to write an article on 'The Evidence of Anecdotes':

> In a limited space which a writer who desires to be read can venture to ask of the patience of his readers, there is no room to argue anything out ... The argument by way of anecdotes is more attractive, more trenchant, and, above all, more summary ... Unfortunately it is singularly inefficient for the purpose of arriving at the truth ... Even in the cases in which the anecdotes are rigorously true, there is a fallacy lurking under them which is fatal to their utility. It is that the facts they relate are generally the exception, and they are almost universally quoted in controversy as if they were the rule ...[25]

And, proceeding to the issue of slavery,

> There are other deeper and truer objections to slavery than casual instances of cruelty to the slave. But it is upon anecdotes of cruelty, upon the delineation of characters like Legree, that a large proportion of the Abolitionist enthusiasm that exists, or did exist in this country has been based.

On other occasions he also expresses distrust of the historical novel and the political novel, in particular the ones penned by Disraeli as a vehicle for his 'mysterious views'.[26] For similar reasons, he also dislikes the vague moralisations of proverbs and of sermons.

Another aspect of Salisbury's empiricism can be seen in his attitude towards the natural sciences. The metaphysicians did not ignore the natural sciences. On the contrary, their researches were just as detailed and minute as those of their empiricist counterparts, and maybe even more so. The difference lay in the fact that their enquiries were all directed towards the confirmation of very general theories at which they had arrived by creative intuition. Salisbury saw no value in such enquiries. By contrast, he was greatly interested in the more specific and more practical experiments which had produced such spectacular benefits for mankind in the nineteenth century. In his article on 'Photography',[27] he shows his excitement in the way in which a series of detailed experiments gradually made photography possible, and removed the difficulties which had made it so complicated.

In a review of Sir Henry Holland's *Essays*,[28] he goes further in his advocacy of patient experimentation, directed towards practical objects. He expresses concern at the tendency of scientists to indulge in 'showy speculation':

> It [science] has made natural laws grander, fewer and more all-embracing, and has increasingly tended to exclude the action of causes whose operation cannot be formulated into a law.

He praises Sir Henry, who was a prominent doctor, for avoiding such general speculation in his Essays.

> The dread of unsafe generalisations, which is so essential an ingredient in the character of a successful physician, is conspicuous in every page of these Essays.

Thus he contrasts useless general theorising with research, altogether more worthwhile, into particular phenomena and into particular problems. Similar opinions are to be found in his Presidential Address to the British Association, which he gave at Oxford in 1894.

His view of the study of history and the social sciences follows in the same sort of pattern. He dislikes the over-romanticised type of historical narrative that is concerned only with kings and queens and battles. The danger of this way of writing history is that the author is prone to let hero-worship dull his judgement and make him unable to take an impartial view. It is largely on the ground that Ranke, unlike so many other historians, was able to resist the temptation of partiality, that the first volumes of his History of England win Salisbury's praise.[29] A further shortcoming of this type of history is that it ignores the condition of the masses—and it is

63

with the fate of the people at large and not just with the fortunes of their rulers that historians should be concerned.

He is also opposed to wide-ranging methods of history which deal not with the acts of individuals but with 'trends' and 'movements'. He explains his opposition at length on several occasions including the review that is quoted below:

> M. Max Wirth has issued the first volume of a new History of Germany from the earliest times. It is written, he announces in his preface, with the object of finding out 'the inner causes of the great events of history', and separating them from the 'outer impulses' to which they have been hitherto attributed. He is an historian of the school who will not believe that great political events can be caused by an individual action, but are always due to some hidden principle, which has been long preparing them. His desire to establish this fatalist view of history gives to his work something of the appearance of a running lecture; and it derives its character still more from his announced desire to make the whole history subservient to the future regeneration of Germany.[30]

The danger of this intuitive history is that one can intuit what one wishes and, if one is painstaking enough, the odds are that it will be possible to find evidence for one's theory. In this way history soon degenerates into propaganda. Salisbury expresses his distrust of the determinist style of history in a review of the fourth volume of Ranke's *History of England*, which covered the period from Cromwell's death to 1674, a period in which he had taken special interest:

> He is a great believer in those personified abstractions which, in the minds of many modern historians, especially among his own countrymen, constitute the chief *dramatis personae* of history—the human beings acting simply as subordinate and involuntary agents. 'Currents' and 'tendencies', 'elements' and 'impulses', 'developments' and 'fermentations', occupy in his pages a position as exaggerated as in the writings of many of his contemporaries.[31]

His dislike of such general, deterministic theory does not, however, indicate a dislike of the socio-economic details which are sometimes used as evidence for 'tendencies'. Quite the opposite. For example, he modifies his criticism of

Wirth's *History of Germany*, which has been quoted above with the observation that

> The work has the great charm of concerning itself more with the actual condition of the people, their laws, customs, and sources of prosperity, than with the details of battles or negotiations.

In another review he comments that 'the annals of commerce are, in truth, much more the business of history than the annals of dynasties'.[32]

Most of these discussions of historiography appear in the monthly surveys of German Literature. One of these articles is of particular interest as it contains two reviews which show side by side, the history of which he approved and the history which he strongly disliked. Of the third volume of von Sybel's *French Revolution*, he says:

> Most historians have tried to convey an idea of the state of things by dint of anecdotes. They have devoted their attention to the representation of individual cases of suffering or guilt. This plan undoubtedly produces a deep impression on the reader's mind, and gives to the history of a stirring period like the French Revolution very much the interest of a novel. But it does not convey anything like the effects produced on the mass of the population. Historians have dwelt so much on the massacres of Paris and Nantes, of Arras and Lyon, that they are apt to leave a half-conscious impression that the miseries caused by the Revolution were confined to such terrible instances. Von Sybel goes to work less in the spirit of the dramatist, and more in the spirit of the Registrar-General. So far as the records of an era of confusion enable him to do so, he tries to give a numerical expression to the misery which anarchy, famine and the universal stoppage of industry . . . had brought.

This favourable review contrasts with the attack on Dr. Fridegar Mone's *Greek History* which, according to the irate reviewer, 'reads more like the performance of some old alchemist'.

> We invite him [the reader] to exercise his powers on the following paragraph. It is part of the chapter on the Laws of the inner Socialistic in the Finance-State:

65

That rank, or that class of Society, or the Individual, which performs a special labour, is rewarded by the totality of the Society. The reward is honour and authority—that is to say, nobility. According to this maxim *virtus nobilitat*, one must seek to answer the questions: I. What was the social labour in the three forms of society among the Greeks? What was the nature of their reward? I will try to make these three maxims evident by an example. Supposing that in the year 490 War-Service (m) was the social labour of Attic society, and supposing the historical nobility (e) were the class who before this date had exclusively performed this labour, then $\frac{m}{e}$ would be the formula for the society; but when in 490 the Burgher-class (p) took part in the social labour, then $\frac{m}{e \quad p}$ would be the formula for the society . . .

This application of Algebra to politics assumes the dignity of a new science. It is much to be hoped that it will be developed. It will be a golden age of repose for journalists when a Ministerial statement can be expressed in a formula, and a debate published in the form of an equation.[33]

The main objection to this last book is yet again the objection against the attempt to take a short cut to knowledge, whereas the former book is praised for the way it builds up knowledge piece by piece from basic facts.

Salisbury's keenness on statistical enquiry is specially pronounced when he deals with economic matters. He is not interested in the theoretical arguments about Free Trade but cares only about its effects on the British economy. In his early speeches at the Oxford Union and at Stamford and in a review of the economic essays published by Tooke and Newmarch in 1857[34] he examines the unemployment figures for the periods before and after the repeal of the Corn Laws, the yearly prices and the imports of Corn. The statistics confirm his view that Free Trade is 'no more than a financial detail'. In the review of Tooke and Newmarch he also regrets the deficiencies in British agricultural statistics. In the article in *Bentley's* on 'The Coming Political Campaign'[35] and in the *Quarterly* article on 'The Income Tax and

its Rivals',[36] he performs a characteristically thorough
analysis of indirect taxation. His method of challenging
Bright's statement that these taxes fell unfairly on the poor is
to go through them in detail, often item by item, and in this
way to make computations of the amounts that people with
low incomes had to pay. In a discussion of an anthology of
essays by Russian writers on political and economic questions, he singles out for praise a study of the Russian system
of fairs:

> Its value is that it deals in statistics and details, and does not
> show that fatal attachment to first principles which dis-
> tinguishes so many of the others.[37]

Several of the long articles, especially those which deal
with Reform, contain detailed statistical analyses of Reform
proposals.[38] In other articles he complains about the lack of
accurate figures, without which, he claims, all Reform Bills
must necessarily be based on conjecture.[39] He eagerly welcomes the use of tinted maps—a novelty at the time—as a
method of condensing statistical material and making it
more easily digestible.[40] He complains at the shortage of
statistics about the condition of the urban poor,[41] and calls
for statistical handbooks on prisons.[42] Repeatedly, he regrets
the absence of statistics that a detailed census of the country
would yield.[43] He also comments on the non-existence of an
English equivalent of the 'Historical Kalender' of political
events which was published each year in Germany.[44]

RELIGION

It is normal to assume that scientific reasoning and religion
do not go together. Thus, the realisation that Salisbury was
deeply religious and that faith was at the very basis of his life
must cast doubt on what has been argued above. An examination of the irrational nature of his belief will intensify these
doubts. Lady Gwendolen Cecil, in the chapter on 'Religion'
in the first volume of her biography, describes a discussion in
which Salisbury said:

> God is all-powerful, and God is all-loving—and the world is
> what it is! How are you going to explain *that*?[45]

The statement was apparently typical and leads Lady Gwendolen to comment:

> It would probably be impossible—it would certainly be beside
> the point—to attempt an analysis in logical form of his accep-
> tance of the Christian revelation. It rested upon a spiritual
> vision which had an existence altogether apart from his
> intellectual processes and which was more compelling of con-
> viction than any evidence which they could produce.[46]

Algernon Cecil, reviewing this passage concludes that 'His
religious opinions approximated, then, in the last analysis to
something near akin to personal mysticism.'[47] A review of the
first volume of Lady Gwendolen's biography which was
published in *The Quarterly Review* is of the same opinion.[48]

But Algernon Cecil is mistaken and is misinterpreting
Lady Gwendolen's views. The first source of his error derives
from her extensive quotations from early letters and a notebook which he wrote as a young man. She draws on these
largely because they give the only solid indications of his
religious views that were known to her: she says that 'neither
in his letters nor in his conversations—even when either were
most intimate—did he indulge in spiritual confidences'.[49]
And, of course, she was not aware of *The Saturday Review*
articles of which he was the author at the time she was
writing that volume. These letters and the notebook were
written at the period when the influence of the Oxford
Movement on him was at its greatest. They show great concern for the details of the sacraments and other such tech-
nicalities. All this gives a surface impression of ritualism which
probably misinterprets his early views and which is quite
absent from the writings on religion which he composed for
the reviews a few years later.

The more general source of error is a general misunderstanding of the words 'irrational' and 'mystical'. In a
celebrated passage in the third book of his *Treatise*, Hume
asserts that normative statements cannot be derived logically
from factual ones; it is impossible to deduce what ought to be

the case from what is the case; to attempt to do this is to commit the 'naturalistic fallacy'. Similarly, it might be said that religious statements also cannot be proved or disproved by factual ones. To say that religion is irrational is thus merely to say that rationality has no application to it: it does not mean that it is positively the opposite of rational. If so, agnosticism in the most precise sense of the word can lead either to the acceptance or the rejection of religious faith; belief and un-belief are equally consistent with rationality, and irrationality consists only in trying either to prove or disprove religion by way of argument from the facts of nature.

When the word 'mystic' is used, it is normally not applied to those—like Salisbury—who refuse to derive belief from fact, but to those who use facts in some way to support a belief or resolution. For example, the Romans used entrails and flights of birds as 'omens' before taking a decision about fighting a battle. In *War and Peace* Bezuhov assigns a numerical value to the letters of Napoleon's name and draws conclusions from the product. In both cases the mysticism consists in the employment of certain natural facts to support conclusions which do not follow from them in the normal way of evidence.

It was precisely this use of natural phenomena in the 'proof' or 'disproof' of belief that Salisbury resolutely opposed. It would thus be quite the opposite of the truth to regard him as any more of a mystic than David Hume. As Lady Gwendolen herself says:

This acquiescence in incomprehension might be compared to the attitude of the pure agnostic.[50]

In a passage that has already been quoted, Rossiter says that 'History is the creator of all the Conservative holds dear, and in the logic of its glacial progress he detects the hand of God.' Now this was what Salisbury, in contrast to many other Conservatives, refused to do. In the notes quoted by Lady Gwendolen there appears the following passage:

> I repeat that I consider this method of arguing, of discerning divine facts from human analogies—of guessing God's ways by what we know of man's ways—is utterly unsound and deceptive.[51]

Later, he wrote a piece entitled 'Judgement-Mongers'[52] in which he ridiculed a clergyman who had pronounced that the cattle plague of 1865 was a divine punishment for horse-racing—he thinks that it is odious to look at events and to see the judgements of God in them. The same theme occurs in a middle called 'An Overruling Providence'[53] in which the conclusion is reached that it is impossible for man to detect the 'meaning' of events or God's 'intentions'. In a review of a book on the Mormons he says that the popularity of Mormonism 'is an instructive recital, as showing how little external evidence has in most cases to do with human faith'.[54]

The period during which Salisbury was writing in the reviews was the time when the whole evolutionary controversy was at its height following the publication of *The Origin of Species* and the position he adopted provides a good illustration of his opinions on the comparative places of religion and natural science. Disraeli's reaction was to dismiss Darwin's theory out of hand:

> What is the question now placed before society with a glib assurance the most astounding? The question is this—Is man an ape or an angel? My Lord, I am on the side of the angels . . .[55]

Salisbury's views were very different. His main message was twofold: that it was premature, on purely scientific grounds, to pass judgement on Darwin's theory, and, that the matter was, in any case, of no religious importance. He complains that people 'have chosen to tie up with the essential truths of Christianity a great many irrelevant opinions concerning the physical history of the earth and of its inhabitants, which, even in the ages when there was a passion for making new dogmas, no Council ever ventured to propound as articles of faith'.[56] He disagrees equally with those who use Darwin as a weapon with which to attack religion and those who hold to the 'dogma of verbal inspiration'[57] of the Bible and thus seek to defend the traditional faith on naturalistic grounds. The Bishop of Natal, Colenso, argued that the dating of the Creation in Genesis was inaccurate. Salisbury thought his pronouncements both irrelevant and pedantic, but he fiercely condemned the Bench of Bishops for the heresy hunt which they carried out against him:

> Does anybody believe that the well-ascertained conclusions of geology are less secure than they were before, because the Bishop of Manchester has declared *ex cathedra* that every line and word of the Pentateuch to whatever subject it may apply, has a supernatural guarantee for its scientific accuracy?[58]

He calls this an 'Episcopal puerility'.

In one of the reviews of German Literature he says of an author:

> He is father of that school of scientific men who go to the scriptures for their natural science, and who have been the pest of science in every age . . .[59]

Professor Weisse's *Theory of Creation* occasions the reaction that:

> To Englishmen, accustomed to intellectual aims of a very different kind, it seems incredible that a powerful thinker should seriously set himself down in the solitude of his study, by the help of his internal consciousness alone, to dissect the nature of the Deity, to draw an account of the progress of creation, and, in doing so, to contradict chemistry on *a priori* grounds.[60]

In another passage he turns his attack on to the showy speculation of scientific men who wish to use their theories to support their atheism:

> As Sir Henry Holland justly remarks, a succession of creations, however numerous, is less difficult of conception than a single creation which should contain in germ such a marvellous series of transmutations.[61]

The point throughout is that science and religion are not to be confused, and that the controversy about evolution has, at base, nothing to do with questions of creed or dogma. This position, obvious and inoffensive as it seems in our own age, was an advanced position for a religious man to hold in the 1850s and 1860s.

In general, the distinction between his personal religious beliefs and his non-religious style of argumentation about all political and social matters is so distinct that one could go through all these writings without being aware of the strength of his personal faith. Even when he deals with Church matters he argues on secular and prudential lines and refuses to talk the language of the faithful. At that time dissent on religious questions and radicalism on political ones went hand in hand, and it was fear that concessions to the Dissenters would prove to be the thin end of the Reform wedge that made him support the Establishment so dourly.

The reason why Lady Gwendolen emphasises Salisbury's religion is not so that it may help to illustrate the logic of his views or his arguments: it is that it may help the reader to understand his motives in putting them forward. 'How was it that he was so little anxious to grasp power?' 'Why did he hold it so firmly and easily when it came his way?' These are the kind of questions that a consideration of his religion will help to answer.

Indeed, Salisbury's faith led him to an unusual degree towards rationality rather than away from it. The faculties of judgement and reason in most men are clouded by a self-interest. Faith led Salisbury towards the wish to serve self-lessly. His general purposes having been thus formed by his religion, the means were left to be worked out by reason and experience.

It is not the aim of this chapter to claim that Salisbury always succeeded in his aim of letting facts lead to theories rather than letting theories lead to a biased view of the facts. Often he came to the facts with strong prejudices and was probably guilty of the *a priori* kind of fault which he condemned in others. At the same time, it must be recognised that his thought was empiricist in style throughout and gave no place to the metaphysical or to the mystic.

CHAPTER IV

Foundations of Politics

UTILITARIANISM

THERE is a close connection between empiricism in epistemology and utilitarianism in ethics and in politics. 'The English Utilitarians' and 'The English Empiricists' are phrases that refer to virtually the same class of people, and this is not coincidental. The reason is that empiricism and utilitarianism share a common atomistic style of thought. The essence of empiricism is that it interprets the meaning of complex words as consisting of more simple ones which represent the experiences of our senses. Words such as 'Constitution', 'State' and 'Liberty' stand for complex ideas whose meaning cannot be ascertained otherwise than by being reduced to their constituent parts. In the same way, the utilitarian refuses to indulge in vague talk about 'rights', 'essences', etc., but insists on translating all political questions—in theory, at least—into questions about the happiness of individual human beings. Having decided that the *summum bonum* is composed of the product of the benefits accruing to individuals, he must go ahead and examine these benefits in detail.

Consider, for example, the question of liberty. The utilitarian tries to give a precise meaning to the concept; what Sir Isaiah Berlin calls the 'negative' notion of freedom:

> I am normally said to be free to the degree to which no human being interferes with my activity. Political liberty in this sense is simply the area within which a man can do what he wants.[1]

73

If asked whether a man was free or not, the reaction of the 'classical English political philosophers' who held this concept would have been to ask 'what is the man able to do and what is he not able to do? Are his movements restricted? Can he say what he wishes? Can he meet with whom he wishes? Is he allowed to use his property as he wishes?' etc., etc. Only after answers had been given to such questions would they give a reply and decide the degree to which he was free.

Contrasted to this is the 'positive' concept, held by the 'rationalist metaphysicians'. Freedom is no longer simply being able to do what one wants; it is 'self-realisation' or obedience to one's 'real self' and to one's real desires which are often in conflict with one's apparent wishes. This concept leads in the hands of Hegel, for example, to the view that the more a man is subject to law the more his 'real self' is free. The point to note for our purposes is that in the transition from 'freedom' to 'real freedom' the precise descriptive meaning given to the concept by the holders of the 'negative' notion is lost. Once freedom is understood in terms of 'self-realisation' or 'national self-realisation' it is no longer possible to have any distinct procedures for deciding whether a nation or an individual is free or not.

It is no surprise, then, that Salisbury, who had no sympathy with 'personified abstractions' or 'corporate entities'[2] rejected metaphysical generalisation in favour of the method of detail. He refused to see in politics the pursuit of high ideals, lofty and remote from the actual needs of the population. The task of the politician was to establish as precisely as possible what social needs remained unfulfilled and to follow the line of action that was most likely to bring a remedy, or a partial remedy.

In politics at least, the old antithesis of principle and expediency is absolutely forgotten: expediency is the only principle to which sincere allegiance is paid. It is true that men often appeal to what they call principles, because it is a traditional habit to do so, and it saves the necessity of thinking; and, moreover, the word, from its frequent use in reference to religion, has a kind of religious flavour about it, and seems to give a dim, shadowy claim to some superhuman sanction. But no one acts on them, or reasons from them . . . The only principle upon which, in the present day, any thinking politician really acts is 'the greatest happiness of the greatest number' . . .[3]

The 'greatest happiness' theme recurs with frequency and he occasionally uses the actual phrase 'the greatest happiness of the greatest number'. At times, he does so tongue in cheek to attack the Radicals on their own ground, as in an article on the Civil War in America in which he condemns the democratic system of government in the United States by denying that it brings 'the greatest happiness to the greatest number'.[4] But he genuinely believed that it was the well-being of the mass of society that formed the rightful object of concern and of activity. In his favourable review of von Sybel's *French Revolution* that was quoted on page 65 the author is praised mainly for his concern with the fate of 'the mass of the population'[5] and not just with princes, battles and isolated events of dramatic interest.

Ultimately Salisbury seeks the justification of action in the Benthamite principle. He also explains the way in which man's moral notions actually develop by reference to a utilitarianism resembling that of Hume. His views of ethics are expanded in two *Saturday Review* articles, the second of which is one of his most notable productions. In a middle entitled 'White Lies', he extols the wisdom of 'disbelieving firmly in all absolute rules'.

> The average human mind yearns for absolute rules in ethics just as it likes broad principles in politics. It is so much pleasanter to avoid the trouble of thought or enquiry by setting up a principle . . . Sharp lines between right and wrong are convenient fictions . . . but they become very demoralising when people try to inculcate a belief in their reality. *Natura non amat saltus* is as true in morals as in physics, and, in practice, the delicacy of the gradations by which right and wrong fade into each other are soon brought home to anyone who scrupulously watches his own conduct.[6]

But although there are in reality no absolute rules, men commonly believe that the ethical precepts they follow are 'good in themselves'. Why? Salisbury gives his own

explanation in an essay written on the occasion of the assassination of Lincoln and called 'Moral Entrenchments'.[7] He
asks why it is that assassination is considered a worse crime
than killing someone in war and explains:

> Opinions upon moral questions are more often the expression
> of strongly felt expediency than of careful ethical reasoning;
> and the opinions so formed by one generation become the
> conscientious convictions or the sacred instincts of the next ...
> Other instances are not wanting of society protecting its most
> important interests by these moral entrenchments. The
> process is, of course, not intentional. It arises necessarily from
> the two facts, that a man has always a strong objection on
> moral grounds to any practice which affects him injuriously,
> and that his children, or other young people who are under
> his influence, grow up attaching the sacredness of a moral
> precept to the opinions so expressed by him, especially if those
> opinions suit their interests as well.

He concludes:

> The rules of conduct, and the hue of moral sentiment which
> will produce happiness and improvement upon the largest
> scale, changes as ages and conditions change. Each society
> must judge of the means best calculated in its own case to
> attain this end. The operation upon public opinion of the selfish
> impulses of individuals may be an ignoble method of giving
> expression to this judgement; but no other would be equally
> effectual, because no other would command an equally general
> assent.

Paradoxically, he turns the method of detail which was used
from the end of the eighteenth century by the Philosophical
Radicals against the Radicals of his own day, accusing them
of clinging to inflexible principles at the expense of a direct
consideration of the utility of their actions. In an article on
the Poor Law, he makes this comment on a scheme for
workhouses:

> It must be recorded to the author's honour, as a remarkable
> fact in this age of doctrinaires, that, much as he loved his
> theory, he loved his fellow creatures more.[8]

In 'The Reform Bill', a contribution to *The Quarterly*

Review of 1866, he complains that Bright and Gladstone have not inquired into the number of working men who are already enfranchised, or the number and class of the extra voters who would be given the franchise by the proposed Reform Bill. He accuses them of wanting to push the Bill through on purely doctrinaire grounds:

> Mr. Gladstone assumes they [the extra voters] will belong to the middle-class. But how he arrived at the satisfactory assurance he does not tell us . . . he may have evolved it from his inner consciousness, as Schelling used to evolve what he called his facts in chemistry and geology. [9]

In an earlier article on 'Theories of Parliamentary Reform' he condemns the 'Symmetrical Reformers', that is, those who support the principle of 'one man, one vote' because of its mathematical simplicity.

> They are children of Abbé Siéyès and the *doctrinaires*: their mania is to introduce the accuracy of a machine and the proportions of a geometrical figure into the institutions which are to secure the happiness and carry out the wishes of capricious, inconsistent, illogical mankind. [10]

Salisbury does not dislike the attempted accuracy and simplicity of doctrine in itself, but he realises that the striving after simplist and theoretically elegant solutions can easily result in a forgetfulness of specific problems and to answers that do not meet social needs. This often leads him to criticise Radical politics for being no more than theories: 'Competitive Examination' has an attractive ring about it as a paper scheme but does not, in fact, select the best civil servants.[11] Tariff schedules are admittedly complex, but simplification for its own sake is purposeless and is harmful in its effects.[12] The intention of Lowe's 'Revised Code' is to introduce administrative simplicity—a useless aim and one which will have serious results on the whole school system.[13] And so on.

While he frequently attacks political opponents for their 'doctrinaire' attitudes, he is equally willing to condemn their lack of principle. If a 'doctrinaire' is merely a person who sticks to set principles, Salisbury is clearly trying to have it

77

both ways: when his opponents are consistent, he accuses them of being 'doctrinaire', when they are inconsistent, he calls them 'unprincipled'. The fact that Salisbury was an active politician and thus inevitably prone to propaganda is certainly a partial explanation of this variety of usage of 'doctrinaire' and 'unprincipled'. But it is not a complete explanation and it is worth examining his understanding of political principles in greater detail. The variety of Salisbury's usage is an indication of the difficulty that faces all pragmatists and utilitarians when they deal with 'principles'. The basic difficulty is this: how can a pragmatist or a utilitarian (i.e. a person who believes that each activity is justified by its effects on social welfare) talk about general principles of action? In Salisbury's writings there seem to be two fairly distinct uses of words and expressions such as 'principle', 'political principle', and 'unprincipled'.

At times it is used to evaluate the motives for which an action is performed, rather than to describe the action itself. This meaning is expounded in an article on 'Political Consistency'. He points out that all the major politicians of the time 'have frequently changed their minds upon the most important issues of the day'. But he does not condemn them all for changing their opinions, for he says that there are sometimes legitimate reasons for doing so. The only ones he attacks are the 'weathercock politicians' who cynically adopt views which are not their own in order to curry favour with the electorate:

> The consistency which is admirable is not that which stubbornly resists argument, but that which is impregnable to fear or ambition.[14]

Accordingly, when he admires Pitt and despises the 'unprincipled' Disraeli,[15] his reason is not that Pitt's policies are more consistent than those of Disraeli, it is merely that he thinks that Pitt's motives are altruistic whereas those of Disraeli are not. In the serpentine[16] career of Disraeli, he can see only the 'oriental cunning'[17] of an 'artless dodger',[18] a 'vulture'[19] whose actions can be explained only by 'unscrupulous ambition'.[20] His judgement of Pitt is the opposite:

[He] was far too practical a politician to be given to abstract theories, universal doctrines, watchwords, or shibboleths of any kind . . . When he thought reform wholesome, he proposed it: when he ceased to think it wholesome, he ceased to propose it. . . .

[He showed] practical good sense and contempt for the reproach of anomaly . . . He always preferred to sacrifice any amount of theory rather than make for his proposals a single needless enemy.[21]

Pitt's motive was 'altruism',[22] and thus he was, in Salisbury's usage of the term, 'principled'.

The word is also used in a descriptive way. In this sense, the meaning is akin to that of consistent, but can be explained more exactly by the use of an analogy from economics. The entrepreneur is bound only by considerations of interest and it is in his short term interest to vary the prices of his goods constantly in accordance with short term fluctuations in costs and in demand. However, there are tactical reasons (ease of administration, the desirability of building up a regular clientele, lack of knowledge about the market, the wish to avoid cut-throat competition with competitors, etc.) for fixing on a constant price for at least a medium length of time. It would be foolish for the entrepreneur to commit himself for too long to any given price, for radical changes in conditions might make this very unprofitable; but there are also the factors, such as those that have been mentioned, which make it unwise for him to change his prices too often.

In politics, according to Salisbury, it is the same. Although his attitude towards politics is pragmatic, he realises that the policy of a person or of a party must be held together by some coherent line of thought if it is to be effective. He is of the view that consistency has a utility of its own. At the same time, just as occasional price changes are necessary for the entrepreneur, so occasional deviations from policy and changes in theory are necessary for the politician: time brings basic changes in circumstance and thus demands changes in theory, and, besides, there will at all times be specific cases which will demand a relaxation of normal standards.

In this way, Salisbury's pragmatism brings him to a

79

'medium' concept of principles; it leads him to regard them as rules which should be obeyed most of the time, but not all the time. He thus criticises both those whose policies show very frequent change, and also those who are inflexible. He argues, for example, that the opportunistic policy of the Conservatives on the question of Reform is not only immoral and in bad faith (i.e. motivated solely by the wish for office), but is also inexpedient.[23] He therefore condemns them on the grounds of volatility. On the other hand, he condemns Gladstone's budget of 1860[24] and Lowe's Revised Code of 1862[25] on the opposite ground. Gladstone's love of mathematical symmetry leads, he says, to a doctrinaire view of taxation, namely

> that it exists principally for the purpose of enabling a Customs officer or an Exciseman to draw up a simple-looking account.[26]

Salisbury's views are summed up in two general quotations: on the one hand a passage in which he opposes undue volatility:

> It is a necessary result of political discussion as carried on in this country that the individual has too large a portion of our thoughts and the principle too little; and controversy is apt to be made up, not so much of political argument, as of a series of political biographies.[27]

On the other hand, a warning that principles cannot remain unchanged for too long:

> No principle cherished by the Whigs of any one generation can be named, which the Whigs of some other generation have not repudiated. Nor is this change of watchwords peculiar to the Whigs. The historical continuity of parties has a political as well as a sentimental value; but it is an absolute delusion if it is applied to measure the tendencies of another statesman in another age. It will only mislead if it is used to give a character of permanence to that which is in its nature fleeting. The axioms of the last age are the fallacies of the present; the principles which save one generation may be the ruin of the next. There is nothing abiding in political science but the necessity of truth, purity and justice. The evils by which the body politics are threatened are in a state of constant change, and with them the remedies by which those evils must be

cured. Such changes operate very rapidly in these days. The concessions that were salutary yesterday may be doubtful today, and infatuated weaknesses tomorrow.[28]

Salisbury's diverse and seemingly contradictory statements about principles can be unravelled in this way: to be 'unprincipled' means either to be self-seeking or to be a victim of indecision. To be 'principled' is to follow a consistent line of policy, which is desirable if that consistency is not adhered to in an excessively dogmatic manner.

His distrust of inflexible ideals and his dislike of abstractions leads Salisbury, in company with Bentham, Hume and other thinkers of the same type, to reject arguments in terms of 'rights': both the 'Divine Rights' normally claimed by opponents to change and the right, such as the right to vote, claimed by Progressives. As the 1850s came to an end, the growing disturbances in the United States brought a renewal in England of discussion about slavery. He violently condemns it on economic and humanitarian grounds, but he refuses to say that the slave ought to have freedom by right.

> Few people are accustomed to denounce slavery on the ground of the inalienable rights of man . . . it is because the degradation and suffering of the negro seems to be inseparable from its working, that so many earnest men have refused to listen to any compromise short of abolition.[29]

His attitude to the principle of national self-government is the same. He refuses to consider the question in terms of basic rights.[30] Similarly, he does not see Reform as a question of 'free-born Britons' being given their 'inalienable rights'[31] and explicitly rejects the claim that all men have a right to equality. He regards it as 'a folly and chimera'. It is a folly because talk of 'rights' is in itself artificial; it is a chimera because it assumes an unrealistic view of the human condition. A fuller discussion of the matter will be found in the section dealing with human nature, which follows.

His refusal to acknowledge the right of national independence and the individual rights of voting and of freedom from slavery leads him, as the other side of the same coin, to the view that no man has any inalienable, God-given privileges

81

over any other man and that no nation has any rights over any other.

Racial theories were popular in the nineteenth century especially among the German metaphysicians. An element of racialism also ran through the work of some British writers—notable among them being Disraeli, whose complex Anglo-Saxon-Judaeo-Christian theories are developed in *Coningsby*, *Tancred* and *Alroy*. In Disraeli's thought there is also the feeling that some men are by birth better than others and form an aristocracy. In *Sybil*, for example, the heroine is a girl of low family and the villains are aristocrats. But it turns out that the 'aristocrats' are in fact impostors, whereas Sybil's noble behaviour is explained by the revelation that she really comes from an ancient line which was unjustly deposed at the time of the Reformation. Salisbury's thought stands out in contrast against this romanticism. He is equally cynical about Disraeli's pro-semitic racialism and the anti-semitic variety that was appearing in Germany. This paragraph comes from one of the reviews of German Literature:

> *Judaism among Strangers* is a curious book. Its reasoning is very similar to that which may be found in *Coningsby* or *Tancred*, only that it is written from exactly the opposite point of view. It is a full acknowledgement of the supremacy to which the Children of Israel are gradually attaining, only in a tone not of national complaisance, but of Gentile terror.[32]

Anti-semitism was still in its infancy at this time and, though Salisbury's wide reading of Continental literature made him fully conscious of its growing force, it remained fairly remote. His visit to New Zealand in 1852 had brought him into contact and close friendship with Maoris and he remained a champion of their cause. In *The Saturday Review* he repeatedly expresses his disgust at the New Zealand colonists in the strongest terms for their 'damned nigger'[33] attitude towards the Maoris:

> Seizing a coloured man's land and giving it to a white man is an operation now generally known as the progress of colonisation.[34]

82

On another occasion (this is one of his favourite hobby-horses) he gives the warning that:

> They [the settlers] are clamouring now—we quote from an influential newspaper—for a general and systematic 'opening of the waste lands to colonisation'. As far as right goes, there are no waste lands, and they might as well talk about 'opening' the Duke of Bedford's park to colonisation'.[35]

He refuses to admit to any form of 'master race' theory and insists that the natives should not be treated in any sub-human fashion:

> There is no sounder test for a high and true civilisation than its dealings with a race of helpless savages. Its office is to rub off prejudices, and there is no prejudice so catlike in its vitality as the prejudice of race . . . and the weakness of savages presents a temptation to rapacity which even liberal politicians and deeply religious men have not always been able to withstand.[36]

At home, also, he opposes the idea that some castes of men are inherently more worthy than others. Although he is a staunch defender of the House of Lords, he does not defend it on grounds of 'natural aristocracy' or 'natural rights'. In a contribution to *Bentley's Quarterly Review*, he approves of the elevation of commercial men to the peerage.

> It is only indeed as representing the wealth of the country that its [the House of Lords'] hereditary character can be in any degree justified.[37]

In a *Saturday Review* article on 'The House of Lords', he supports the hereditary principle, not for its own sake, but 'as a rough security for the predominance of the wealthier and more educated classes'.[38] He does not regard peers as more than human beings, although they may be better educated and richer than most. At the other end of the social scale, he refuses to regard workers or paupers as anything less than human. The following quotation comes from an article on 'Miss Rye's Emigrants' in which he favours emigration as a way of easing the unemployment problem in the cotton industry which was caused by the Civil War in America. He complains—and could this piece have been penned by Marx or Engels?—that, although two thousand of the unemployed girls had applied to the Poor Law Guardians for assisted passages, these had been refused:

> They [the Guardians] are afraid—such is Miss Rye's account of their motives—that some of their best mill hands may leave them . . . They cannot get rid of the notion that these factory girls are 'hands', not human beings. They are merely a portion of the machinery by which cotton fortunes are made. As such they are to be preserved from actual starvation; but they are with equal care to be held back from any improvement in their condition which shall render them unavailable for the future manufacture of calico. The guardians are, probably, strong opponents of slavery; but it is only the slavery which is imposed by direct enactment. The force of circumstances, stronger than law, binds these unhappy girls to the soil on which they live, and the employment to which they have been brought up; and the guardians decline the exercise of their legal powers, rather than help to free them from that practical serfdom. The mill-owners, it seems, will not bate one jot of the calculation by which their human machines are to yield them the largest possible profit for the smallest possible outlay. As they closed their mills that they may be freer to speculate in the raw material, instead of working it up—as they withhold subscriptions, in order to force a grant from the exchequer— so they resist emigration, lest they should have to pay for the mitigation of present distress by some slight deduction from their future profits.[39]

Although he did not believe in caste differences, he did find it difficult at times to dismiss class prejudices from his mind. There is an interesting middle on 'Flogging at Public Schools' in which he argues against the practice of caning the pupils:

> If it is inflicted, as it often will be, on a sensitive boy, it will infallibly make him reckless. He will not care what disgrace he incurs when he has been made to pass through such a disgrace as that.[40]

Nevertheless he considers flogging to be a necessary punishment in the Army and Navy because the men are 'coarse and brutal' and 'can be tamed by no gentler measures'. One gets the feeling that he could not completely convince himself that the public schoolboy and the naval rating of the same age were not in some way different creatures, but this feeling probably corresponded to the realities of the Victorian age. Even Mill, writing at the same period, was unable to recommend complete manhood suffrage in the realisation that some men were just not ready to have the vote. The most salient feature of Salisbury's views on this question was not the occasional feeling that there were basic differences between men, but the general conviction that all men were human, no more and no less.

The evidence of his writings is confirmed by Lady Gwendolen, who distinguishes his opinions sharply from those of the pre-Reform or eighteenth-century Tory: 'He had no respect whatever for the privileges of birth whether as shown in the distinctions of rank or in the right to exercise power independently of the interests of the community at large. He believed, it is true, that the authority enjoyed by the governing classes in the past had promoted those interests and that these would be best served in the future by its continued maintenance; but only as long as these classes continued to display the qualities of energy, industry and self-sacrifice which the profession of government demands.'[41]

Consideration of Salisbury's utilitarianism can be completed by an examination of his view of liberty. He was a subscriber to the 'negative' concept. In one of his philippics against the Radicals, he asks 'What does freedom mean to these men [Cobden and Bright]?'

> We used to think that freedom meant being free: but that definition is evidently very wide of the mark . . . These men who preach freedom to us have no real desire for it in its literal sense. The protection of each individual human being from more interference than is indispensably necessary to protect the freedom of his neighbours is what we used to understand as the meaning of freedom.[42]

He complains that the Radicals believe in the divine right of majority tyranny and says:

> The fact that you possess the thirty-millionth part of a right to elect your own ruler does not give him any right to oppress you, or afford you much consolation when he does so.[43]

85

In a late *Saturday Review*, he deals with the same subject when he condemns the intolerant Sabbatarianism found in Boston, Massachusetts, and also in Glasgow:

> The melancholy feature about these absurdities is that both at Glasgow and at Boston the people who commit them imagine themselves to be the friends of religious liberty . . . If religious liberty only means the liberty to practise the religion which in the eye of the lawgiver is divine, there is no part of the world, not even Madagascar and Japan, which has not been immemorially in the enjoyment of that inestimable blessing . . . A great disadvantage of the haste and turmoil in the midst of which all political thinking is conducted in our day, is that even reflecting men scarcely ever stop to define to their own minds the meaning of their cries. Thus the phase 'religious liberty' . . . is employed to express anything and everything except its simple meaning of letting people do as they like in matters of religion.[44]

His view, then, is the classical empiricist one. It does not commit him to support a policy of freedom in all cases, but it does commit him to acknowledging any restrictions of freedom without dressing them up as accretions of 'real' freedom.

To sum up: with Salisbury, as with other thinkers of the same type, empiricism is connected with utilitarianism. This utilitarianism can be seen in his regard for the equal moral worth of all human beings, in his pragmatism, his rejection of 'rights' and in his negative concept of liberty.

HUMAN NATURE

Some utilitarians are conservative, others are progressive: where does the difference between them lie? In the view of Berlin,

> Philosophers with an optimistic view of human nature, and a belief in the possibility of harmonising human interests, such as Locke or Adam Smith and, in some moods, Mill, believed that social harmony and progress were compatible with reserving a large area for private life over which neither the state nor any other authority must be allowed to trespass. Hobbes, and those who agreed with him, especially conservative or reac-

tionary thinkers, argued that if men were to be prevented from destroying one another, and making social life a jungle or a wilderness, greater safeguards must be instituted to keep them in their places, and wished correspondingly to increase the area of centralised control and decrease that of the individual.[45]

We can extend Berlin's analysis of liberty and say that it is in their views of human nature that Conservatives like Salisbury differ from progressive utilitarians.

Hobbes is a paramount example of an empiricist whose pessimistic estimate of human nature leads to an authoritarian, conservative view of government. According to Hobbes, if men were controlled by no external force, they would be led by their instinctive wishes for competition, security and glory to fight with each other. This unrestrained condition, which he calls a State of Nature, would make life nasty, brutish and short. Most political shortcomings in the life of a country can thus be excused with the explanation that, people being what they are, troubles are only to be expected in the natural order of things, and that any attempt at change might easily produce a worse state of affairs. Furthermore, there is always the danger that the upheaval accompanying any basic changes might allow man's uncontrolled instincts to come again to bring chaos and destruction.

The view of a revolutionary thinker (like Marx for instance, or maybe Rousseau) is likely to be the opposite. In order to support his revolutionary conclusions, he must argue that evil in society is external to man himself and is caused by defective social institutions; and from this follows the conclusion that the destruction of those artificial institutions will allow men's natural goodness to come to the fore and a natural, happy way of life to be regained.

Human beings are, after all, the raw materials out of which societies are formed, and no social engineer can proceed without forming some estimate of what those materials are like. Thus, the questions about human nature and the 'State of Nature', although they seem at times to be pedantic and complex, are basic to political thought.

Salisbury's views of human nature bear a striking resemblance to those of Hobbes. Unlike Hobbes, he was writing during a time of peace and great prosperity, but nevertheless he was full of fears for the future. The Victorian Age has often been called the 'Age of Improvement' and the idea of Progress (a fixed concept with a capital 'p') was widespread. But Salisbury was highly cynical. Lady Gwendolen Cecil recalls the 'peculiar horror' with which he regarded the word 'optimism'. To him it meant a propensity for seeing things as you wish to see them instead of as they are. There was no fault which he held to be more common in public life or which he condemned more repeatedly or more unsparingly.[46]

In a *Quarterly Review* article on America called 'Democracy on its Trial', he gives an account of the development of democratic theory, mentioning and quoting, among others, Sidney, Locke, Milton, Sismondi, Sydney Smith and Tocqueville:

> One of the most conspicuous *shibboleths* by which this new school was distinguished, was their peculiar use of the word 'Progress'. They asserted, with the air of men who have made a great discovery, that the age was an age of progress, and that our policy ought to be progressive.[47]

Salisbury calls this a truism, but:

> Whether that progress is to be looked on as progress towards good or towards evil, will depend very much on each man's notion of the *summum bonum*.[47]

These theories of progress are 'intoxicating' and 'well intentioned' and dangerous:

> In itself there are few theories more charming than the natural perfectibility and perfection of the human race. It commends itself so heartily to sanguine youth, to think that evil is no necessity in the world, but that it is caused, or largely enhanced, by the corrupt imbecility of a handful of privileged families.[48]

In a later contribution to the *Quarterly* (dealing again with the Civil War in America), he repeats the warning against 'delusive optimism'[49] and he develops his pessimistic opinions in a *Saturday Review* middle written at the same time:

> Many changes have passed over the world in the last fifteen

years. We are all colder, more prosaic, less hopeful, than we were. A generous theory, based on a belief in the perfectibility of man, was as certain then to evoke a cheer as it is now to be scouted with a scornful laugh. In those days men believed in an extended suffrage, and external peace, and the possibility of extirpating crime by reformatory prisons. Some went so far as to believe in an approaching union of all Christian Churches. Others, of an opposite turn of mind, had persuaded themselves that a drab-coloured millennium was dawning on the other side of the Atlantic. Rude facts have roughly woken us from these luxurious dreams, and taught us that the antagonism which divides sects and classes, the ambition which embroils nations, and the love of a good dinner which animates the garotter, are passions as rife and powerful as they ever were before at any period of human history. It is the melancholy but complete collapse of optimism. We are compelled with heavy hearts to give up our aspirations after ideal churches and ideal common-wealths, and content ourselves with patching a little here, and altering a bit there, in the hope that the systems under which we live may at all events furnish us shelter for our time. Practical philanthropy, which has abandoned all other hope but that of being a temporary palliative for ills it cannot cure, is useful, but little fascinating. The flood of evils wells up ceaselessly; and it requires no small philosophy to labour on, baling it out little by little, with the certainty that no exertions that we can make will ever materially abate its flow.[50]

Human nature does not admit of the possibility of per-manent progress. It is possible to give men a veneer of civilisation, but it will require very little to rub it off. Man is motivated first and foremost by self-interest. In addition, he has a wish for glory: he likes to claim distinguished ancestry; he has a lust for self-importance which he satisfies by jobbery and patronage; he loves exclusiveness. Salisbury describes this craving in an amusing middle on 'Moral Game Preserves':

> Whatever philosophers may say, there can be no doubt that the impulse which leads to the preservation of game is one of the most deep-seated instincts in our nature.[51]

Accordingly, the Corporation of London insists on keeping its own police force and the clergy are intensely attached to the parochial system, even when, in large towns for instance, it becomes impractical:

> In each case the motive power is the pleasure which is the mainspring of so much human exertion—the satisfaction of possessing something which nobody else, or at all events nobody else in the neighbourhood, possesses.

Then, 'There are many people who look upon their friends as a species of preserve . . . They warn off poachers with all the terrors that a spiteful tongue can hold out.' They like to be the focus of all their friends' interests, and resent these friends becoming independently friendly with each other. All these habits are the result of 'the delusion of self-importance'.

In more serious vein, Salisbury is painfully aware of all the wars and the destruction which fill the pages of history. This consciousness of the long sufferings of mankind is treated most fully and clearly in the article on 'Poland'[52] written for *The Quarterly Review*. When he wrote the essay in 1863, the Poles were in revolt against the Russians and the Russians were in the process of putting down the rebellion with the greatest brutality. Salisbury shows in detail that the brutality of the Russians is merely a continuation of a series of atrocities that has lasted for over a thousand years and that more often than not the Russians have been on the receiving end. In a review of 'Pictures of German Life', an anthology of German literature of the fifteenth to the seventeenth century, he remarks that:

> In selecting most of his descriptions from periods of war, the author unfortunately represents the general colouring of German history with only too exact a fidelity.[53]

Salisbury then gives a gruesome description of the tortures used during The Thirty Years' War and gives some casualty figures. For example, in the domain of Hennenburg (population 8,000) 82 per cent of the population, 85 per cent of the horses and cattle and 63 per cent of the houses were destroyed. Elsewhere there are other descriptions of torture. He quotes several of the accounts in detail and they seem to have filled him with a mixture of fascination and horror.[54]

He returns repeatedly to the sentiment that civilisation is only skin deep. In a *Quarterly Review* article on 'The Political Lessons of the War' (the Franco-Prussian War) he says:

> They [the Prussians] have shown us that the highest education, the most advanced civilisation, do not stifle the original passions of the noble savage—that if you scratch the cultivated German Professor, you will find the nature which made the lanzknecht of the middle ages or the 'marauders' of the Thirty Years' War.[55]

The view recurs in a *Saturday Review* leader ('The War Christians of New Zealand') on the atrocities committed by the colonists against the Maoris:

> The state of things in New Zealand, like the state of things in America, furnishes instructive evidence of the small extent to which civilisation has power to tame the natural savagery of mankind.[56]

His attitude is well summed up in a review written in 1857 on the slave problem in Kansas. He starts the article by describing the lawless and corrupt state of politics in Kansas and the selfish motives of the slave-owners and those who had campaigned for the extension of slavery into that State. He then concludes:

> This is a sad tale to repeat of men of our own kin, in their own spheres, persons of education and refinement, nursed in our institutions, and assuming to be the vanguard in the march of freedom. But the lesson is not without its use. It teaches us how thin is the crust which the habits of civilisation, however ancient and unbroken, draw over the boiling lava of human passion. Whenever the Anglo-Saxon race has been free for a few years from any movements of open violence, there have always been certain philosophers eager to catch at the belief that the need of curbing human nature has gone by, and that the millenium of 'enlightened selfishness' is dawning. And their theories only formulate the belief that 'all men are born good', which lies deep in the breast of the present generation. Such follies are best answered by the spectacle of one of the freest and most educated communities that the world has yet seen, plunging into anarchy, rapine, and bloodshed in order to perpetuate the unspeakable degradations of slavery.[57]

Under circumstances such as these, utopianism is not only mistaken, but is criminally so. The most that man can hope for is the avoidance of conflict and the establishment of peace. In the works of Salisbury, as in those of Hobbes, the avoidance of conflict becomes the major aim of political activity, both domestic and foreign. He calls peace 'the greatest of all blessings'[58] and war 'a wholesale system of killing, despoiling and deceiving'.[59] His final judgement on the career of Castlereagh—a judgement which involved Salisbury's highest praise—was simple:

> It can only be said of him generally that he found Europe at war and that he left it at peace.[60]

In Castlereagh's political priorities are reflected Salisbury's own:

> He cared for nationality not at all; for the theoretical perfection of political institutions very little; for the realities of freedom, a great deal; and for the peace, and social order and freedom from the manifold curses of disturbance, which can alone give to the humbler masses of mankind any chance of tasting their scanty share of human joys—for the sake of this, he was quite ready to forego all the rest.[61]

The fear of war and disturbance also led him to the ardent support of toleration of all kinds, and especially of religious toleration. He opposed excessive proselytising[62] and condemned the misplaced zeal with which the Pilgrim Fathers prosyletised the American Indians: 'They sought to Christianise the country by the simple expedient of slaughtering those who were not Christians.'[63] He described the witch-hunts in New England and also those in Westphalia[64] and called them a 'plague'. Indeed intolerance was the worst facet of religion: it led to persecution which not only hindered civilisation but also brought about the kind of violence which Salisbury so dreaded.

Like Hobbes, Salisbury believed in the basic equality of men. But, also like Hobbes, he did not conclude from this that political equality was feasible. On the contrary, he was convinced that it was incompatible with the basic aim of peace. Hobbes argued that the basic equality of men would lead to conflict and Locke was of the view that in time inequalities would inevitably entrench themselves. In a review of a book on ancient local institutions in Germany, Salisbury writes:

> It is curious to watch how naturally and how confidingly men start with institutions of absolute equality, and hold their lands in perfect community, and how surely, in the lapse of centuries, the inevitable operation of natural laws centres the common power in a few persons, and divides the common lands among a few owners. First, the natural attachment of mankind for the spot on which they have lived confines a commoner's labour and that of his children to one piece of land; then long use ripens into the exclusive right to use; then the right to use is held to imply the right to allow others to use, or the power of alienation. This once granted, the natural differences in the thrift or fortune of various families soon obliterate all traces of the original equality of property; and the equality of property once gone, the equality of power will not long survive it.[65]

In a late middle on 'Equality' he speaks with foresight on the effects of technical advance:

> Taking only real independent power into the calculation, men stand pretty much on a level in a state of society in which muscle is the main source of force. But it is clear that the levels begin to be altered the moment that science is called in to furnish forces which shall take the place of muscle. The application of science involves accumulated wealth, and in the long run, whatever temporary difference ingenuity may make, the resources of science will be most available to those who have the most wealth at their command . . . The simplest illustration of the comparison is furnished by the instance of firearms . . . the success of the scanty forces of the Western Powers against the vast population of China . . .[66]

The same is true internally:

> Governments are becoming more and more successful to set insurrection at defiance.

Having shown that equality is not feasible, he also seems to suggest that it is undesirable. Here again the argument is reminiscent of Hobbes. It will be remembered that Hobbes supports a system of government by an absolute ruler. He does not maintain that the absolute ruler will be any better than his fellow men, but says that his elevated position will make it his selfish desire (through his love of glory) to be of benefit to them.

In the same way, Salisbury does not believe that aristocrats and captains of industry are basically better than other men. But he does believe that a tiger is at its most dangerous when it has an empty belly and that men are most rapacious when they are in need. If the rulers are those who already have the wealth, it is at least possible that their ease of circumstances will mellow their harsher instincts.[67] Prosperity and education usually go together and it is likely that the wealthy and the noble will have been trained in the techniques and virtues of government; and, however small the value of education, it is at least better than nothing. There is a final point—and this is perhaps the crucial one: if the penniless mob has political power, it will naturally try to take away the wealth from the rich minority; the result will be civil conflict. This conflict will not occur if power is held by those with the biggest existing stake in the country.

It is on grounds such as these that he is opposed to any extension of the franchise giving a majority of votes, and thus political power, to the working class. They are only human, he argues, and their rapacious instincts must prevail if temptation is put in their way:

> My own feeling with respect to the working men is simply this —we have heard a great deal too much of them, as if they were different from other Englishmen. They spring from the same race. They live under the same climate. They are brought up under the same laws. They aspire to the same historical model which we admire ourselves; and I cannot understand why their nature is to be thought better or worse than that of other classes. I say their nature, but I say nothing about their temptations . . .
>
> The franchise has a direct money value to those who do not care much about public affairs in the way of bribery, it has an indirect value to those who do not care about public affairs in the way of encouraging unjust and special class legislation.[68]

THE PROBLEM OF CHANGE

The problem that was the most important and fundamental of those considered by Salisbury in his writings was the problem of political change. In the case of many Conservatives one is left with the feeling that their reluctance to envisage change is grounded in the last resort in a sentimental regard for antique ceremonial and established political forms and social ways. This feeling for *mores maiorum* is one of the most powerful bases of political conservatism, just as emotional revulsion against established ways is a base of radicalism.

Yet no such sentiment inspired Salisbury's conservatism. If he wished to preserve old political institutions, it was because he thought on rational grounds that they were better than anything that could be put in their place. It is true that he had an emotional fear of the mob and of the crudities of democratic politics. But he also disliked the traditional classes of society, the knights of the shires and the hearty aristocracy of which his father was a loyal member, and he showed very little attachment and considerable rebellion against the ancient as such.

He realised that there could be no finality in politics[69] and felt nothing but contempt for the '*nolumus leges Angliae mutari*'[70] class of politicians: their conservatism was the result of nothing other than 'stagnation of mind'. There are several passages in which he turns roundly on the squires, the specimens of 'the political dodo'.[71] He condemns them, not because he always disagrees with their views, but because their opposition to change comes from instinct rather than from reason. For example, he acidly comments on their inability to enter into intelligent discussion of Indian affairs. The Indian names are complicated and

> a country gentleman can never get out of his head that a ryot is something that he ought to suppress; and though he may give an intellectual assent to the fact that a ryot is a sort of peasant, his sympathies towards the unhappy bearer of so ominous a name are inevitably chilled.[72]

95

His lack of emotional attachment to old forms is well illustrated by his attitude towards state ceremonial. He grudgingly admits that the mass of the people expect a show, and that there is no reason to disappoint them.[73] But he thinks that English attempts at pageantry are always 'ridiculous',[74] and he condemns Lord Mayor's Day as being 'not the type of old custom or ancient usage which it is worth keeping'.[75] His articles also contain several middles in which he debunks ceremonies such as the Opening of Parliament.[76]

In more than one article, he appeals to the Queen (then in retirement following the death of Prince Albert) to 'resume the ceremonial duties of her station'.[77] But it is noteworthy that his reason is not his like of monarchical pomp but the down to earth fact that this pomp played a function in maintaining the influence of the monarchy, which could then be used in 'the defence of order'. His attitude towards pageantry and its ancient forms is strictly utilitarian.

Another aspect of his thought relevant to this point is its surprising lack of patriotic feeling. At a later period of his life he showed signs of being moderately infected by the nationalism and imperialism which was then becoming prevalent. During his earlier life, however, such ideas played little part. In this respect, Salisbury's thought contrasted directly with that of many other conservatives and especially with the national-racial theories of Disraeli.

Indeed, he was in some ways in favour of change for its own sake. He thought that power corrupts and thus said:

> A little Radicalism is a very useful thing for the purpose of keeping in check the natural selfishness of the classes who are the tenants of power. A feeling that their own overthrow is possible, if not probable, keeps jobbing within bounds, and provokes occasional attempts at practical reform.[78]

He also realised that 'old laws get out of gear with new realities'[79] and condemned in particular the outdated structure of municipal institutions and of the legal system (in this he was, of course, following directly in the Benthamite tradition).[80] His general frustration at the difficulty of innovation is expressed in his *Quarterly Review* account of 'Photography':

> Newcomers are seldom popular with those whose room they occupy. And the feeling appears to be peculiarly bitter in cases where the old-established favourite has to give way to some new-fangled device, which has been introduced in the natural course of things, as the world advances. [81]

And yet this same Salisbury, who had no attachment to the established order but felt distrust of it, was also capable of such statements as:

> It [Palmerston's ministry] has done that which it is most difficult and most salutary for a parliament to do—nothing. [82]

How is it possible to reconcile the progressive views that have been quoted with his conservative policies?

The reason why he followed 'do nothing' policies was that, although he thought that inaction was bad, he was also convinced that usually the only alternative to inaction was recklessness, and that this was worse. This pattern of argument can be illustrated by an account of his analysis of revolution.

Salisbury seems to distinguish two different types of revolutionary cycle which will, for the sake of convenience, be called the 'stable' revolutionary cycle and the 'explosive' revolutionary cycle. The 'stable' cycle comes into operation in the following way. (i) An abuse exists. (ii) The abuse leads to revolutionary disturbance. (iii) Revolution leads to the removal of the abuse. (iv) Once the abuse is removed, social harmony is restored.

The 'explosive' cycle comes into operation in the same way, but it has very different results. (i) An abuse exists. (ii) The abuse leads to revolutionary disturbance. (iii) Revolution leads to the removal of the abuse. (iv) Even though the original abuse has been removed, the revolutionary violence develops a momentum of its own and continues to intensify until (v) a total reaction is produced and the original government is restored in such a way as the original abuse is brought back into being.

Salisbury believes that explosive cycles are very much more common than stable ones, and it is this judgement that leads him to his conservative views. He does, however, deal with several examples of stable revolutionary cycles. Three of these (the American Revolution, the Italian Revolution under Cavour and the First Reform Bill) are considered below.

Although Salisbury is no admirer of the American democracy that had developed by the mid-nineteenth century, he has nothing but praise for the American Revolution. In a review article of a book entitled *Diary of the American Revolution*, he says:

> The feeling with which most Englishmen will rise from the perusal of this book will be one of sorrowful but profound contempt for the Government under which their ancestors flourished in the good old days. Nobody, except perhaps Washington, appears in very noble colours; but the only actors who make a thoroughly despicable figure are the English Ministers and their favourite generals.[83]

On another occasion he calls Washington the 'great American hero'.[84] As far as the Revolution as a whole is concerned, he has to admit that it is a case of a violent upheaval that produced a viable political system. In the review of the events of 1860 which appeared in *The Saturday Review* of 29 December 1860, he indicates that revolutions are not all violent, and writes with generous praise of the movement for Italian Independence.

> The extravagances of revolution have often been defended on the plea that powerful tyrannies could not be overthrown without them. A comparison of 1860 with 1848 ought to dispose of that reasoning for ever. . . . [He proceeds to describe the transient successes of the 1848 revolutions and says that they were unsuccessful 'because the public opinion of Europe was not with them'. Thus, 'The reaction began to work.' . . .]
> A very different course, with, apparently a very different set of results, has been followed in 1860. Nothing has been trusted to the perilous chances of a street mob. It has not been attempted to found an edifice of political regeneration on the fatal triumphs of the *classe dangereuse* in arms. Thoughtful and

experienced statesmen have initiated the movement, and have watched over it at every step. The right moment was patiently waited for, and the outbreak was not precipitated, as before, for the sake of realising the mad dreams of a vain and weak monk who had just attained to the tiara . . . A revolution begun with so much forethought and so many guarantees for success could command leaders of a very different calibre from those who are tossed to the surface by a revolution that springs from a street row . . . the guiding spirits of the revolution, especially of the reconstructive part of it, have been, not mob leaders, but great statesmen. Accordingly, it has taken its character from those who conducted it. It has not started one single abstract idea, or consecrated any new theory of government or of society. It has done nothing to terrify the owners of property or the friends of order in any part of the world. It has simply carried out the practical object—the only one at which it aimed—of transferring Italy from the domination at once absolutist and foreign to liberty under an Italian king.[85]

Perhaps his most important account of the working of the stable cycle is in the article he wrote for *The Quarterly Review* in 1869 on 'The Past and Future of Conservative Policy':

While the world lasts there must still be old institutions to upset, there must always be a large class of men whose condition no disturbance could deteriorate, and there will never want an ample supply of enthusiasts to dream new social theories. Social stability is assured, not by a cessation of the demand for change—for the needy and the restless will never cease to cry for it—but by the fact that change in its progress must at least hurt some class of men who are strong enough to arrest it. The army of so-called reform, in every stage of its advance, necessarily converts a detachment of its forces into opponents. The more rapid the more formidable will the desertion become, till at last a point will be reached where the balance between the forces of conservation and destruction will be redressed and the political equilibrium be restored.[86]

He repeats the same analysis when he writes about the 1832 Reform Act:

Except when fired by genuine oppression, the working classes alone cannot make a revolution. The middle-class has often fought its way to power by their help; and on such occasions very democratic theories have found their way into very exclusive company. But as soon as the middle-classes are inside the citadel instead of outside, their former allies find that democracy goes with marvellous rapidity out of fashion.[87]

This analysis implies that revolutionary agitation usually arises from some just sense of grievance and that the established rulers will be wise if they give concessions to such agitation. As he says in 'Theories of Parliamentary Reform',

Changes that are really wholesome are only made noxious by being put off. The stream is not arrested—it is only dammed into a flood.[88]

But Salisbury does not think that the stable cycle is anything more than a rare case. It will occur only if the quality of the revolutionary leadership is especially high (as in the American and Italian examples) or if the grievance is a fairly minor one and is dealt with under conditions of general stability. In cases other than these, agitation—even if it is in a patently good cause—will lay bare explosive emotions and ambitions, 'the revolutionary demon' will be unleashed and extremism will reign supreme. An account of this explosive cycle is given in Salisbury's first article in *Bentley's Quarterly Review*. He describes the typical revolutionary pattern of events on the Continent. Monarchical tyranny leads to revolt. The reaction of the monarch is to make concessions and so:

a troop of unwashed ministers is invested with high-sounding offices and absolute power, and is loaded with the confidence and favour of the court . . . But the time of popular triumph and monarchical dirt-eating is short. The mob of the ignorant and half-starved to whom the revolution is due, and whom, therefore, its leaders dare not curb, looks upon its emancipation from law as the only solid fruit of victory. They plunge into excesses compared to which the previous tyranny was innocent, and soon bring on the reaction—that dreaded rebound from revolutionary fervour which a revolution rarely survives. On the wave of the reaction the monarch, complacently swallowing his oaths, floats back to absolute power . . . Thus tyranny begets resistance and resistance begets tyranny. At last the cup is once more full; the camel's back is broken; the rage and scorn of the sufferers have accumulated to that point that they are no longer amenable to the usual restraints of physical fear: and then the whole edifying spectacle of mob excess and court duplicity is played out again for the edification of the world.[89]

The general conclusion to be drawn is that concessions to rioters and violent revolutionaries will encourage disrespect for law and order, and this will bring unavoidable chaos and disaster. Salisbury illustrates this when he investigates the causes of the French defeat by Germany in the Franco-Prussian War. He attributes the defeat to the debilitating effect of the constant political instability and revolution which had plagued France:

> It is feebleness of the very principle of Government, caused by chronic revolution, that has mainly brought about these vast disasters . . . The principle of submission to an established authority has disappeared; and every attempt to restore it has been baffled by the spirit which originally destroyed it.[90]

He explains how uncertainty begets uncertainty. Businessmen invest only speculatively, for it is not safe to tie up money for long periods; the governed live only for the day. The rulers also suffer in the same way, for when there is insecurity,

> they will eschew far-reaching statesmanlike schemes as a sowing of seed which they may never reap. Their policy will be showy, hollow, unreal—designed to gain the applause or appease the ill-humour of the moment.

On another occasion, he compares revolution to an epidemic and he several times points out that, although many political agitations start out with moderate and reasonable demands, it is 'the professors of extreme opinions who always in the end profit by revolutions'.[91] And he gives the warning that 'there must always be Girondins to pave the way for Jacobins'.[92]

Under circumstances such as these, the upholders of established order can make no greater mistake than that of supposing that revolutionaries will be satiated by concessions. Rather than weakening themselves by the offering of palliatives, they should offer 'the deadening resistance of a sandbag to dangerous forces of political fanaticism'.[93] Not only is the policy of resistance to all change in the interest of the established powers but it is also in the interest of the oppressed masses. The only way in which revolution affects the masses is to make them suffer by buffeting them between two sets of rulers—the established government on the one hand and the leading elite of the revolution on the other.

The general result of all this is a dismaying one. Salisbury admits that the *status quo* is rarely satisfactory and also admits that revolution can on occasion be successful and beneficial. At the same time, he fears the evils of disruption to such an extent and rates the uncertainties of revolution so highly that he is led to the conclusion that it is better in all but the most exceptional circumstances to bear those ills we have rather than fly to others we know not of.

Fears such as these account for his policies on Reform and on Church matters in the 1860s. In his writings he admits the anomalies in the system of Church Rates;[94] he agrees almost completely with the complaints against the Establishment in Ireland;[95] he is even in partial agreement with those who point out the anomalies of the constituency system produced by the 1832 Reform Act. But he opposes reforms in all these cases and invariably uses the same argument: reform will not bring contentment, it will merely bring renewed agitation. In other words, he is arguing that the stable cycle is not at work in Britain. As he writes in *The Quarterly Review* article 'Democracy on its Trial', 'Once the dyke is breached by small concessions, all will be lost.'[96]

Looking back at Salisbury's analysis from the vantage point of one hundred years of history, how does it appear to the modern reader? It should be acknowledged from the first that the analysis itself is a good one: the distinction between the occasions on which agreement to change will ease the demand for further change, and the occasions on which it will merely stimulate a further demand provides a useful framework. But Salisbury's application of the theory is possibly one-sided. The analysis gives no foolproof way of deciding whether any given situation is 'stable' or not;

it remains a matter of judgement, and Salisbury's pessimism seems to have led him to the position in which he was much too willing to diagnose an explosive situation. His argument against the extension of the franchise, for example, was that mild reform was merely a palliative and that renewed agitation would force through reform bill after reform bill until total power lay in the hands of the working classes. He was correct when he predicted that the Act of 1867 would not be final. But he was wrong in predicting a total and violent transfer of power to the working classes. Indeed it could be said that a stern and unbending policy of the kind proposed by Salisbury would have had the very effect of damming up the stream of discontent into the revolutionary flood that he so feared and of leading to disturbances and disruption of the Continental type.

This remains a matter of hypothesis, as Salisbury's central policy was cut down by the Act of 1867. But his reaction to the passing of this measure illustrates an important difference between Salisbury's view of change and that of romantic and 'Divine Right' Conservatives. The romantic Conservative supports his chosen form of government not only because it is established or viable but because he believes it is hallowed. If it is overthrown, his position demands that he work for the restoration of his divine government. After the establishment of a republic, for example, the believer in the Divine Right of Kings must be committed to the restoration of the monarchy. He becomes a reactionary and in extreme cases he is willing to foment revolution and disruption for his purposes. The implications of Salisbury's conservatism are quite different. His dread of conflict and disorder makes him fear the process of change in itself. Once changes have taken effect—even changes that he opposed before the event—the logic of his position is that he must accept the new situation in all but the rarest of circumstances, as the shortcomings of the new state of affairs must now be weighed against the misery that will probably result from an attempt to revert to the *status quo ante*.

CHAPTER V

The Theory of Balance

HOBBES was convinced that conflict between individuals could best be eliminated when one person or group of persons was put in a position of absolute and undisputed authority over the rest. But Salisbury's views were like those of the eighteenth-century thinkers of whom David Hume was the most prominent English representative: the evils of conflict would be ended by the diffusion of power rather than by its concentration. Therefore, the most desirable form of state was one that produced an 'equilibrium' so that no individual or group of persons had the power to oppress others.

Like many other political thinkers, Salisbury divided states into three categories. He classified them into:

1 The despotic state.
2 The democratic state.
3 The constitutional state.

He criticised the first two forms of state on the ground that they failed to embody the desired equilibrium and recommended only the third.

DESPOTISM AND DEMOCRACY

At the time when Salisbury was writing his articles, most of Europe was still ruled by dynasties which were little more than feudal in character. He was totally out of sympathy with these regimes and there are several passages in his writings which indicate that he fully approved of the Continental Liberals who were struggling to establish constitutional governments. Salisbury saw that dynastic rulers could rarely resist the temptation to take advantage of their great and unchecked powers. The result was that their regimes were inefficient, indolent and corrupt. Absolute power led them to an attitude of 'luxurious apathy'[1] and to a concern for their personal interests at the expense of the well-being of the mass of the people. In addition, the 'mechanical and unerring unity of despotism'[2] prevented any free flow of ideas and led to the eventual drainage of all intellectual energy on the part of the ruling group.

One of the main shortcomings of despotic regimes was that the execution of policy had to be entrusted to a bureaucracy and, as there were no means whereby the people could control this bureaucracy (or, at least, to have some channel of appeal against its actions), injustices abounded. The lack of any outside control of the officialdom also meant that inefficient procedures were bound to crystallise. In 1861, the English newspapers carried the story of a trivial incident concerning a British tourist, Captain Macdonald, who had been involved in a minor quarrel with a German passenger in a train in Prussia. Allegedly, he had been the innocent party, but the station-master had treated him roughly and when Macdonald complained, he was imprisoned for insulting an official (station-masters in Germany were government officials). Salisbury wrote a middle and spoke in Parliament about the incident, which he regarded as a typical result of a despotic system. He complained about the unchecked power of the bureaucracy and pointed out that, had diplomatic pressure not been applied, Macdonald would have been subject to a term of imprisonment of two years for insulting a civil servant:

> The person of the official is absolutely sacred. His sensitive feelings are guarded by the law with most anxious care. As far as the subject is concerned, he can do no wrong and say no wrong.[3]

In a review article written a few months later, he complained that the German police force lacked 'facility and pliancy of organisation'.[4] Consequently,

> it [has] degenerated into a stupid, pedantic, dilatory despotism—too helplessly smothered in its own forms to contribute anything to the effectual repression of vice and crime, and only serviceable as a means for persecuting political antagonists.[4]

In another review article, he deplores the power of the Russian imperial officials, the Tchinovnicks. The strictly hierarchical structure of the Russian bureaucracy gave great amounts of independent power to the Tchin, who naturally used it to govern Russia for their own interests with the result that

> the Emperor is practically an absentee landlord, knowing nothing of his estate except what the tchin is pleased to tell him; and the seventy million subjects fare at the hands of the tchin much as the cotters fared at the hands of the middleman.[5]

The lack of balance in the despotic system resulted in inflexible, inefficient, unjust government. Its injustice was bound to lead to insurrection and its inefficiency meant that the despotism had little chance of controlling it. Unchecked government was inevitably unstable and, as power centred geographically round the court of the emperor or tyrant, it required only a single, well-directed mob riot to endanger the regime.[6]

The disadvantages of the democratic state were, in Salisbury's opinion, very similar—but probably more serious. The mistake of democratic theorists was that their estimate of human nature was unrealistically generous.

> The first impulse of any good man . . . is to believe everyone else to be as free from evil passion or blind selfishness as himself; and an over-belief in the goodness and wisdom of mankind is the 'first falsehood' of a sincere democratic reasoner.[7]

Salisbury admitted that there were exceptional circumstances in which government by the people was workable. 'It was essentially a fair-weather system':[8] when things were going well, democratic government would stimulate commerce. It was also likely to work in countries like America in which there was no shortage of land and raw materials and in which there was therefore not likely to be a hungry urban mob. As long as prosperity kept man's rapacious instincts dormant, democracy would survive.[9] But:

> The great danger of democracy is, that it places supreme power into the hands of those who may be misled by hunger into acts of folly or of wrong. In an old country, no excellence of institutions can ensure that such periods of maddening want shall not occasionally occur. Where the bounty of Nature is wellnigh exhausted, and multitudes exist on no other resources than the prosperity of trade, it must be that sometimes one precarious resource will fail. When such periods of distress do come, it is vain to hope that argument will restrain hungry men from relieving their own and their children's misery by any measures which the institutions of their country give them power to take.[10]

Salisbury assumed that in all societies, at least in those of the nineteenth century, a preponderant amount of wealth would be in the possession of a minority of the citizens. He also thought that it was impossible to control the trade cycle and to avoid periods of depression. These two assumptions led him to the conclusion that democracy (i.e. the rule of the poor majority) led inevitably to the confiscation of the property of the rich—and this was in his mind tantamount to revolution. In times of great need, it would prove impossible for a popular government to resist the rapacious demands of the urban mob and it would thus have to acquiesce in its actions. An example of the kind of thing he feared is given in a leader on 'The Rights of Labour at the Antipodes'. The European miners were jealous of the Chinese workers, so they gathered together, marched on them, treated them brutally and stripped them of every shred of property.

> Against this oppression there is no appeal for them. The utter impotence of the law in the face of any mob, which is the mark of all democratic constitutions, has been brought painfully to light.[11]

Democracies are especially liable to crowd violence:

> Passion is fostered equally by the two main characteristics of the democratic sovereign—ignorance and numbers.[12]

The riots will spawn mob leaders, and, once they are in power, these ochlocrats will become despots. He comments that universal suffrage and the ballot 'have been found on the other side of the Channel to be as faithful ministers of one man's will as the sword and halter were in other days'.[13] Indeed, Salisbury claims that there is an 'essential identity between the democracy and the despotism ... the same universal equality under one strong, unfettered, unrestricted government'.[14] There is another danger. The democratic despot will constantly have to protect his home position by a reckless foreign policy that will rouse the imperial passions of the mob and will satisfy the dreams of glory of his own praetorian guard:

> Those who have reached their eminence by violence or craft have no other defence against the indignation which their success arouses than in the appeal to some strong passion by which all other passions may be swallowed up ... Cromwell could appeal to religious fanaticism; a French usurper has no other course but to invoke that unscrupulous worship of military glory which has been the besetting sin of the French nation in every period of their history. [The Bonapartes were, for Salisbury, central examples of the democratic despot; in the above piece, he is discussing the foreign policy of Louis Napoleon.][15]

But even when there is no danger of mob rule or of democratic despotism, the democratic form of government is a prey to other vices. Salisbury fears that democratic government will put too much power in the hands of the legislature and not enough with the executive. This legislature will be too greatly influenced by capricious shifts in public opinion and will suffer from chronic instability. In conditions such as these, able political leaders will not be prepared to come forward but will prefer to pursue other occupations. Politics will thus be left in the hands of mediocrities. He follows Tocqueville in showing how this process had occurred in America and he also gives examples of the same tendency in England. He argues that the large urban constituencies with several thousand electors give an indication of the pattern that will become general if the franchise is extended. He gives lurid descriptions of politics in Finsbury, Tower Hamlets and St. Marylebone[16] and says that only characterless men will demean themselves by agreeing to come forward as candidates.

> Marylebone is precisely in the condition to which an unrestricted suffrage has brought America. There is something so filthy in the humiliation that a Marylebone candidate has to undergo that none but mere political adventurers will stand . . . The refined and educated population who give to Marylebone the wealth of which its demagogues boast, who are the fountains of all its outward show of luxury and prosperity, hold themselves as much aloof from the filthy turmoil of borough politics as if they lived in New Orleans or New York . . . The pewter-pot alone remains supreme.[17]

A further disadvantage—one which also results from the attention that democracies must pay to public opinion— is that democratic government will inevitably be costly government.[18]

In other words, democratic government is—almost by definition—weak government. The danger of this weakness is that it is liable to lead to conditions of uncertainty in which it is especially easy for despotism to establish itself.

> It is in its nature to produce Governments of exaggerated weakness in times of calm and of exaggerated strength in times of tumult.[19]

At another point he examines 'The Politics of Marylebone' and makes the general conclusions:

> In strong times, when some physical privation presses, or some contagious passion excites them, they will be ungovernably tyrannical and reckless of the rights of others. In times of calm, public questions upon which they are appointed arbiters will lose all interest for them, and their whole political energies will be devoted to hindering a railway, or setting up a bathing-place in a fish-pond.[20]

The definition of 'democracy' that Salisbury uses is 'absolute government of the numerical majority'.[21] The absolute government of the numerical majority has another systematic disadvantage: it gives no guarantee for the rights of minorities. Salisbury quotes at length from Tocqueville on the subject of Majority Tyranny and is fully aware of its excesses in America.[22] He also considers the subject in a leading article on the 'Representation of Minorities' and thinks that ingenious schemes of proportional representation (such as the one proposed by Hare) are bound to be ineffective:

> It is to little purpose that the minority are protected from the strength of the majority at the hustings, if they are made to feel the full force of it in the division lobby.[23]

The only protection for minorities is to be found in a 'mixed' form of government:

> So long as men sit by a number of tenures, a tyrannous majority is improbable. One man sits because he is locally popular; another because he is friends with the powerful men of his district; a third because he has sat for a long time, and does Parliamentary business well; a fourth because he is a good Catholic; a fifth because he is a good Protestant; a sixth because he understands the particular trade of his locality.[24]

The danger of majority tyranny is also great in countries with racial divisions. (Mill showed in 'Representative Government' that he also was aware of this point.) These divisions constituted one of the greatest difficulties that faced Britain when the time came to give a form of popular government to such countries as New Zealand.[25]

Through most of these varied criticisms of democracy there runs a common theme. Democracy is a dangerous form of government because it is unbalanced. It provides no compromise between the need for stable government and the need for flexibility and pliancy to public opinion. This lack of balance is expressed institutionally in the inability of democracies to divide power between the legislative and executive branches of government. Power is not shared by different classes, but it is in the hands of one class. There is no division of power between majority groups and minority groups. Similarly, in foreign affairs, the democracy veers giddily between policies of weakness and policies of aggression. At home, the masses mix long periods of apathy about politics with short outbursts of feverish mob activity. As a

system of government it is not viable and tends to lead sooner
or later to a despotism of a Bonapartist kind and, when there
is a reaction against this, to a dynastic regime of the old type.

THE CONSTITUTIONAL STATE

A passage in the last article which Salisbury wrote for *The
Quarterly Review* gives the essence of his thought on institutional matters:

> There is a general disposition among those who in the con-
> stituencies are opposing the party now in power to substitute
> the word Constitutional for the word Conservative in their
> political language. It is the fruit of a true instinct. The object of
> our party is not, and ought not to be simply to keep things as
> they are. In the first place, the enterprise is impossible. In the
> next place, there is much in our present mode of thought and
> action which it is highly undesirable to conserve. What we
> require is the administration of public affairs, whether in the
> executive or the legislative department, in that spirit of the
> old constitution which held the nation together as a whole, and
> levelled its united force at objects of national import, instead of
> splitting it into a bundle of unfriendly and distrustful
> fragments.[26]

The way in which he proposes to hold the nation together is
to apportion power between difference groups. His view is
that the national interest will emerge when there is a balance
between conservative and innovatory forces; between the
dangers of stagnation and the dangers of recklessness; and
between the vices of weak government and the vices of
absolutism. This requires a political system which will ensure
the existence of a balance between classes; a balance
between the interests of the town and the interests of the
country; and between the majority and the minority. And
this will only be achieved when there is a balance between
central government and municipal government; between
the House of Commons and the House of Lords; between the
legislature and the executive; and between the government
on the one hand and the press on the other.

Key words throughout the articles are 'balance',

'equipoise', 'checks' and 'equilibrium'. A typical expression of his thought is a paragraph in the article on 'The Conservative Surrender', written in 1867.

> There can be no finality in politics. Whatever the actual state of things may be, the spirit of innovation always must exist. The world would grow very stagnant if it disappeared. The appetite for change can never be glutted . . . The long periods of political repose which communities enjoy from time to time, are due, not to the disappearance of the *rerum novarum cupidi*, but to the establishment of an equilibrium between the Conservative and the innovating force . . . The two forces are complementary to each other; the paralysis of either makes the other ruinously strong.[27]

This equilibrium requires a balance between town and country, but, much more than this, it requires balance between the interests of different classes. Accordingly, he praises the system whereby

> in the country, the boards of guardians [of the Poor Law] are generally composed of different classes, who check each other's selfishness. In London the whole management is in the hands of a class who make their fortunes by scraping together petty profits and petty earnings.[28]

In political terms, Salisbury sees the balance between classes as implying an electoral system in which no single class has sufficient voting power to enable it to make attacks on the property of any other class. This leads him to propose that voting power should be related to wealth.

> The State is a joint-stock company to all intents and purposes. It is the combination of a vast number of men for well-defined objects—the preservation of life and property. But it has this monstrous and unheard-of peculiarity, that it is a joint-stock company in which the shareholders vote, not by shares, but by heads.[29]

He proceeds to agree that all lives are equal, but argues that property is not equal and thus suggests the possibility of a graduated franchise.

The piece just quoted comes from 'Theories of Parliamentary Reform'. The argument is repeated in an article on 'Parliamentary Reform', in which he maintains that the tendency of Russell's demands of 1865 seems ultimately to be complete democracy and says that this must be rejected outright. But he continues to suggest as an alternative that

> They [the working classes] may not ask for supremacy . . . But they may ask for a share of political power proportioned to the share which their labour gives them in the country's wealth. Such a claim, if it be advanced, must be met in a very different tone from that which has justly been used to repel the intolerable claim of supremacy. It is probably in view of some such contingency that the Conservatives have always abstained from meeting any of the bills for the extensions of the suffrage with a direct negative . . . Their doctrines are not adverse to the claims of any particular class, except when that class is aiming to domineer over the rest. And, therefore, there is nothing inconsistent with their principles in any system of representation, however wide its scope may be, so long as it does not ignore the differences of property which exist in this country, and maintains with an even hand, the balance of power among the various classes of which the nation is made up.[30]

It is not only by a balanced system of voting that domination by a particular class can be avoided, but also by a machinery of government which is in equipoise. There must first of all be a balance between municipal and central government. In practice, this means that there must be some limits on the powers of the central government and that certain powers should be reserved for the local authorities. It also means that municipal government must be streamlined and modernised so that it is fit to fulfil its functions. Considerations such as these made Salisbury attribute great importance to the task of recasting the structure of local government when he became Prime Minister, and led to the legislation of 1888. He explains some of his fears of overcentralisation in a middle which he wrote in 1863:

> Village Hampdens are, in practice, fussy, greasy sort of people, very narrow-minded, very fond of jobbing, and endowed with a praeternatural thickness of cuticle in order to enable them to endure patiently the mortifications incident to a life passed in parochial contested elections. [He proceeds to explain that they are inefficient and refers to the current scandals concerning

the administration of highways and the Poor Law. But, he continues . . .] the real comfort is, that other systems do not in reality work better. [He compares decentralised England with centralised France . . .] On the first blush of the matter, efficiency certainly does seem to be the result of centering power in the hands of individual officers responsible only to the Executive. But the plan has its drawbacks—drawbacks so serious as to reconcile an Englishman to the inconveniences of being governed by squabbling juntas of shopkeepers and tenant farmers. [The centralised managers are too ambitious . . .] and they are fearfully liable to the disease of a fixed idea. [He gives an example of a mayor of a seaside town in France who preferred building holiday homes to dykes. The results were disastrous.][31]

This does not mean that he opposes every kind of centralisation. For example, he welcomes proposed schemes for taking the administration of the Poor Law out of the hands of parish Boards of Guardians and transferring it to a larger body.[32] What he wishes to avoid is a system in which all power in all matters is in the hands of a single authority. He has two main fears: that over-centralisation will breed a system in which policy is too rigid and unrealistically simplist; and that a concentrated government will be at the mercy of an urban mob. He attributes the instability of French politics largely to the fact that it is centred geographically in Paris. In a review article on 'Provincial Liberties in France', he notes that both the *Ancien Régime* and the Revolutionary Regime favoured centralisation and that both suffered as a result at the hands of the Paris mob, and draws the moral that:

> The only possible basis for a secure and progressive freedom lies in that very local autonomy to which the Revolution was so relentlessly hostile.[33]

Revolution is only possible when

> The government is so centralised that the mob of the capital is able to dispose of it at will.[34]

A second type of institutional balance which he advocates is a balance between legislature and executive. His aim is to find a compromise between the evils of unchecked autocracy on the one hand and unstable mob rule on the other. Some of his writings foreshadow those of 'Elite Theorists' of the twentieth century: he maintains that it is impossible to work a system where there are no leaders. Thus, the desirable system cannot be a leaderless one; rather, it must be that in which the leaders are subject to effective control. The argument is propounded in the *Quarterly Review* article on 'The Confederate Struggle and Recognition'.

> Political equality is not merely a folly—it is a chimera . . . Whatever may be the written text of a Constitution, the multitude always will have leaders among them, and those leaders not selected by themselves. They may set up the pretence of political equality, if they will, and delude themselves with a belief of its existence. But the only consequence will be, that they will have bad leaders instead of good . . .
>
> Always wealth, in some countries birth, in all intellectual power and culture, mark out the men to whom, in a healthy state of feeling, a community looks to undertake its government. They have the leisure for the task, and can give to it the close attention and the preparatory study which it needs. Fortune enables them to do it for the most part gratuitously, so that the struggles of ambition are not defiled by the taint of sordid greed . . . They are the aristocracy of a country in the original and best sense of the word. Whether a few of them are decorated by honorary titles or enjoy hereditary privileges, is a matter of secondary moment . . .
>
> Unlimited power would be as ill-bestowed upon them as upon any other set of men. They must be checked by constitutional forms and watched by an active public opinion, lest their rightful pre-eminence should degenerate into the domination of a class. But woe to a community that deposes them altogether.[35]

His view of the functions of the House of Commons is similar to that of John Stuart Mill. It should function as a check on the executive, but it should have no further powers. Salisbury's fear was that the extension of the franchise would put so much power in the hands of the elected representatives of the people that they would be able to exercise capricious control over the executive. He was writing his articles in the period between the First and the Second Reform Bills and it was during this period that the power of the House of Commons was at its height; he felt that this predominance would only increase with a large extension of the franchise:

> The House of Commons would undoubtedly be a singularly unfit body to exercise executive power. Its proceedings are too slow, its policy too uncertain, and too dependent on the numerical majority of the moment. And the very publicity which is the breath of life to it would be fatal to functions requiring accurate and often secret information . . . But it is in the power of the House of Commons to extend this executive authority to whatever it thinks fit . . . The control which it possesses, if it pleases to exercise it, is quite absolute. By a simple vote it can paralyse any single department or all the departments of the civil service.[36]

He repeats this view in the *Quarterly Review* article 'Disintegration' when he complains that

> All confidence in fixed principles or a determinate policy is gone.[37]

The reason is that for the first time Parliament is completely supreme. It can dismiss a ministry at will. The same sentiment is mentioned with great frequency in *The Saturday Reviews*.[38]

A check on the precipitate use by the House of Commons of its powers can be provided by the House of Lords. Salisbury fully realises that the popular chamber, the House of Commons, must normally wield legislative powers. What he fears, however, is that public opinion will sometimes be led into temporary extremism and that this will be reflected in unwise legislation. The House of Lords should on these occasions exercise a delaying power which will give the public the opportunity of deciding whether the original legislation was really what they wished or whether it had just been a passing whim.

> In times of storm, the Peers form a breakwater over which the waves of popular fury may harmlessly break, and which may secure, until the agitation has subsided, institutions that would have been otherwise swept away.[39]

In times of calm it provides an opportunity of mending any

careless legislative workmanship of the Commons and it also
gives a public platform to men of prominence. Salisbury was
dismayed by the failure of the existing House of Lords to
fulfil its functions adequately. This led him on several
occasions to propose reform of the Lords by the appointment
of new Peers taken from the world of business and other such
spheres.[40]

Finally, he was a keen advocate of a free press and laid
great emphasis on its constitutional role. He points out at
least two functions of the press. It provides a forum for the
discussion of public issues and can thus act as the medium
through which new issues can be brought to the attention of
the public and of Parliament.[41] This, in turn, might have the
effect of inducing the government to introduce legislation. A
more important function is that of providing a detailed
check on the administration and the judiciary. He calls the
press 'one of the surest guarantees by which [governmental]
efficiency can be secured'.[42] He considers at length the case
which formed the subject of the St. Giles enquiry of 1865.[43]
The matter originated in a letter received by a magistrate
from a pauper who claimed protection for a brother pauper
who was dying as a result of treatment he was receiving in a
workhouse. The resulting enquiry brought to light the scan-
dalous treatment which paupers habitually received in
workhouses and it also demonstrated how difficult it was for
them, in their deprived condition, to use the recognised
channels through which they could complain of their treatment. Salisbury recognises that there will always be a tendency for Poor Law nurses to become callous to the sufferings
of the paupers and concludes that the nurses should be constantly supervised. The only method which he considers
stands a chance of success is the threat of exposure by an
ever-vigilant press.[44] He takes the same position in a leader
on 'The Press and the Bench'. The article was written on the
occasion of an attack on the press by the Lord Chief Justice,
Lord Cockburn.

> The Press, as the organ of opinion, has fought its way to the
> position it now holds, not under the protection of the Courts of
> Law, but in their teeth.[45]

He continues with the observation that, of all public authorities, the Judges—appointed virtually for life—need the kind of check that the press provides.

> Most of us have been used to think that public men are all the better for being well looked after, and that a searching criticism of their actions is the best security that those actions will be kept free of a corrupt or selfish taint.

Salisbury's predictions about the results of extended franchise did not come to pass. He thought that the result would be the strengthening of Parliament *vis-à-vis* the executive. Exactly the opposite happened. The extension of the franchise was accompanied by the extension of the organisation of political parties and the concentration of power in the hands of their leaders. This meant that Cabinets, formed out of the leading members of the majority party in the Commons, experienced less difficulty in controlling the back-bench M.P.s than the Cabinets of Salisbury's time had done. But here, as in the last chapter, a distinction must be made between Salisbury's analysis and the sense of judgement with which he drew specific conclusions from it. Some of those conclusions have been falsified by events; his general analysis has not. Indeed, current discussions on the Reform of Parliament are based on a recognition of Salisbury's main point: that a position must be found where the government and the administration under it are not constantly endangered by Parliament, but where their actions are kept constantly under a healthy check.

CHAPTER VI

International Relations

To say that Salisbury's ultimate goal in international affairs was to obtain peace is to state the obvious. Or so, at least, it may seem. For are not all policies directed in the long run towards the establishment and maintenance of peace? This is unfortunately far from the case, for there is a whole school of thought which welcomes international conflict and war itself as an arena of national glorification and aggrandisement. It is worth quoting at some length from Hegel's paragraphs on 'Sovereignty viz-à-vis foreign states' which come from the section on 'The Ethical Life of the State' in the *Philosophy of Right*.

. . . The State has individuality . . . Individuality is awareness of one's existence as a unit in sharp distinction from others. It manifests itself here in the State as a relation to other States, each of which is autonomous vis-à-vis the others. This autonomy embodies the mind's actual awareness of itself as a unit and hence it is the most fundamental freedom which a people possesses as well as its highest dignity . . .

It is the individual [person's] substantive duty . . . to maintain this substantive [national] individuality, i.e. the independence and sovereignty of the State, at the risk and sacrifice of property and life, as well as opinion and everything else naturally comprised in the compass of life . . .

War is not to be regarded as an absolute evil . . . War has the higher significance that by its agency, as I have remarked elsewhere, the ethical health of peoples is preserved in their indifference to the stabilisation of finite institutions; just as the blowing of the winds preserves the sea from the foulness which

119

would be the result of a prolonged calm, so also corruption in nations would be the product of prolonged, let alone 'perpetual' peace.

For Salisbury, 'national individuality' is not a positive object of policy. And, in so far as the pursuit of it is likely to lead—as Hegel and many others recognise—to international conflict, it is positively pernicious. For if a result of social and political organisation is that men fight each other as groups or as nations instead of individually, then internal peace will have been of little avail. His aim is to achieve a situation that combines internal harmony with international peace and, in general, the principles guiding his views on dealings between nations are similar and complementary to the principles of national organisation which have been outlined in Chapter V.

Glory is not a goal of foreign policy. Instead, this policy is to be guided totally by a calculus of the interests of the citizens of Britain, and must constantly recognise that the ultimate evil that can befall them is war.

Accordingly, he is resolutely opposed to the 'principle of nationality' and has little sympathy with the nationalist movements that were forming and increasing in virulence in the Europe of the nineteenth century, movements both of the left and the right. He has two main objections to nationalism: that it tends to be essentially artificial, and that it leads to aggressive foreign policies. It is his opinion that there are very few organic political units which can be called 'nations' and can reasonably be said to possess a distinct and unified will. Admittedly there are small cultural and ethnic groupings throughout Europe, but it is impractical to divide existing states into their constituent racial and cultural divisions (i.e. *nationes* in the strict Latin sense of the word), for the resulting units will be too small.

> The triumph of nationalities, the uprooting of all ancient landmarks, and the splitting up of mankind into a multitude of infinitesimal governments, in accordance with their actual differences of race, would be to undo the work of civilisation

and renounce all the benefits which the slow and painful process of consolidation has procured for mankind.[1]

However, nationalism in the sense of the term that was becoming current involved the creation of new, and in Salisbury's view, synthetic units. For example, German nationalism arose only in the period subsequent to the Napoleonic Wars and 'had never existed before'.[2] What had only recently been a series of 'mere local traditions'[3] had now been supplanted by a new 'national German feeling'.[4] He is also convinced by the nationalist claim that the people of various countries should be allowed to determine their own fate. It is useless, for instance, to look into history to divine a national will of the Polish people:

> The Poland that contrived by weakness or corruption to lose its independence was a Poland consisting of a hundred and fifty thousand souls. Such, at the time of the partition, was the number of the Polish nobility, who alone bore a share in conducting that ceremonious anarchy which was called a Government.[5]

On the same lines, Salisbury replies to the criticism that the statesmen at the Congress of Vienna had taken no account of the wishes of European national groups:

> It was impossible for any statesmen to consult the wishes of the peoples, for the simple reason that the peoples had no enduring and settled interests to consult.[6]

When a sense of national feeling is consciously forged—and several of the reviews comment on the use of folklore and language in Germany for this purpose—the effects are often bad, for national feelings will so often be strengthened by the intentional encouragement of aggressive xenophobia. In the twentieth century there have been a large number of cases in which this process has been apparent—notably in the Nazi Germany of the 1930s. In the 1860s also Salisbury followed the expansion of Germany and its military victories in 1864, 1866 and 1870 and was quick to connect Germany's new territorial and imperial ambitions with her new-found nationalism. He accounted for Bismarck's aggressive foreign policy by saying that it was a means of giving an outlet to passions that would otherwise have been spent in democratic societies and associations opposed to his rule. It also acted as cement for Germany's shaky national unity. In short, he wrote, 'it adjourns all internal controversies'.[7]

In a world of different nations, some of whose interests were in conflict, and some of whom wished to attack others merely for vainglory, how could any country—a country, say, like Britain—ensure that it avoided destructive conflict with other nations? Such a question posed in terms of nations is more difficult than the same problem put in terms of individuals. For individuals can be controlled and kept from anti-social actions by the establishment of a higher and more powerful authority. But no supra-national body regulates international conflict. Salisbury expresses the difficulty in its classical form in a late contribution to *The Quarterly Review*.

> Those who reflect little on political difficulties, confuse the code of morals which applies to an individual with that which applies to a nation; and in any case in which it would be morally wrong for an individual to use force, they speak as if it would be equally wrong for a nation to use it. They entirely omit to consider that individuals are protected against wrong by an organised government . . . As a collection of individuals, we live under the highest and latest development of civilisation . . . As a collection of nations we live in an age of the merest *Faustrecht*, in which each one obtains his rights precisely in proportion to his ability, or that of his allies, to fight for them.[8]

And he concludes elsewhere: 'it is obvious that an eighth commandment for nations would be a very difficult code of morality to construct'.[9]

The lack of any higher mediating authority makes the dangers of international misunderstandings very great. Salisbury is convinced that conflict between nations is often against the basic interests of all the participants and results from avoidable tangles. His general response to the problem is guided by the principle of stated national objectives.

As a basic formula, the aims of Britain should be limited: they should be of national scope, and there should be no attempt at aggrandisement or territorial expansion; at the same time, no other country should be allowed to be in a position in which it might be tempted to attack Britain. In view of these limited objectives, and conscious of the ease with which accidental misunderstanding sometimes produces needless conflict—for there is no international method of arbitration to prevent such misunderstanding—Salisbury is an unyielding advocate of frank, guileless diplomacy. British diplomats cannot afford to ignore the possibility of intrigue on the part of other nations, but they should not indulge in it themselves. The principle of stated objectives implies total opposition to the use of bluff, bluster or threats in the conduct of international relations, and to the undertaking of commitments which a country does not fully intend to fulfil.

He disapproves of all forms of irregular diplomacy, such as the use of private individuals in negotiations, on the grounds that they can lead to dangerous misunderstandings. In a leader published in *The Saturday Review* in 1862 he describes the disadvantages of 'diplomacy through pamphleteers' as conducted by Louis Napoleon.[10] Misleading articles had appeared in *La France*, a journal which was accepted as a semi-official organ of the Emperor's views. The initial advantage of such a medium for the Emperor was that he could use his pamphleteers as a mouthpiece but could at the same time reserve the freedom to disclaim their assertions if changing situations made it advisable to do so. The drawback was that if one of the pamphleteers went out of hand, no denials would be sufficient to convince people that the views expressed in the semi-official journal were not his own, and he might in this way be drawn into involvements and troubles which were quite unnecessary.

Similarly, he attacks the use of social diplomacy, 'the system of after-dinner manifestoes':

Statesmen are but human, after all, and bad wine is generally strong. Then, endurance of three hours of oppressive weakness creates an intense desire to relieve the nerves by some vigorous display of energy, which will show itself in the phrases even of a practised orator.

. . . Even experienced speakers are apt to drop expressions of which they would have preferred, in cold blood, to modify the force. But the dinner-manifestoes involve many more elements of danger. A good orator always has some sympathy with the audience to whom he is speaking. There will always be a tinge of recklessness in the phrases even of a calm and sober speaker, when he is addressing an excited, hallooing, thumping, half-drunk mob of guests.[11]

A constant source of complaint is the policy of Lord John Russell, Foreign Secretary in Lord Palmerston's government; a policy of 'fierce notes and pacific measures'.[12] He criticises Russell for getting involved in petty incidents like the Macdonald Affair (see page 105) when Russell intervened on behalf of a British traveller who had been arrested in Germany. In spite of the justice of the case,

> it is a great mistake . . . to treat of this affair as if it affected higher questions of diplomacy. Until the official world of Prussia is much reformed, the more the facilities of travelling bring the two nations into contact the less good-will is likely to be generated. But these feelings are not calculated to influence to any perceptible extent the policy of the Government. If national hatreds could make war, we should have been at war with France and America many times during the past forty years.[13]

Russell's readiness to resort to gunboat policy was a special object of Salisbury's wrath, especially when it was exercised in the interests not of the nation but of adventurers and assorted drunks who happened to be English.

> We do not desire to be made ridiculous or odious in the eyes of the rest of the world by an extravagant exhibition of arrogance.[14]

He describes some of the more flagrant uses of gunboat diplomacy in the celebrated *Quarterly Review* article on the 'Foreign Policy of England' (1863), and, in particular, the case of the 'Forte':

> No Englishman can recount the circumstances which brought this country to the verge of war, for a cause of offence so apocryphal and so paltry, without feelings of mortification and

shame. The facts are shortly these: Three officers—two mid-
shipmen and a chaplain—went out from Rio for an excursion
into the country. In the afternoon they dined at a country inn
of which the amount has been the subject of some controversy
. . . They travelled on their road until they came to a certain
guardhouse on their way to Rio, and at this guardhouse they
found a sentry. What passes between gentlemen who have
dined and the guardians of the public peace is always a matter
of some dispute . . . The sentry's account of the matter is that
they came up to him flourishing a stick in his face and making
an uncomplimentary remark about his trousers—and that he
took them up because they tried to take hold of his legs and
throw him over the parapet. . . . Accused of intoxication, and
unable . . . to give a good account of themselves, our heroes
were locked up. But their sorrows were not of long duration.
They obtained writing materials and contrived to communi-
cate with the English Consul; and as soon as their rank was
explained to the authorities by somebody who did understand
Portuguese, they were released at once.[15]

'It is evident,' the article continues, 'the British Government
had no case at all: they had not the shadow of a grievance.'
Russell thought otherwise. 'He did not wait for a moment to
investigate the circumstances of the case. He did not even
write to demand an explanation. He did not propose that the
subject should be submitted to arbitration. He accepted at
once, in its most exaggerated form, the statement of the
three young officers, and sat down without delay to write a
despatch in his most hectoring style to the English Minister at
Rio.' Salisbury quotes from the despatch:

Her Majesty's Government cannot submit to have such an
outrage unatoned for, and you will therefore embody the
foregoing remarks in a note to the Brazilian Government,
warning them at the same time of the serious light in which
Her Majesty's Government have viewed the case, and you
will demand:
  1. That the Ensign of the guard be dismissed from the
service.
  2. That the sentry who commenced the attack shall be adequately punished.
  3. That an apology be made by the Brazilian Government for
this outrage on British naval officers; . . . [and so on].[16]

Leaving questions of right and wrong to the side, behaviour of this kind is bound to lead to a reputation for cowardly and overweening diplomacy, especially when it is seen that Britain is not willing to carry out her threats when she is dealing with any of the larger powers. In her relations with Germany over the question of Schleswig-Holstein and with Russia at the time of the Polish rising, Britain showed that she was not willing to keep to her word if it meant conflict with a more powerful country. Russell's kind of policy was thus shown to combine the actions of the bully with those of the coward:

> It is only when the two qualities of heroism and meekness are cunningly combined that they earn unmitigated contempt . . .
>
> But, upon the least ideal and most commercial views, it is not convenient to be despised. The defence of a high reputation is, after all, a cheap one. A nation which is known to be willing as well as able to defend itself will probably escape attack. Where the disposition to fight in case of need is wanting, or is dependent upon some casual and fleeting gust of passion, the political gamblers who speculate in war will naturally be inclined to invest in the venture of aggression. The policy which invites contempt seldom fails to earn a more substantial punishment. It is rarely permitted to take refuge in the cynical adage that hard words break no bones. Contempt is soon followed by open insult, and insult meekly borne draws injury quickly after it. And there is a point where injury becomes intolerable, and even the most submissive must turn . . . The time must come at last when aggression must be resisted, and then, when it is too late, the expensiveness of a name for cowardice forces itself upon every apprehension.[17]

Russell's fault in regard to his policy towards Denmark and Poland was not that he did not go to their aid. It was merely that, having made pronouncements on their behalf and having given assurances to Denmark and Poland, he did not carry these promises to the point of action when it became apparent that it would involve sacrifice to do so. Salisbury makes the following conclusions:

> Lord Russell's entire inability to perceive the connexion between advice and action is the true cause of the discredit

into which, as regards Europe at least, he has brought his country.

Those who attempt to defend the conduct of the Government usually make an effort to transfer the discussion to another question. They insist that England had no sufficient interest in the restoration of Poland, or in preserving the integrity of Denmark, to outweigh the manifold horrors of war. No doubt this is an interesting subject to discuss; and arguments of a forcible character might be advanced upon the side of peace, especially in regard to the question of Poland. But that is not the issue that has been raised by those who call the Government to account for the discredit they have brought on England. Non-intervention, in the abstract, may be good policy or bad: it is non-intervention heralded by threats to one side, and promises to the other, that we condemn. It is the attempt to secure the advantages of action by blustering diplomacy when there was no real resolve to fight that we deplore. It is not in the policy itself, which for the moment we pass by, but in the language by which it is introduced, that we find the deep offence that the Government has committed against English honour.[18]

In all these varied criticisms of Russell's foreign policy, he is making the same basic point. A diplomat must avoid needless aggravation on matters that are of less than national importance; he should never indulge in empty threats that debase the currency of his words, but should state his central objectives and should hold to them.

His attitude to treaties further reflects the principle of stated national objectives. The absence of a higher authority to mediate between nations makes it imperative that nations should stand solidly by their contractual obligations with other countries so that chaos and bloodshed can be avoided. In external affairs, much more than internally, there is a clear long-term utility in a consistent policy. The fulfilment of treaty obligations admittedly involves sacrifices and dangers in the short term—but in the long run, if foreign nations know that England's word is solid, they will not take the chance of attacking her interests as covered by her treaties. A corollary of this determination to honour international obligations, even at great cost, is that statesmen should exercise the greatest caution in entering into such agreements in the first place.

The 'balance of power', the second staple rule of his theory of international affairs, is the application to foreign policy of the principle of 'equilibrium' used by Salisbury in home affairs. He recognised that sometimes 'great wars come from little causes'[19] and these wars—the unnecessary ones—he aimed to avoid by an application of the principle of stated objectives. But he also realised that some conflicts were not accidental but were the result of deeper causes and disapproved of the style of diplomacy that attempted to conceal not only cracks but deep cleavages as well. Once a direct confrontation of interests had developed, it had to be played out; 'diplomacy' would only make things worse in the long run. In his article on 'The Danish Duchies' he makes it plain that

> The quarrel is not one of misunderstanding, or which is likely to be appeased by compromise. It is that perpetual form of quarrel which, in its nature, is irreconcilable, and which must always exist between those who mean to eat and those who are averse to being eaten.[20]

And he warns against the dangers of a policy which refuses to recognise the seriousness of the situation. Faced by such a state of affairs, England has no alternative but to stand by her treaty obligations, even if this entails fighting. For the alternative must be even more serious in its effects. In the long run, though, the general objective is to prevent a situation of such direct conflict from developing. This can best be achieved by blocking the emergence of any one nation so powerful that it might be tempted to attack its neighbours. The basis of English foreign policy is summed up by Salisbury in his first contribution to *The Quarterly Review*.

> England had once a traditional policy which was not very difficult to fathom or to apply. She did not meddle with other nations' doings when they concerned her not. But she recognised the necessity of an equilibrium and the value of a public law among the states of Europe. When a great power abused its superiority by encroaching on the frontier of its weaker neighbours, she looked on their cause as her own. But a change

has come over the spirit of our policy in recent years. It is no longer dictated by any single principle, but it is the confused and heterogeneous resultant of two conflicting elements.[21]

In several of his finest articles he traces the application of the principle of a balance of power by Pitt and by Castlereagh.

In the spring of 1792 Pitt, as is well known, neither wished nor looked for war . . . As long as English interests were untouched, he pursued the wise policy of non-intervention. But English interests could not remain untouched very long. After victory over Austria, the French came to the banks of the Scheldt, and the Revolutionary Government intimated their intention of opening the navigation of the river to armed vessels for the purpose of investing Antwerp. At this point it became impossible for England to continue to look on in silence. The closing of the Scheldt was guaranteed by treaty with Holland . . . Nor was this the only point where this aggression upon neutral rights concerned us. England has ever watched the Scheldt with an especial jealousy. It has always been one of the cardinal maxims of her policy to secure that it should not fall into the hands of any power who she had need to fear.[22]

Castlereagh followed a similar policy:

During the war his aim was to overthrow Napoleon, and to reduce France within her ancient limits. After the war his aim was to uphold the balance of power, and so to secure lasting peace to Europe.[23]

In his writings on contemporary foreign affairs, Salisbury uses the same principle. At the end of the 1850s, the expansionist power in Europe seemed to be France. In a violent article ('France and Europe', *Bentley's Quarterly Review*, October 1859), he gives a warning against French 'Imperialism', asserts that 'love of Empire is inevitably a love of war',[24] and predicts that Louis Napoleon will attack 'some neighbour whose territory is easy to conquer, and near enough to keep—some Naboth'.[25]

Accordingly, his European sympathies are with Germany and he expresses regrets that the Treaty of Vienna left Germany so divided, thus weakening the only real bulwark against France. He concludes as follows:

129

In the storm which is impending over Europe, and of which we have already felt the preliminary gusts, it is to Germany alone that we can look for the alliance of a people—the only alliance that will avail us now . . .

The Germans must always be our natural allies for they are the only great people besides ourselves who harbour no schemes of European conquest, and whose welfare is bound up with peace . . . The course of events has linked our interests together.[26]

But the course of events was to change rapidly in the years which followed the writing of this article, and as Germany became more powerful, the equilibrium principle demanded that English favour veer towards France. It was not that the regime of Louis Napoleon became any more attractive to Salisbury. It was simply that there was more to fear from the newly powerful Germany than from France in a state of enfeeblement. As he writes in a *Quarterly Review* article on the Franco-Prussian War ('The Terms of Peace', October 1870),

the diplomatic science of modern times must be recast. There is no portion of the European equilibrium in which the power of France does not form an important element, and that element must now be struck out of every calculation.[27]

The preservation of a balance of power could be achieved, England's word respected and her treaties assured only if she were able to defend her interests when they were attacked. This meant that a standing army was necessary. At the same time, as Salisbury realised full well, a standing army becomes restless if it is not given any fighting to do, and is not easily amenable to civilian control. Furthermore, its very existence constitutes a provocation to other nations and thus acts as a threat to peace. So, here again, Salisbury demands a sense of proportion and favours a middle position. He calls for a standing army, but insists that it is not huge and repeatedly advocates some form of control of army organisation, though he never quite decides which form of control is most realistic. His main plea is for a stable and long-term policy towards the army. For it is the sudden cutting of defence estimates at times of economic retrenchment that is so dangerous, and the sudden build-up of forces—rather than their absolute level—which is provocative to other nations.

The article he wrote in December 1862 on the 'Reduction of Estimates' is typical of several he wrote on the subject. It was written after the Government had set up an economy committee at the Horse Guards.

> The evil days of retrenchment are coming on us fast. We have indulged in a financial revel, and we are awakening to the retributive headache.
>
> The first idea of a perplexed financier always is to cut down the army. It is looked upon as a sort of luxury, like a private gentleman's carriage, which is naturally 'put down' when times are bad. The philosophy of this plan is not easy to understand. The army is either an indispensable necessity or an intolerable waste . . . Defence is an article of the first necessity.[28]

He complains about 'capricious guests of parsimony'[29] and gives the events of 1853 as an example of how parsimonious finance and a balanced series of Estimates were followed by military disaster in the Crimea.

He puts the case against huge establishments of arms in an article on 'Scientific Warfare'. If one nation can outproduce others, tyranny will be easier. If no nation can outproduce others, an arms race will be the result:

> A constant state of preparation for war will, of course, be more necessary than ever, and the millenium of reduced armaments will be even more distant than it is now. As long as contests were decided by men, active enlistment might extemporise an army in a few months; but sudden preparations will be impossible if contests are to be decided by machines of vast cost, requiring themselves an enormous apparatus and specially-educated labour for their production.
>
> There is, of course, another possibility which is even less satisfactory to contemplate. It is conceivable that invention may take another turn, and that some missile may be discovered, cheaply and easily procurable, and so fearfully destructive that it will be to modern armour-plates what gun-powder was to medieval armour . . . Progress in such a direction is hardly to be hoped for. Mutual slaughter goes on quite fast enough, and needs no new facilities; and the Americans

have by their example wholly falsified the doctrine that such facilities, by sharpening war, also shorten it.[30]

He does not examine this problem in more detail in any other of his articles, but the logic of his position would imply that he would favour an attempt at negotiated disarmament in order to ensure that a balance was preserved as all the powers were in the process of reducing their armaments.

Salisbury's clinical approach, almost totally lacking in appeal to patriotism and chauvinist feelings, and his anxiousness to avoid unnecessary international responsibilities is most noticeable in his writings on colonial affairs. He rejects the argument that colonisation is a sacred mission for the white man in general and for the Briton in particular. His cynical attitude towards 'master-race' theories has already been quoted in Chapter IV:

Seizing a coloured man's land and giving it to a white man is an operation now generally known as the progress of colonisation.[31]

On another occasion, he partially acknowledges the Imperialist argument that

It would be impossible to lay down that any barbarous nomad tribe is at liberty to lock up the most productive regions of the earth, or that no extent of misgovernment can justify the forcible release of the oppressed from the oppressor.[32]

But he is unwilling to follow this view to its logical conclusion. For,

to assume the reverse of these propositions would be to wipe away the law of nations altogether.

His view is that Britain had been landed with colonies, not in the pursuit of the general interest or of conscious Government policy, but because it was in the private interest of merchants, land sharks and missionaries. 'Except in the case of convict colonies, the British Government has scarcely ever taken the initiative in colonisation.'[33]

The colonists' arguments about their colonial mission were transparent excuses for the exercise of greedy self-interest. He comments roughly on the Maori War in New Zealand.

On the settlers' side, the 'damned nigger' principle with which we are so familiar in India and the United States, is showing itself more and more distinctly through a thin veil of commonplace professions. It is easy to see, by the tone of argument employed, that treaties and the rights which rest on them are looked on as of very small account compared to 'the advance of civilisation' and the 'prevalence of the stronger race'.[34]

In actual fact, he points out that 'the colony was formed by the first colonists as a commercial speculation'.[35] And Australia was little different, for its inhabitants were merely the 'poor gentility' and the 'starving clerkdom' who had emigrated because they thought 'gold was to be had for the picking up'.[36]

In most of the colonial settlements, the newly arrived emigrants had drawn up land agreements with the natives which they had later ignored. With his stringent views about the keeping of treaties, Salisbury condemned this behaviour outright.

Emotion and international law apart, the factor which settles Salisbury's attitude towards colonisation is expense. And his attitude here is a good illustration of his general 'balance-sheet' approach. For he does not consider that far-off colonies vitally affect British interests. Writing in 1861, he says that the colonies 'can no longer claim the first or even the second rank among the subjects of the day'. Accordingly,

the account between us and them is now a very simple one. On their side they furnish us with a market for our exports, which some economists think would be straightened, and others think would be widened, if their connexion with England were to cease. On our side, we spend about a million and a half yearly on their defence—an expenditure which enables us to furnish an agreeable variety of station to our soldiers, and to indulge in the sentiment that the sun never sets on our Empire.[37]

So the account is in debit. The constant difficulty is that the colonists start wars without the permission and against the will of the British Government and then expect British troops to extricate them from the difficulties that follow. Salisbury maintains that it is the interest of the British population as a whole that must determine national policy and he expands on his discontents in an article entitled 'Prodigal Sons'. He writes that any family contains a ne'er-do-well whose object it is to spend as much of the family fortune as possible. And it is the same with England: the colonists from New Zealand and South Africa are the 'black sheep in our colonial flock'.

> It would be madness, they think, to undertake any expenditure which can be successfully shifted upon the shoulders of anyone else. So long as England is foolish enough to pay, they are not foolish enough to refuse . . .
>
> If the next refusal [by the colonists] to contribute were followed by an immediate withdrawal of troops, the colonists might possibly arrive at the conviction that a rather more equitable policy was a better investment for their money.[38]

In another article, dealing this time with Canada ('Canada and its Cost'), he welcomes the mood of a debate in the House of Commons when 'the sentimental view was at a discount, and hard material considerations formed the staple of the argument'.[39] The root of the trouble with the colonies is that it is impossible to control the settlers because they are too far away, but it is impossible to leave them to face the consequences of their actions unaided. This leads to the conclusion that colonies are undesirable. In 1864, there is an article in which he writes in opposition to Britain's involvement in further Ashanti and Maori wars, 'Little Wars' as he sarcastically calls them:

> We are attempting to conquer what we cannot possibly hold.[40]

The occupation of New Zealand requires the permanent garrison of a whole regiment 'at the expense of the mother country':

> A genuine Empire is a very grand thing. But a sham Empire, consisting chiefly of titles and professions of allegiance heavily paid for in hard cash, is rather a *parvenu* counterfeit of the real thing.

He concludes with a lesson 'which England needs to learn by heart'—that if the centre of an empire be vulnerable, 'ships, colonies and commerce are rather a source of peril than of strength'.[41]

But, in spite of his disapproval of colonisation for both sentimental and materialistic reasons, he is resigned to the extension of England's colonial burden. An example of this fatalism is found in an article on 'The Revolution in Japan' (1863). He fears that a consequence of the weakness of Japan which was likely to be a result of the revolution might be the forced opening of Japan to foreign trade. And if France and Russia make a grab for Japan,

> will England stand idly by as an indifferent spectator? It will scarcely be in human nature for her to do so. It is easy to philosophise about the vanity of extended territory, until we see it grasped by others ... The instinct of the nation will never be content without a share in the booty which it sees its neighbours greedily dividing. Yet of all the burdensome acquisitions England can possibly make, any portion of the Empire of Japan must needs be the most burdensome.[42]

He ends the article with the hope that the government of Japan will re-establish its strength so that England might avoid the dilemmas that a scramble for Japan would pose.

Salisbury's international politics with regard to colonies and foreign nations alike is conservative in the most direct sense of the word. He is fully aware of the explosive cycle whereby aggression invites counter-attack, conquest leads to attempts at reconquest and war produces a momentum of its own. It is always his aim to block these cycles of events before they begin and to break their momentum where they already exist. The simplest way of doing this is to recognise the *status quo* in all but the most exceptional of circumstances. Territorial wars, in particular, can be avoided only by the recognition of existing boundaries by all countries.

As the Franco-Prussian War was coming to its close, Salisbury wrote an article recommending the following terms of peace:

> The arrangements which statesmen ought to contemplate must be those which will tend to make the two nations, equal in bravery and scarcely dissimilar in numbers, live side by side in industry and peace. They will be very blind if they base their plans on the assumption of a permanent inferiority in French military talent; and nothing but such an assumption would,

even in Prussian interests, justify conditions that will act as a
permanent defiance . . .[43]

He maintains that Germany's alleged need for Alsace-
Lorraine as a defence against France is a specious excuse for
aggrandisement:

> 'Pacific Germany' is a mere diplomatic commonplace. There is
> nothing in history to justify such a pretension . . .
> If Europe were sufficiently united to force the belligerents
> into reasonable terms, its best interests would be served by
> absolutely prohibiting any change of frontiers. The first object
> of a treaty of peace should be to make future war impossible . . .
> a ceded territory would be a constant memorial of humiliation.

It is not only in his attitude towards territorial change, but
in all facets of his foreign policy that Salisbury shows his
desire for stability and lack of change. Indeed, the corollary
of the principle of stated national objectives is that these
stated objectives should remain constant: for if a given policy
were liable to capricious change, it would not provide the
desired confidence and the necessary warning to other
nations. And the aim of a policy of balance is not just to
create an equilibrium between nations, but to create an
equilibrium that ensures stability. It is on similar lines that
he thinks there should be no sudden changes in the size of a
country's standing army.

The reasoning throughout is that action on the part of a
state is bound to produce a whole series of reactions, and this
chain reaction might well produce entanglements and
misunderstandings that will end in conflict. The evils of an
existing but stable situation are thus normally to be preferred
to the uncertainties and dangers of change.

If criticism of this willingness to accept the *status quo* is to
be offered, it must be on the grounds that it sometimes leads
Salisbury to a static and unnecessarily fatalistic approach. An
example of this, perhaps, is his colonial policy. He regrets
colonial expansion which in his view hinders the prosperity
of the mother country. But, though he opposes any active
extension of the Empire, he is willing to acquiesce in any
extension once it has been made.

In general though, he was fully aware of the fact that, in spite of attempts at stabilisation, international situations do sometimes change, and that when they change, they require a changed response.

A more general criticism of Salisbury's attachment to the *status quo* as a principle of international relations is that it is an easy principle for a satisfied island state like the England of the nineteenth century to hold. The burdens it imposed on some of the European nations were greater. Salisbury would probably have been willing to acknowledge cases in which the general principle did not apply and when a stable cycle was at work, so that the redress of an existing grievance would satisfy rather than provoke the parties involved.

Inevitably it will be asked whether Salisbury's foreign policy favoured 'isolation'. It did not.

His theory of international relations is certainly a theory of limited activity, and a view that holds that permanent alliances are impractical and undesirable. But Salisbury does not think of isolation as something splendid: he writes that it is a 'foolish' policy.[44]

He disliked the meddlesome conduct of diplomacy. Meddlesomeness, at best, was aggravating. At its most serious, it was downright dangerous. It was for this reason that he did not consider that petty matters concerning the welfare of individuals lay within the province of national policy. The central aim of diplomacy was the avoidance of war, an aim which should not be endangered or obscured by the pursuit of other insignificant objects. His approach also involved limited activity in so far as he strongly held the view that there should be no intervention in the internal affairs of foreign states. His grounds were that this served only to aggravate those internal disturbances and to endanger international peace. He considers the question in some detail in his *Quarterly Review* article on Castlereagh. He is discussing the Treaty of Vienna:

> All the failures that have taken place have arisen from one cause: the practice of foreign intervention in domestic quarrels. There is no experience which the experience of nations more uniformly condemns, and none which governments more

consistently pursue. Domestic discord is bad enough; but the passions which provoke it burn themselves out at last, and the contending parties are eventually schooled by each other into the moderation which alone makes the co-existence of freedom and order possible. But if foreign intervention on either side be once threatened, much more if it be carried out, a venom is infused into the conflict which no reaction weakens and no revenge exhausts . . . The history of the last seventy years is strewn with the wrecks of national prosperity which these well-meant interventions have caused. Often they ruin at once the party on whose behalf they are made; and even if they bring it to a seeming victory at first, they ruin it not less effectively in the end. Incurable impotence and decay is the almost certain punishment of civil triumphs won with foreign arms.[45]

However, it is not his general advocacy of limited activity that leads Salisbury to oppose permanent alliances. His reason is simply that alliances are based on interests and not on historical sentiment, and the fact that the interests of two nations coincide at any given time cannot guarantee that they will continue to do so far into the future. He maintains that an essential principle of England's traditional policy is

that in the views of a statesman charged with government, an absolutely paramount place must be reserved for the interests and the honour of the country whose force he is directing. In every case in which the claims of his own country come into competition with those of another, he is bound to remember that he is not an arbitrator between the two, but a trustee for the interests of the one.[46]

In other words, there can be no alliance so firm that a foreign secretary ceases to owe his fundamental duty to his own country but owes it to the alliance collectively. Interests change. And alliances must change with them. The maintenance of equilibrium, for instance, demanded that England moved away from her support of Germany as Germany became more powerful. He also viewed permanent alliances with disfavour as he realised that the internal politics of a country like England (and this he blamed on her democratic constitution) were inevitably liable to change. He preferred to make no treaties rather than to store up trouble for the future by signing treaties which risked being broken.

But to say that he opposed permanent and total alliances is not to say that he was opposed to alliances of all sorts. And to argue that he advocated a policy of limited activity is to argue quite a different view than that which maintains that Salisbury's external policy was one of complete inactivity.

CHAPTER VII

Thought into Action (1854–68)

SALISBURY, especially during his early career in the House of Commons, stood out from his Party in his apparently unbending resistance to change in all its forms, and some historians—and even numbers of his contemporaries and friends—have been tempted to regard his politics at this period as a purely emotional reaction to a reality he found unpleasant. According to F. B. Smith, for example, Salisbury's arguments, though often rational in form, were inspired by 'an unreasoning fear of the masses' and constituted 'a dangerous call to preserve a caste system of government'.[1] He contrasts Salisbury's arguments against Reform with the coldly intellectual orations of Robert Lowe who 'gave the case against Reform a universality and consistency that transcended the narrow interest arguments of the gentry'.[2] Smith's contrast is unwarranted. Salisbury's actions as a Member of Parliament may have been ill-judged on occasion or lacking in finesse, but they were a direct and conscious application of the view of politics which he propounded in his writings.

As early as 1853 Salisbury put forward the programme and the approach which was to occupy him for fourteen years in Parliament. His first election address and speech to the electors of Stamford starts with a pledge to a zealous and undeviating adherence to Conservative Principles. This does not necessarily imply opposition to all changes, for he has no objection to 'cautious change', but he says he will resist 'any such tampering with our representative system as shall disturb the balance of reciprocal powers on which the stability of our constitution rests'. This view of change and equipoise controls his attitude not only to reform of the franchise but to other allied questions as well; he favours full religious toleration but opposes any 'Ultramontane' interference with the Established Church which is 'at variance with the fundamental principles of our constitution'; he opposes the secularisation of education and deplores the income tax as tending to upset the balance between classes. The address ends with a pledge of support for 'measures tending to social and sanitary improvements and the amelioration of the conditions of the labouring classes'.

In writing his address, Salisbury was influenced in part at least by the patron of the Stamford seats, the Marquis of Exeter, but it is an accurate expression of his platform and one to which he was to refer repeatedly in later years. It was clear by 1853 that the Reform Act of 1832 would not continue to be accepted as final and Conservatives were 'now called upon to enter another struggle'.[3] Until 1866 the reform issue remained for the most part under the surface and was fought out indirectly in a variety of battles centring in particular on the position of the Church. In his maiden speech, Salisbury spoke against the Oxford University Bill on the ground that it interfered with University endowments and constituted an attack on the Establishment.

> ... they were at present asked to reform the final Reform Bill of 1832; and it further appeared, that although the main argument adduced in favour of the Roman Catholic emancipation in 1829 had been, that it would set the Roman Catholic question at rest for ever, they were in this very Session called upon to pull down the last bulwark left by that measure against the attacks of the most relentless foes of the Established Church.[4]

The speeches he gave in the 1850s on the Marriage Law Amendment Bill[5] and the Church Rates Bill[6] were of the same form; he normally made out a case for the injustice or disadvantage of the particular measure under discussion and then proceeded to his real fear, that it was just a 'first blow' motivated by a desire to separate the Church from the State and consequently to subvert the constitution. The merits of the individual Bills were beside the point; partial success would not satisfy the Radicals but would spur them on; the best chance of forestalling their ultimate aims was to block them at each step they chose to make. This Salisburian reasoning appears clearly from his opposition to the Jew Bill of 1858. Hitherto their refusal to swear 'on the true oath of a Christian' had prevented practising Jews from sitting in Parliament. Salisbury admitted that Jews were unlikely to conspire against the State,[7] and that oaths penalised only the sincere. He opposed the Bill solely because the admission of Jews would mark a further stage in the secularisation of the House of Commons and would therefore increase the difficulty of upholding the Established Church.

Such a negative strategy would, of course, store up trouble for the future. Salisbury thus combined indiscriminate opposition to Radical proposals with a search for less disruptive ways of improvement.

He was seriously dissatisfied with the shortcomings of the Church of England and seems to have made attempts in the 1850s to increase its effectiveness. As he placed little confidence in the use of legislation for purposes such as these, his efforts were normally made outside Parliament, but his attitude is illustrated by a speech of 1856 on the Bishops of London and Durham Retirement Bill in which he attacked the 'ridiculously large' retirement grants to Bishops and complained that Church endowments were being directed excessively towards the Cathedrals at the expense of the Parishes.[8] The aim of forestalling the Radicals also led him in 1857 to move for a Select Committee to enquire into the use of voting papers at elections. The use of these papers would enable people to vote without going in person to the hustings. This would reduce the costs of elections and would also 'relieve us from the scandal of those occasional outbursts of riotous and disorderly conduct which were a disgrace to our political system'. In fact, he believed the adoption of the system of voting papers would remedy many of the defects in the existing condition of the electoral franchise of which reformers complained.[9]

The fullest account of his strategy in the 1850s is contained in a speech on National Education which he gave to a Mechanics' Institute at Stamford in 1856.[10] The occasion for the education controversy was the move by Russell, Milner Gibson and Pakington to abolish the existing system of grants for education by which the amount given to each school was proportionate to the amount it raised privately, and to institute a new system for raising money by an 'Education Rate' as a part of the local rates. The Liberal argument was that the existing system directed grants where they were least needed—to those schools which were in any case able to raise money of their own. In consequence, they argued, fewer children attended school in England than in America and the Continent.

Salisbury's reply starts with a typically thorough and critical examination of the Liberal statistics. He does not deny that the evil of which they complain exists, but he certainly does not believe that it is so serious, or at all events so permanent, as it has been represented to be. He agrees that action is called for, but this need not imply the abandonment of the whole system of Privy Council grants.

Special regulations for specific cases would alleviate hardship and remove cause for complaint while leaving the basic structure intact. The overriding advantage of the Privy Council system is that 'You follow a rigid unbending rule, whose equity no one can dispute, and whose application no one can mistake', and he opposes any interference with the principle of proportional grants on the ground that abandonment is bound to raise the question of the denomination of the schools to which the new grants are to be given. The only way out of 'the religious difficulty' is the alternative of non-sectarian education, which is just as bad for it also tends towards the separation of Church and State. The proposed 'Education Rate' emerges as 'the thin end of the wedge of disestablishment' and must actively be resisted.

This first period of Salisbury's parliamentary career came to an end with the defeat of Palmerston's Liberal Government and the formation of Derby's second ministry in 1858. Salisbury's jaundiced attitude to the new Ministry should not be attributed to the fact that his request for office was unproductive; his distrust in particular of Disraeli who led the Conservatives in the House of Commons was of longer standing. They were politicians of a different species. Salisbury stood firmly by his 'Conservative Principles', which meant above all opposition to any fundamental reform of the Constitution. A Conservative government strong enough to carry through a Conservative policy was all well and good. What he feared was that some leading Conservatives with Disraeli in the forefront would be so tempted by the lust for office that they would agree to form a minority administration, even if this meant governing with Radical support, and on Radical terms. If this was the only alternative to a Whig government, it was preferable to keep the Whigs in power for it was in this way that Conservative Principles would best be served. In his first speech at Stamford in 1853 he had said that the agitation for Reform was a result of a party system in which each side was tempted to 'bribe the democracy'.[11] Now, in 1858, Disraeli's policy was clear: 'it was to buy the Radical support in the enterprise of ousting the Whigs'.[12] To Salisbury this was foolish as well as unprincipled:

> If Conservative has any meaning at all, it means anti-Radical ... Hostility to Radicalism, incessant, implacable hostility, is the essential definition of Conservatism.[13]

The willingness of the Conservatives to form a minority movement meant that the day of working majorities and, therefore, of anything like systematic legislation was at an end:

> It is this chaotic, unorganised, capricious mass, looking upon politics as a game of skill in which office is the only stake, treating a party division as a means of excitement which holds a middle place between a horse-race and a thimble-rig that is called upon to face one of the most difficult crises the country has yet been summoned to go through.[14]

He extended the charges in the article in *Bentley's Quarterly Review* which appeared in July 1859:

> When Mr. Disraeli gave notice that on the last day of February

he should bring forward his Reform Bill, there was no mistaking the feeling which animated the vast majority of the House of Commons. They felt that the unscrupulous ambition of public men had pledged them to a Reform Bill, which was neither called for by the practical necessities of the country nor desired by the nation at large.[15]

In the event, the Bill was much milder than Salisbury had expected, 'Lord Aberdeen's Bill carefully strained and filtered',[16] and as he subsequently declared to the electors of Stamford, he thought it was more straightforward on his own part to follow the defects of the Bill in Committee rather than oppose it outright. But its very moderation led directly to the passing of a wrecking amendment by Lord John Russell, who favoured a different and much more far-reaching measure, and to the end of the Conservative Ministry. Salisbury was probably quite relieved.

His criticism of the Conservative Government was heightened by his view that its unnecessary preoccupation with politicking had diverted it from the most pressing problem of the day, which was the danger of French expansionism. For a number of weeks in 1859, he thought that Europe was on the brink of war. He did not believe that England was in immediate danger of attack, but it was in her interest to give active assistance to Germany which was the most likely candidate for attack by Louis Napoleon. But England's defences were totally inadequate—the result of 'the dream of security into which two generations of peace had lulled them',[17] and her influence among foreign nations had been weakened by the frequent changes of ministry which prevented her from exercising the restrained but consistent policy that was in her interest.

The international crisis passed as quickly as it had come, and in 1860 Salisbury resumed the task of blocking any reforming legislation that might be proposed by the new Palmerston Ministry. The flux of the 1850s had resulted in stalemate: the Conservatives no longer attempted to dislodge Palmerston because they could not hope to form a viable ministry of their own; in return, Palmerston kept a check on the reforming spirits among his followers. For Salisbury the

145

situation was ideal, for the immediate momentum of Radicalism, depending as it did on the inconclusive party battle
between the Conservatives and the Whigs, was checked, and
Palmerston remained willing to keep in office by governing
with a loose hand and was receptive to amendments that
Conservatives like Salisbury might bring forward.

During the 1860 Session the new Government made a half-
hearted gesture by introducing its own Reform Bill. Salisbury's argument against it remained unchanged:

> This was a measure which affected the legislating body, and,
> therefore, contained within itself the germ of further progress . . .
> When this measure had passed there would be a far different
> House of Commons—one far less inclined to resistance and
> much more disposed to make common cause with the poor
> class of society, and to push on more rapidly the stone which
> they had set rolling.[18]

Of more immediate importance, though, were the financial
measures introduced by Gladstone, the new Chancellor of
the Exchequer. The simplification of the tariff and the repeal
of the Paper Duty were aimed at substituting direct for
indirect taxes. In Salisbury's view 'such a plan of finance was
really a plundering finance'.[19] Indirect taxes fell on all classes
in equal proportions, but the income tax penalised particular
sections of the community and shifted the burden away from
the classes represented by Cobden and Bright. Salisbury did
not attribute to Gladstone himself the class motives of the
Radicals—Gladstone was following what he mistakenly
thought were Peel's principles of finance, and 'the dogmas of
political economy' which indicated that indirect taxes
infringed the public interest by distorting the laws of supply
and demand. Bright's support for the income tax derived
from his 'unscrupulous devotions to the interests of one
class':[20]

> To shift on to the owners of realised property all the burdens of
> the State, and to secure to the trading and manufacturing
> community an enjoyment of the blessings of government
> together with a perfect immunity from their cost, is the point
> towards which all his manifest agitations converge.[21]

146

In this period the Radicals also attacked the Constitution through their attacks on the Church Rates. Salisbury placed himself firmly in 'the "no surrender" class'.[22]

> The original ground taken by the Dissenters was that it was a grievance to them to be called upon to support a religious establishment to which they did not belong; and everybody would acknowledge that that was an objection which was worthy of very great attention . . . The speech however of the hon. Member for Birmingham [Mr. Bright] on Wednesday last, had shown that that grievance was a mere sham. The hon. Member, with his usual boldness, gave an account of the real motives which animated what he would term the political Dissenters . . . His object was not merely to put down Church rates, but the Church . . . dissent was made a mere cloak for political designs.[23]

He was not fully confident that the supporters of the Establishment would gain a lasting victory, but

> they had kept church rates alive for thirty years, and with their numbers they could keep them alive ten years longer; at any rate, they might keep tithes twenty years after that, and endowments twenty years longer still. That brought them to fifty years, and that period was something in the life of a nation.

It is clear, then, that Salisbury's rigidity was based on grounds of policy and was not doctrinaire. By 1868, when the position of the Church was much weaker following the passing of the Reform Act, Salisbury moved away from his unbending position, and he urged the acceptance of a compromise Bill as an alternative to total abolition of Church Rates:

> What shall we gain if we adhere to the principle of 'No surrender' upon the subject? . . . I am bound to say, taking the most impartial view that I can upon the subject, I do not think that the Church will gain anything by prolonging this contest. I do not conceal for a moment the reluctance with which I give up anything that the Church possesses; but I am bound to look to both sides of the question, and not to content myself with stolid opposition, and refuse to give way to that tendency by which it seems to me so many of us are apt to be affected, of pursuing for many years a steady obstruction, and then giving way to an

unreasonable panic. I think, therefore, it is wiser to accept the terms now offered, because I am distinctly of opinion that we may go further and fare worse.[24]

Salisbury saw the Revised Code of Regulations for Education, introduced at the beginning of 1862, as an attack on the Establishment which resembled the National Education proposals of the 1850s; he therefore attacked it on similar grounds. On the same principle, his sympathies with the Southern States in the American Civil War derived, in part at least, from his positive dislike of the North and his interest in demonstrating the failure and despotism of its democratic government.

Salisbury had every reason to be satisfied by the success with which Conservative forces blocked Radicalism in the early 1860s. As he claimed in his Election Address of 1865, it had been the task of the Conservative Party 'to resist a large number of measures . . . tending dangerously to impair the stability of our institutions in Church and State. That resistance has been in almost every case victorious.' In their battle against the Radicals, they had not been unaided: Palmerston had also opposed the Financial Reformers and the Dissenters, not with enthusiasm, but with the 'far more effective resistance of a sandbag'.[25]

The main failure of the Conservative Opposition cited by Salisbury was their inability to moderate Russell's foreign policy, especially in regard to the Danish Duchies. Salisbury had very strong views on the subject and deeply resented Russell's unnecessary interference with the matter in the first place and the inconsistency and cowardice which then prevented him from fulfilling his undertakings. He pursued the question by speeches in Parliament, in a number of articles (one of which was translated into French and published under his name), and in a polemical correspondence in *The Times*. It was one of the first Salisburian campaigns to catch the notice of the general public, but it does not seem to have had any noticeable effects on Russell.

In 1865, the term of the Ministry came to a finish and there was a General Election. Shortly after, Palmerston died. The political stalemate was at an end. Salisbury realised that he could no longer hope to apply the policy of 'No surrender' with the success it had enjoyed while Palmerston was alive. Accordingly, he moved away from his previous position that it was necessary to 'change enormously or not at all'.[26] In his 1865 Election Address he declared:

> We are not in any way bound to adhere to the provisions of the Reform Act of 1832, and if any alterations in it can be made which will extend the suffrage more widely without giving undue power to any single class I shall welcome them gladly; but I should be sorry to run any risk of destroying the balance of power by which the freedom of the various classes of the community is at present maintained.

The same position appears in the articles he wrote at the time, For example, his article on Parliamentary Reform which appeared in April 1865 opposes any measure that implies complete democracy. 'But there is another alternative':

> [The working classes] may ask for a share of political power proportioned to the share which their labour gives them in the country's wealth. Such a claim, if it be advanced, must be met in a very different tone from that which has justly been used to repel the intolerable claim of supremacy.[27]

When Gladstone brought forward his Reform Bill in 1866 Salisbury was active in opposing it, maintaining that it had been introduced in such a way that it was impossible to tell what its effects would be:

> The information supplied to the House is defective in two particulars. In the first place, the House is not told by the Statistics how far the agricultural population would be swamped by the urban; and, secondly, how far, in boroughs and counties, the middle and upper classes will be swamped by the working classes.[28]

When he had made a reckoning of his own he concluded that the Bill did not provide for the requisite balance between different classes. But his speeches suggest that he would have been willing to accept, albeit reluctantly, a Bill that guarded the constitutional equilibrium by such devices as fancy franchises which would have prevented the country from being ruled by the working classes which formed the numerical majority.

In the event, Gladstone's Ministry, weakened by the revolt of Robert Lowe and the Adullamites, did not last beyond the summer of 1866. For Salisbury the lesson was plain. Gladstone had made the mistake of formulating a Bill to suit the more extreme sections of his Party while ignoring the views and claims of the nucleus. Now that the Conservatives were back in power they should take notice of the moral and attempt to pass only a moderate Bill, aimed at remedying specific anomalies in the existing system, by such means as a change in the registration procedure and the introduction of voting papers. Even such a limited measure should only be introduced if the Ministry felt it was strong enough to pass the measure through the House of Commons without amendment. Above all, the Conservatives must avoid the temptation of introducing a general Reform Bill which would then be liable to alteration in debate until a Radical measure finally emerged.

The fears he had expressed during the Conservative Ministry of 1859 all re-emerged as Derby returned to office: that an inconclusive scramble for power by the Whig and Conservative teams would again be of benefit to the Radicals who would hold the balance between them in Parliament. Ideally, Salisbury would have preferred to see an alliance, or co-operation at least, between the Conservatives and the Whigs directed against the Radicals. He was as convinced as he had always been that neither the Conservatives nor the Whigs favoured Reform and were only led to unwilling support by the artificialities of the party battle:

> Party allegiance and a blind obedience to tradition have done many wonderful things; but they never achieved a more remarkable triumph than that of driving into the ranks of Mr. Bright's battalions the representatives of some of the leading houses of the English aristocracy.[29]

Salisbury did not feel any involvement in the factional strife between the great political clans:

> Party allegiance is but a means to an end; it can never determine the decision of questions more important than itself. No true patriot can become a party man without reserving to himself the liberty of independent action upon measures which

our national life, and the very continuance of our form of society is affected.[30]

These pleas had no effect. A Conservative Reform Bill was introduced at the beginning of the Session of 1867 and some weeks later Salisbury resigned from the Government in which he was Secretary of State for India. Most of his contemporaries seem to have regarded his resignation as an honourable but worthless moral gesture. As it turned out, they were probably right, but this was certainly the opposite of what it was intended to be. He thought that resistance was folly or heroism, virtue or vice, in most cases according to the probabilities of its being successful; and he protested to an old Oxford friend who had written to criticise his action:

> I have opposed it [the present Bill] because I think it a bad and dangerous Bill. I am not 'testifying' or any nonsense of that kind, I am trying to kill the Bill—or failing that to take the sting out of it: and I shall continue to take any opportunity that offers for contributing to that end.[31]

The claim accords with his actions before and after his resignation. He did not resign at the beginning of the 1867 Session when a Bill of the 'general' kind he had been determined to avoid was announced. It was only when definite proposals had been presented to the Cabinet, when he had worked out their implications in detail and come to the conclusion that they would upset the Constitutional equilibrium if they were passed that he made his continued membership of the Cabinet dependent on their withdrawal. While there was hope of keeping the proposed Bill within bounds, he preferred to remain within the Cabinet and exercise an influence from the inside. Following his failure in Cabinet, Salisbury preferred to see the fall of the Conservative Government to the passing of its Bill. As it happened, only two other members of the Cabinet resigned with him and after some initial uneasiness Derby and Disraeli pressed on untroubled. But hindsight tends to obscure the fact that the dissolution of the Ministry was a distinct possibility at the time of his resignation.

Even this failure to topple Derby and Disraeli did not drive Salisbury into inaction. The year that passed between his return to the back-bench and his removal to the House of Lords was the busiest of all those he had spent in Parliament. It was useless now to put forward yet again the case for a Bill that preserved the equipoise of the Constitution, for the case had in effect already been lost as both sides of the House had agreed to abandon it. Instead, he directed his general arguments against the dubious political morality of the Conservatives in bringing in a Bill more extreme than one they had themselves rejected a year previously, as well as the inexpediency of their activities. Above all, he concentrated his efforts on criticisms of particular clauses and amendments: he joined with Mill among others in support of the multi-member constituency as a protection for minority rights,[32] spoke on behalf of a clause by which his old scheme for voting papers would pass into law,[33] favoured the retention of hustings expenses for candidates,[34] and so on.

The passing of the Bill left deep scars and it is an eloquent commentary on his approach that, despite a few emotional outbursts, he never seriously considered leaving politics. On the contrary, the passing of the Reform Bill was for Salisbury a beginning rather than an end: the beginning of the struggle to defend the remaining bulwarks of the Constitution, weakened as they were by the new measure. In the article he wrote for *The Quarterly Review* in October 1867 bitterness mixes with defiance and resolve:

> It is the duty of every Englishman, and of every English party, to accept a political defeat cordially, and to lend their best endeavours to secure the success, or to neutralise the evil, of the principles to which they have been forced to succumb.[35]

And he called upon the Conservative Party to prepare their defences against the next wave of the Radical assault which was likely to be directed against the Church. The attack duly came in the Session of 1868 and it is perhaps fitting that the last speech he gave in the Commons before the sudden death of his father took him to the Lords was a defence of the Established Church in Ireland against the mounting attacks that were to lead to the fall of the Conservative Government later in the year.

Salisbury's career in the House of Commons ended in the failure of the objects for which he had been striving all the time he had been an M.P. But this is not necessarily a reflection on the quality of his thought for the success of a politician must inevitably depend on his skill, judgement and personality, on outward circumstances and chance as well as on his principles and his thought. It is clearly wrong to exaggerate the rigidity of his position. He was frightened of the snow-ball effects of even moderate changes, and ideally he opposed all reforms. But he carried through this opposition in a variety of ways: when 'No surrender' appeared most likely to be effective, he adopted the stance of total resistance; when circumstance dictated that he had no alternative, he modified his position.

There are times when an enveloping defeatism makes people acquiesce in changes they do not desire, and when the consciousness of success makes the supporters of innovation step up their demands. It was such a situation that Salisbury diagnosed in the 1850s and the 1860s. He hoped that a publicly declared position of complete rigidity would stem the fatalism of the Conservatives and Whigs and would also moderate the hopes of the Radicals. But when the pressure for change became so great that the attempt at complete blockage was no longer realistic, he altered his tactics and tried to weaken its force by agreeing selectively to some of the demands for reform. And if this more limited policy failed he showed an unhesitating resilience and a willingness to work in the new situations created by previous failures.

Most striking of all are the terms in which he chose to state his policies and the contrast between the Conservatism of a Burke which stood by ancient institutions as the expression of a divine will and that of Salisbury which recognised that stability as well as change had to be justified continually in terms of the social benefits they were likely to bring; between a Conservatism that regarded the State as an 'organism' and one which likened it to a 'joint-stock company'.

APPENDIX ONE

Published Writings of
Lord Salisbury

Published Writings of Lord Salisbury

I. ELECTION ADDRESSES (1853–1865)

1. August 1853 (*Lincoln, Rutland and Stamford Mercury*, 19 August 1853)
2. March 1857 (*Lincoln, Rutland and Stamford Mercury*, 27 March 1857)
3. April 1859 (*Lincoln, Rutland and Stamford Mercury*, 15 April 1859)
4. June 1865 (*Lincoln, Rutland and Stamford Mercury*, 16 June 1865)

II. LETTERS TO *The Times* (1863–1867)

1. 31 December 1863 (On the Danish Question)
2. 22 January 1864 (On Denmark and Germany)
3. 26 January 1864 (On Denmark and Germany)
4. 10 April 1866 (A protest against Gladstone's mis-quotations of his speeches on Reform)
5. 5 August 1867 (Correction of Speech)

III. ARTICLES IN PERIODICALS (1856–1894)

Oxford Essays

Vol. IV pp. 52–79, 1858. 'Theories of Parliamentary Reform' (Reform Bills have to be judged according to whether they ultimately bring the greatest happiness of the greatest number. No measure of Reform is possible that will not bring a monopoly of power to the majority: i.e. to the working classes. Such a monopoly will upset the equipoise of the Constitution and will bring chaos and unhappiness.)

National Review

N.R. 1, Vol. II, pp. 1–16, Nov. 1883. 'Labourers' and Artisans' Dwellings' (The housing-problem of the town poor results mainly from the low wages of the worker. Parliament should give low-interest loans for the building of inexpensive dwellings.)

N.R. 2, Vol. IV, pp. 145–62, Oct. 1884. 'The Value of Redistribution: A Note on Electoral Statistics' (The proportion of Conservative seats in the 1880 Parliament was less than their percentage in the elections.

Thus it would be in the Conservative interest to accept Liberal proposals for an extension of suffrage in the Counties, as long as such an extension was accompanied by a redistribution of seats which took away the built-in bias against them.)

N.R. 3, Vol. XX, pp. 289–300, Nov. 1892. 'Constitutional Revision' (The effect of a rejection of a Liberal Home Rule Bill by the Lords would be to give the choice to the electorate in a new general election. In all foreign Constitutions, there are barriers to precipitate Constitutional Revisions, in the English Constitution such a necessary barrier is provided by the House of Lords.)

N.R. 4, Vol. XXIV, pp. 450–59, Dec. 1894. 'Lord Rosebery's Plan' (It is impossible to reform the House of Lords in such a way as to make it pliant to Liberal policies without at the same time effectually destroying it.)

Bentley's Quarterly Review

B.Q.R. 1, Vol. I, pp. 1–32, Mar. 1859. 'English Politics and Parties' (By entering into an auction with the Whigs for Radical votes, the Conservatives have reduced politics to a quest for office regardless of principle. The resulting instability is especially dangerous in view of the danger of an attack from France.)

B.Q.R. 2, Vol. I, pp. 343–74, Jul. 1859. 'The Faction Fights' (An attack on Disraeli's attempt to attract Radical support by introducing a Reform Bill. Salisbury interprets his motives as those of pure selfishness.)

B.Q.R. 3, Vol. II, pp. 1–32, Oct. 1859. 'France and Europe' (Louis Napoleon's uncertain hold of power in France must make him seek to bolster his position by military conquest. His next victim is probably Germany, and a German alliance is thus in England's interest.)

B.Q.R. 4, Vol. II, pp. 303–34, Jan. 1860. 'The Coming Political Campaign' (The see-saw between Conservatives and Whigs will only benefit the Radicals. This is very dangerous, for Bright's speeches show that the Radicals aim at robbing the rich by revolutionary measures of direct taxation.)

Quarterly Review

Q.R. 1, Vol. 107, pp. 514–54, Apr. 1860. 'The Budget and the Reform Bill' (An attack on Gladstone's Budget of 1860: Salisbury claims that the gradual substitution of direct for indirect taxation will lead to graduated income-tax and the 'spoilation' of the propertied class. Bright's motive in pressing for extended franchise is to give the poor majority the power of spoliating the rich by taxation, and Disraeli is helping him along by bidding for Radical support in his effort to oust the Whigs.)

Q.R. 2, Vol. 108, pp. 265–302, Jul. 1860. 'The Conservative Reaction' (From 1858–1860 neither Conservatives nor Whigs nor the general public wanted Reform. Both parties pledged themselves to support it only because they thought it was inevitable; but at last the Radical bubble has burst.)

Q.R. 3, Vol. 108, pp. 568–605, Oct. 1860. 'Competitive Examinations' (The evils of the patronage system have been exaggerated; and, in any case, written examinations are a totally unsuitable way of selecting Civil Servants.)

Q.R. 4, Vol. 109, pp. 212–47, Jan. 1861. 'The Income Tax and Its Rivals' (A detailed defence of the merits of indirect taxation. Salisbury says that it is Gladstone's love for theoretical simplicity that leads him to favour direct taxation; Bright's motive in advocating it is his narrow interest in the welfare of the trading classes.)

Q.R. 5, Vol. 109, pp. 531–65, Apr. 1861. 'Lord Stanhope's Life of Pitt' (Salisbury attributes Pitt's great political success to his 'lofty forgetfulness of self' and his wish to represent the whole nation rather than one faction.)

Q.R. 6, Vol. 110, pp. 247–88, Jul. 1861. 'Democracy on Its Trial' (The outbreak of the Civil War marks the failure of the democratic experiment in the United States and should give the warning to English politicians against introducing such a system in England.)

Q.R. 7, Vol. 110, pp. 544–78, Oct. 1861. 'Church-Rates' (The Church Rate is anomalous in many ways, but it must be retained for political reasons. The attack of the 'Political Dissenters' on the Rate is part of a general attack on the Establishment, and the attack on the Establishment is part of an attack on the institutions of the country as a whole.)

Q.R. 8, Vol. 111, pp. 201–38, Jan. 1862. 'Lord Castlereagh' (A defence of Castlereagh against the charge that he favoured absolutist governments. His first aim was to cement the anti-Napoleonic alliance. After 1815 he aimed to secure peace by achieving a balance of power that would bar any future French expansionism.)

Q.R. 9, Vol. 111, pp. 516–61, Apr. 1862. 'Stanhope's Life of Pitt' (A defence of Pitt's conduct of the war against France and of the later parts of his career in general.)

Q.R. 10, Vol. 112, pp. 236–70, Jul. 1862. 'The Bicentenary' (Salisbury argues that the ultimate aim of the Dissenters—or at least the aim of the dominant faction—is the spoliation of property.)

Q.R. 11, Vol. 112, pp. 535–70, Oct. 1862. 'The Confederate Struggle and Recognition' (A further account of the failure of democracy in the United States and an argument for the recognition of the Confederacy.)

Q.R. 12, Vol. 113, pp. 253–88, Jan. 1863. 'Four Years of a Reforming Administration' (It is by making piecemeal concessions to the Radicals that Palmerston has managed to remain in office.)

Q.R. 13, Vol. 113, pp. 448–81, Apr. 1863. 'Poland' (Poland's historical claims to independence are weak; furthermore, Polish independence is a chimera. Salisbury urges the signatories of the Treaty of Vienna to concentrate on assuring the fair treatment of the Poles by the Russians according to the terms of the treaty, rather than giving the Poles empty hopes of independence. The article was written at the time of the great Polish uprising.)

Q.R. 14, Vol. 115, pp. 236–87, Jan. 1864. 'The Danish Duchies' (Germany's motive in attacking Denmark is to gain an outlet to the sea, which is necessary for the fulfilment of her imperial ambitions. England is in honour and in interest bound to support Denmark.)

Q.R. 15, Vol. 115, pp. 481–529, Apr. 1864. 'Foreign Policy of England' (Russell's policy is one of bullying small countries, and of aimlessly annoying large ones. Salisbury warns that a reputation for cowardice and a consequent loss of influence will be the result of a policy of 'fierce notes and pacific measures'.)

Q.R. 16, Vol. 116, pp. 245–81, Jul. 1864. 'The House of Commons' (Salisbury expresses gratitude that Palmerston's ministry has done nothing in the way of Reform. He argues that the English Constitution has gradually grown up into a workable system and that it would be dangerous to tamper with it. The article contains a long theoretical discussion of the right to vote.)

Q.R. 17, Vol. 116, pp. 482–519, Oct. 1864. 'Photography' (An account of the technical development of photography and an estimate of its great uses. He also argues against those who say it is not art.)

Q.R. 18, Vol. 117, pp. 449–86, Jan. 1865. 'The United States as an Example' (The end of the Civil War will not bring an end of trouble. The South will continue to smoulder with discontent. The Civil War should have taught Cobden and Bright that majority tyranny is as bad as any other.)

Q.R. 19, Vol. 117, pp. 540–74, Apr. 1865. 'Parliamentary Reform' (Salisbury expresses himself willing to consider any Reform that does not tend to bring the domination of the working class.)

Q.R. 20, Vol. 118, pp. 193–224, Jul. 1865. 'The Church in her Relations to Political Parties' (Church Endowments and Test Acts are a necessary part of the Church of England without which its manifold benefits could not be obtained. But Churchmen will have to enter the political arena if they want to defend these benefits: for example, they should vote against Gladstone's re-election as member for Oxford University.)

Q.R. 21, Vol. 118, pp. 280–95, Jul. 1865. 'The Elections' (A warning that Palmerston is in decline and that a vote for Palmerston will, in effect, be a vote for the radicalism of Russell and Gladstone.)

Q.R. 22, Vol. 119, pp. 250–80, Jan. 1866. 'The Coming Session' (Palmerston's death means the probable introduction of a Reform Bill: while emphasising that Conservatives have no doctrinaire objection to Reform, he suggests a Conservative-Whig coalition directed against any precipitate measure. But he fears that Whig party loyalty will make such a coalition impossible.)

Q.R. 23, Vol. 119, pp. 530–59, Apr. 1866. 'The Reform Bill' (The Whigs do not want Reform. They realise that what is ultimately involved is the spoliation of the rich. But they hope that the Bill will

be killed by Conservative opposition alone, thus saving them from
the necessity of voting against their party. Salisbury warns them that
these are dangerous tactics.)

Q.R. 24, Vol. 120, pp. 259–82, Jul. 1866. 'The Change of Ministry'
(Gladstone made the mistake of supporting the extremists of his party
and leaving the moderates in the lurch. Salisbury is not averse to a
moderate measure of Reform, but urges the Conservatives to learn
Gladstone's lesson and not to introduce any general measure.)

Q.R. 25, Vol. 123, pp. 533–65, Oct. 1867. 'The Conservative Surrender'
(The 1867 Reform Bill effectively gives over political power to the
working classes. But even more traumatic than the Bill itself is the way
in which it was introduced.)

Q.R. 26, Vol. 127, pp. 538–61, Oct. 1869. 'The Past and Future of
Conservative Policy' (The Conservatives have found that success has
not been brought by a flirtation with Radicalism. In the future they
should keep to their principles: even if this means exclusion from office
in the short run.)

Q.R. 27, Vol. 129, pp. 540–56, Oct. 1870. 'The Terms of Peace' (He
blames the military intoxication of the Germans for the Franco-
Prussian War and regrets that Britain's stock has fallen so low that
she has not been able to act as an honest broker.)

Q.R. 28, Vol. 130, pp. 256–86, Jan. 1871. 'Political Lessons of the War'
(The Prussian King was not beholden to the whims of Parliament or
Public Opinion—he was thus able to plan systematically for war and
defeat the French.)

Q.R. 29, Vol. 131, pp. 549–80, Oct. 1871. 'The Commune and the
Internationale' (The Commune shows the brutalities that result from
the assumption of power by the urban working classes. The regime
was brutalised by the socialist, revolutionary ideas with which it was
infused. Salisbury warns that the English Radicals might become
infected with the same ideas, with the same results.)

Q.R. 30, Vol. 133, pp. 558–93, Oct. 1872. 'The Position of Parties' (The
tide is turning against the Liberals. The Conservatives should wait
patiently and refuse to take office until they are assured of a solid
majority.)

Q.R. 31, Vol. 135, pp. 539–74, Oct. 1873. 'The Programme of the
Radicals' (The ultimate aim of the Radicals is an attack on the
Church and on property. The moderate Liberals should not let their
wish for office let them become unwilling partners in such a programme.)

Q.R. 32, Vol. 151, pp. 535–67, Apr. 1881. 'Ministerial Embarrassments'
(Liberal vacillation has led to the trouble in Transvaal, Afghanistan
and Ireland: the Cabinet has been divided between the policy of
coercion and the policy of conciliation, and their final acts have
resulted in the worst of both.)

Q.R. 33, Vol. 156, pp. 559–95, Oct. 1883. 'Disintegration' (Both
Conservatives and Whigs stand for the same central policies of uphold-

ing the Empire and property. They should thus amalgamate, or, failing this, the Whigs should refrain from playing into Radical hands by an over-fierce opposition to the Conservatives.)

Saturday Review
   Volume II, Jul.–Dec. 1856

S.R. 1, p. 779(R), 27 Dec. 'Letters of Queen Henrietta Maria'

   Volume III, Jan.-Jun. 1857

S.R. 2, p. 38(R), 10 Jan. 'History of the Scotch and Irish Poor Laws'
S.R. 3, p. 60(R), 17 Jan. 'Christianity and Hinduism'
S.R. 4, p. 83(R), 24 Jan. 'Robertson's Church History'
S.R. 5, p. 130(R), 7 Feb. 'An Evangelical Novel' (A protest against religious argument clothed in literary garb.)
S.R. 6, p. 152(M), 14 Feb. 'The House of Commons Mare's-Nesting' (Description of a House of Commons scene during a dull speech by Disraeli.)
S.R. 7, p. 156(R), 14 Feb. 'Letters from Canterbury, New Zealand'
S.R. 8, p. 180(R), 21 Feb. 'The Friend of Robespierre'
S.R. 9, p. 197(M), 28 Feb. 'Red-Hot Cannon Balls' (A sarcastic attack on 'the political dodo': the squires on the Tory back benches.)
S.R. 10, p. 203(R), 28 Feb. 'Manifest Destiny'
S.R. 11, p. 221(M), 7 Mar. 'Independent Members' (For the back bench squirearchy, 'independence' means 'irresponsibility'.)
S.R. 12, p. 240(M), 14 Mar. 'The Death-Rattle' (In the Commons, the squires have come to the defence of the Church.)
S.R. 13, p. 247(R), 14 Mar. 'Slavery; and its Remedies'
S.R. 14, p. 249(R), 14 Mar. 'Freida the Jongleur'
S.R. 15, p. 272(R), 21 Mar. 'Long Vacation Rambles'
S.R. 16, p. 293(R), 28 Mar. 'The Puritan Commonwealth' (An exposé of the intolerance of the Massachusetts Puritans.)
S.R. 17, p. 297(R), 28 Mar. 'The Days of My Life'
S.R. 18, p. 361(R), 18 Apr. 'Kerr's Blackstone' (A review of changes in the Constitution since the time of Blackstone.)
S.R. 19, 364(R), 18 Apr. 'The Life of Martin Luther'
S.R. 20, p. 383(R), 25 Apr. 'Mr. T. Gladstone on Kansas' (A support of the Northern Position over the extension of Slavery to Kansas.)
S.R. 21, p. 398(M), 2 May. 'A New Speaker'
S.R. 22, p. 425(M), 9 May. 'Party' (An analysis of the functions of political parties.)
S.R. 23 p. 432(R), 9 May. 'Tooke and Newmarsh on Prices' (A review of the free-trade controversy in light of subsequent agricultural statistics.)
S.R. 24, p. 433(R), 9 May. 'Journal of Barbier' (Comments on the *Ancien Régime*.)
S.R. 25, p. 458(R), 16 May. 'The Future of Slavery'

S.R. 26, p. 481(R), 23 May. 'The Valley of the Amazon' (American schemes to colonise the Amazon with slaves.)

S.R. 27, p. 506(R), 30 May. 'Walpole's Letters'

S.R. 28, p. 556(R), 13 Jun. 'Mr. Recorder Hill on Crime' (An attack on the philanthropical reformers.)

S.R. 29, p. 575(R), 20 Jun. *'Le Cadet de Colobrières'*

S.R. 30, p. 593(M), 27 Jun. 'The Bores of Supply' (The Committee of Supply in the Commons.)

S.R. 31, p. 599(R), 27 Jun. 'Fides; or Love-Making à la Belgravienne' ('This amalgamation of Dr. Pusey and Lord Byron is not to our taste.')

Volume IV, Jul.–Dec. 1857

S.R. 32, p. 8(M), 4 Jul. 'An Ancient and Undoubted Privilege' (House of Commons' Committees.)

S.R. 33, p. 18(R), 4 Jul. 'A Word for Slavery' (A scathing review of a novel which purports to 'answer' *Uncle Tom's Cabin.*)

S.R. 34, p. 44(R), 11 Jul. 'Weld's Vacations in Ireland'

S.R. 35, p. 66(R), 18 Jul. 'Nightshade'

S.R. 36, p. 139(R), 8 Aug. 'The Rival Suitors'

S.R. 37, p. 238(M), 12 Sep. 'Bloomeriana' (Opposition to political rights for women.)

S.R. 38, p. 249(R), 12 Sep. 'Reade's Poems'

S.R. 39, p. 267(R), 19 Sep. *'La Ferme aux Pommiers'*

S.R. 40, p. 284(R), 26 Sep. 'Germaine'

S.R. 41, p. 325(M), 10 Oct. 'Saxon Ideas of Anglo-Saxon Manners' (Review of *Martha*, a German opera set in England.)

S.R. 42, p. 328(R), 10 Oct. 'M.M. Sue and Quinet on the Religious Situation'

S.R. 43, p. 330(R), 10 Oct. 'Russian Views of English Policy' (Salisbury admits that English foreign policy is not as clean as most of the English think it is.)

S.R. 44, p. 375(R), 24 Oct. 'Religious Novels in Germany'

S.R. 45, p. 451(R), 14 Nov. 'Seymour and His Friends'

Volume V, Jan.–Jun. 1858

S.R. 46, p. 20(R), 2 Jan. 'A Pious Tale' (An attack on moralistic novels that succeed, at the same time, in being salacious.)

S.R. 47, p. 45(R), 9 Jan. 'French Novels' (Salisbury regrets the 'imperious pruriency' of the novel-reading public.)

S.R. 48, p. 167(R), 13 Feb. 'Oriental and Western Siberia' (A travel book.)

S.R. 49, p. 193(R), 20 Feb. 'Antiquarian Novels'

S.R. 50, p. 197(R), 20 Feb. 'Metaphysics at Manchester' (An unfavourable review of a botany book which purports to show a teleological pattern in nature.)

S.R. 51, p. 212(M), 27 Feb. 'The Amusements of a Crisis' (The fall of Palmerston's Government.)

S.R. 52, p. 274(R), 13 Mar. 'The Morals of Mayfair'

S.R. 53, p. 298(R), 20 Mar. 'The Factory Movement' (Salisbury points out that it was the Tories who passed the Factory Acts.)

S.R. 54, p. 345(M), 3 Apr. 'Free Trade in Letters' (An article in support of Government subsidy of transatlantic mail packets.)

S.R. 55, p. 377(R), 10 Apr. 'The Moors and the Fens'

S.R. 56, p. 403(R), 17 Apr. 'Cousin Harry'

S.R. 57, p. 452(R), 1 May. 'The Three Chances'

S.R. 58, p. 468(M), 8 May. 'How to Dispose of Well-Meaning Men' (How the House of Commons deals with boring Private Members' Bills.)

S.R. 59, p. 643(R), 19 June. 'Local Tales'

Volume VI, Jul.–Dec. 1858

S.R. 60, p. 238(R), 4 Sep. 'German Classics for Competitive Examinations' (He welcomes the introduction of German into the school curriculum, but says that literature is not a suitable subject for Competitive Examinations.)

S.R. 61, p. 288(R), 18 Sep. 'Cardinal Mezzofanti'

S.R. 62, p. 357(R), 9 Oct. 'A Chinaman's Journal in Japan'

S.R. 63, p. 402(R), 23 Oct. 'The Reformers of Italy and France' (Salisbury refuses to subscribe to 'historical fatalism'.)

S.R. 64, p. 620(R), 18 Dec. 'The Late Baron Alderson' (A review of a book by Salisbury's father-in-law.)

Volume VII, Jan.–Jun. 1859

S.R. 65, p. 190(R), 12 Feb. 'The Bloated Haristocracy'

S.R. 66, p. 270(M), 5 Mar. 'The New Appointments' (Disraeli's Cabinet includes several patronage appointments of effete aristocrats.)

S.R. 67, p. 272(M), 5 Mar. 'The House of Commons at the Dentist's' (The introduction of Disraeli's Reform Bill.)

S.R. 68, p. 429(M), 9 Apr. 'Constitutional Illusions' (A complaint against the sleepy sessions of both Houses of Parliament.)

S.R. 69, p. 557(M), 7 May. 'Horse Guards Mandarins' (He ridicules Competitive Examinations.)

S.R. 70, p. 588(M), 14 May. 'Plump for Penates' (The democratic constituencies are likely to choose mediocre local candidates.)

S.R. 71, p. 661(R), 28 May. 'German Thieves'

S.R. 72, p. 709(M), 11 Jun. 'The Artless Dodger' (An attack on Disraeli.)

S.R. 73, p. 744(M), 18 Jun. 'And is Old Double Dead?' (An attack on the inconsistencies of Sir James Graham's political career.)

S.R. 74, p. 752(R), 18 Jun. 'Emile de Girardin on Reform' (The French experience of universal suffrage was not an encouraging one.)

S.R. 75, p. 776(M), 25 Jun. *'Fiat Experimentum in Corpore Vili'* (A comparison of the politics of a democratic urban constituency with those of a small rural one.)

Volume VIII, Jul.–Dec. 1859

S.R. 76, p. 12(M), 2 Jul. 'Political Vendetta' (An attack on the Conservative opposition to Gladstone's election as member for Oxford University.)

S.R. 77, p. 71(R), 16 Jul. 'Flannel Petticoats and No Surrender' (Lord Haddo has introduced a petition to ban the use of 'nude female live models' by the Royal Academy.)

S.R. 78, p. 107(R), 23 Jul. 'Cousin Stella' (An account of slavery in Jamaica.)

S.R. 79, p. 133(R), 30 Jul. 'The Handbooks' (i.e. travel-guides.)

S.R. 80, p. 222(M), 20 Aug. 'Pity the Sorrow of a Poor M.P.' (The discomforts of an M.P.'s life will soon mean that only petty social climbers will be tempted to put themselves forward as candidates.)

S.R. 81, p. 250(M), 27 Aug. 'The Swiss Excursionist' (The vicissitudes of family holidays abroad.)

S.R. 82, p. 280(M), 3 Sep. 'Odorous Comparisons' (Salisbury dislikes British admiration of things French.)

S.R. 83, p. 332(M), 17 Sep. 'The Geography of Dirt' (An article on travel in Europe.)

S.R. 84, p. 390(M), 1 Oct. 'The Doves of Doon' (He praises Derby's tough Irish policy.)

S.R. 85, p. 400(R), 1 Oct. 'The History of New England'

S.R. 86, p. 421(M), 8 Oct. 'The Flogging Question' (A criticism of 'sentimental' opposition to flogging.)

S.R. 87, p. 455(R), 15 Oct. 'A Frenchman's View of England'

S.R. 88, p. 542(M), 5 Nov. '*La Maratre*' (Review of a Balzac play.)

S.R. 89, p. 552(R), 5 Nov. 'M. l'Abbe Mullois and the Papacy' (Salisbury criticises the temporal power of the Catholic Church.)

S.R. 90, p. 577(R), 12 Nov. 'Our Future Rulers' (An attack on outrages committed by Trades Unionists.)

S.R. 91, p. 616(R), 19 Nov. 'The March of Intellect in Heavy Clays' (It is unwise to attempt to educate country squires.)

S.R. 92, p. 672(M), 3 Dec. 'St. Pancras Workhouse' (The St. Pancras Workhouse has illegally been turning away applicants for aid.)

S.R. 93, p. 815(R), 31 Dec. 'The History of Brazil'

Volume IX, Jan.–Jun. 1860

S.R. 94, p. 11(M), 7 Jan. 'Clerical Philandering' (Too many sermons are directed towards the sentimental emotions of female congregants.)

S.R. 95, p. 19(R), 7 Jan. 'The Story of New Zealand' (The colonists have treated the Maoris unfairly.)

S.R. 96, p. 41(M), 14 Jan. 'The Triumphs of Private Enterprise' (Private enterprise is just as inefficient as Governmental enterprise.)

S.R. 97, p. 52(R), 14 Jan. 'The Late Bishop Wilson' (He criticises his simplist, doctrinaire attitude.)

S.R. 98, p. 83(R), 21 Jan. 'Liberty Hall'

S.R. 99, p. 85(R), 21 Jan. 'Australian Facts and Prospects'

S.R. 100, p. 107(M), 28 Jan. 'Parliament' (The Debate on the Address.)

S.R. 101, p. 112(R), 28 Jan. 'Letters of Shleiermacher'

S.R. 102, p. 145(M), 4 Feb. 'The Wild Oats of the Session' (A description of the ineffectiveness of Parliamentary Committees.)

S.R. 103, p. 150(R), 4 Feb. 'Guesses at Truth' (Salisbury condemns 'proverbial' knowledge and says it is no substitute for reason and logic.)

S.R. 104, p. 178(M), 11 Feb. 'The Despatch of Business' (The difficulties that face back-bench Bills.)

S.R. 105, p. 210(M), 18 Feb. 'The Entr'Acte' (The main political activity is in the drawing-rooms and clubs, where pressure groups are putting forward their budgetary claims.)

S.R. 106, p. 215(R), 18 Feb. 'The Life of the Duke of Wellington'

S.R. 107, p. 217(R), 18 Feb. 'German Literature'

S.R. 108, p. 241(M), 25 Feb. 'The Financial Debate'

S.R. 109, p. 251(R), 25 Feb. 'Natal' (An appeal for an end to colonial expansion.)

S.R. 110, p. 276(M), 3 Mar. 'The Reform Bill's Farewell Season' (By now, the introduction of a Reform Bill is merely a ritual formality.)

S.R. 111, p. 279(R), 3 Mar. 'Diary of the American Revolution' (He is full of praise for the Revolution.)

S.R. 112, p. 312(R), 10 Mar. 'Von Sybel's History of the French Revolution'

S.R. 113, p. 338(M), 17 Mar. 'A Parliamentary Bashi-Bazouk' (Salisbury fears the expansionist aims of France.)

S.R. 114, p. 347(R), 17 Mar. 'German Literature'

S.R. 115, p. 370(M), 24 Mar. 'Flogging the Dead Horse' (Bright and his Reform Bill.)

S.R. 116, p. 400(M), 31 Mar. 'The Gods of Epicurus' (M.P.s are more interested in personal quarrels than in settling important issues.)

Volume X, Jul–Dec. 1860

S.R. 117, p. 553(M), 3 Nov. 'The Casus Belli in New Zealand' (The 'nigger-despising' temper of Governor Browne has thrust an unnecessary and an unjust war on the British taxpayer.)

S.R. 118, p. 562(R), 3 Nov. 'Sources of the Nile'

S.R. 119, p. 586(M), 10 Nov. 'Protection to Foreign Industry' (An attack on Gladstone's Budget.)

S.R. 120, p. 595(R), 10 Nov. 'Remains of Richard Rush' (The papers of an illiterate U.S. Ambassador to England.)

S.R. 121, p. 620(M), 17 Nov. 'Beggars and their Dupes'

S.R. 122, p. 632(R), 17 Nov. 'German Literature'

S.R. 123, p. 658(M), 24 Nov. 'Mr. Gladstone and the Hop-Planters' (Gladstone has made concessions to the hop-planters who were objecting to the provisions of his Budget.)

S.R. 124, p. 695(R), 1 Dec. 'Urquhart on the Lebanon' (Salisbury laughs at the Russophobia of the author.)

S.R. 125, p. 726(M), 8 Dec. 'An Expensive Governor' (A further condemnation of the reckless disregard of Maori rights by the New Zealand settlers.)

S.R. 126, p. 727(M), 8 Dec. 'Private and Public Schools' (He prefers the character-building freedom of the public school to the 'mock utopia' of the private school.)

S.R. 127, p. 768(R), 15 Dec. 'German Literature'

S.R. 128, p. 833(M), 29 Dec. 'The Year' (An analysis of the Year's events.)

Volume XI, Jan.–Jun. 1861

S.R. 129, p. 12(M), 5 Jan. 'The Province of Charity' (A systematic Poor Law is better than sporadic bursts of charity.)

S.P. 130, p. 34(M), 12 Jan. 'The Blunders of Benevolence' (A cynical look at Charity Committees.)

S.R. 131, p. 43(M), 12 Jan. 'The Glee and Madrigal Union' (Salisbury prefers simple English ballads to complex foreign anthems.)

S.R. 132, p. 75(R), 19 Jan. 'A German Defence of the Papacy'

S.R. 133, p. 78(R), 19 Jan. 'German Literature' (Includes an important analysis of the study of history, and a review of a pamphlet by Karl Marx.)

S.R. 134, p. 94(M), 26 Jan. 'The Hop Agitators' (An account of pressure-group activity.)

S.R. 135, p. 100(R), 26 Jan. 'Canada'

S.R. 136, p. 119(M), 2 Feb. 'The Protestant Auto-da-Fe' (A Catholic Civil Servant has been hounded out of his position.)

S.R. 137, p. 124(R), 2 Feb. 'Lord Colchester's Diary' (An account of the increase of power of the House of Commons following the 1832 Reform Act.)

S.R. 138, p. 140(R), 9 Feb. 'Ladies Spiritual and Temporal' (Salisbury maintains that the English have not the character to make pageants successful. He describes the Opening of Parliament.)

S.R. 139, p. 161(M), 16 Feb. 'The Uses of Insincerity' (The Radicals pay only lip-service to Reform.)

S.R. 140, p. 173(R), 16 Feb. 'Lord Colchester's Diary: Second Notice'

S.R. 141, p. 175(R), 16 Feb. 'German Literature'

S.R. 142, p. 190(R), 23 Feb. 'The Eton Defence' (An attack on Eton's narrow classical curriculum.)

S.R. 143, p. 193(M), 23 Feb. 'The Turnbull Deputation' (Same subject as No. 136.)

S.R. 144, p. 217(M), 2 Mar. 'The Church-Rate Debate'

S.R. 145, p. 228(R), 2 Mar. 'Tchinovnicks' (Even the Czar is ruled by his officials.)

S.R. 146, p. 242(M), 9 Mar. 'Lord Palmerston's Conversion' (Palmerston has become like an 'anile parson'. (Same subject as No. 143.))

S.R. 147, p. 251(R), 9 Mar. 'Ranke's English History: Second Notice'

S.R. 148, p. 270(R), 16 Mar. 'The Real Anti-State-Church Association' (The Bench of Bishops bring the Establishment into disrepute by their misuse of Church patronage.)

S.R. 149, p. 277(R), 16 Mar. 'German Literature' (Includes a condemnation of German intuitive philosophy.)

S.R. 150, p. 291(M), 23 Mar. 'Public Committees' (They are powerless.)

S.R. 151, p. 313(M), 30 Mar. 'The Beginning of the End' (Palmerston's central position means that he is the only man who can bring stability. Salisbury fears that an attack by the Radicals will bring about his downfall.)

S.R. 152, p. 324(R), 30 Mar. 'Thoughts on Preaching' (Episcopal malpractices have led to a lowering of the standard of talent entering the Church.)

S.R. 153, p. 336(M), 6 Apr. 'Marriage Settlements'

S.R. 154, p. 348(R), 6 Apr. 'Cochin China' (Salisbury is strongly opposed to gunboat diplomacy.)

S.R. 155, p. 364(M), 13 Apr. 'The Second Tenth of April' (Another Reform Bill has been 'talked out'.)

S.R. 156, p. 374(R), 13 Apr. 'The Prisoner of Burmah'

S.R. 157, p. 392(M), 20 Apr. 'Officialism in Prussia' (The experiences of a British traveller have developed into a diplomatic incident.)

S.R. 158, p. 405(R), 20 Apr. 'German Literature' (Includes the exposition of an 'iron law of oligarchy'.)

S.R. 159, p. 416(M), 27 Apr. 'The Two Rivals' (Quixotic Private Members' Bills.)

S.R. 160, p. 422(M), 27 Apr. '*Le Prophète*' (Review of an opera by Meyerbeer.)

S.R. 161, p. 442(M), 4 May. 'Parliamentary Rhetoric' (The Budget Debate.)

S.R. 162, p. 456(R), 4 May. 'Universal Restoration' (Review of an Industrial epic set in Huddersfield.)

S.R. 163, p. 470(M), 11 May. 'Am I not a Beast and a Brother?' (He mocks private bills in general and those of Lord Raynham in particular.)

S.R. 164, p. 473(M), 11 May. 'Baron de Schlernitz's Apology' (Development of No. 157.)

S.R. 165, p. 497(M), 18 May. 'Tear 'em Rehabilitated' (Salisbury distinguishes 'fits of extreme depression' from madness, and attacks Roebuck for his inability to do likewise.)

S.R. 166, p. 506(R), 18 May. 'Adventures in Equatorial Africa' (A discussion of evolution.)

S.R. 167, p. 512(R), 18 May. 'German Literature'

S.R. 168, p. 527(M), 25 May. 'Count-Outs' (Salisbury regrets their excessive use.)

S.R. 169, p. 538(R), 25 May. 'Proverbs of the German Jews'

S.R. 170, p. 553(M), 1 Jun. 'The Ragged School Controversy' (A warning about the evil effects of charity.)

S.R. 171, p. 563(R), 1 Jun. 'Arminius' (The Germans are anxious to build up national identity and to find historical folk heroes.)

S.R. 172, p. 581(M), 8 Jun. 'Maynooth' (Salisbury is not opposed to the Maynooth grant.)

S.R. 173, p. 589(R), 8 Jun. 'A New System of Nature' (About the 'supposed conflict between science and scripture'.)

S.R. 174, p. 604(M), 15 Jun. 'Servants and Tradesmen'

S.R. 175, p. 620(R), 15 Jun. 'German Literature'

S.R. 176, p. 632(M), 22 Jun. 'The Speaker's Vote' (The Church-Rate debate ended in a tie.)

S.R. 177, p. 649(R), 22 Jun. 'La Beata'

S.R. 178, p. 663(J), 29 Jun. 'Philanthropic Jurisprudence'

S.R. 179, p. 672(R), 29 Jun. 'Queensland' (He complains about the ban against Chinese labour in Queensland.)

Volume XII, Jul.–Dec. 1861

S.R. 180, p. 9(M), 6 Jul. 'Marriage Market and Belgravian Intelligence' (Match-making mammas are looking only for rich eldest sons.)

S.R. 181, p. 25(R), 6 Jul. 'Captain Forbes on Iceland'

S.R. 182, p. 43(M), 13 Jul. 'Festive Enjoyment' (A graphic account of the boredom of the 'At Home' and the public dinner.)

S.R. 183, p. 50(R), 13 Jul. 'Jerome Bonaparte'

S.R. 184, p. 63(M), 20 Jul. 'Fashionable Factory Girls' (i.e. debutantes.)

S.R. 185, p. 66(M), 20 Jul. 'The Advantages of Expeditious Legislation' (The Bill by which the government of India was taken out of the hands of the East India Company was over-hasty.)

S.R. 186, p. 75(R), 20 Jul. 'German Literature'

S.R. 187, p. 89(M), 27 Jul. 'Red-Tape Retrenchments' (He objects to Gladstonian 'cheese-paring'.)

S.R. 188, p. 97(R), 27 Jul. 'Schlagweil's India and High Asia'

S.R. 189, p. 113(M), 3 Aug. 'The House of Lords' (He deplores the low attendance at debates.)

S.R. 190, p. 136(M), 10 Aug. 'The Session' ('A session of little things.')

S.R. 191, p. 146(R), 10 Aug. 'Merivale on Colonisation' (Salisbury says that the subject is no longer of political importance.)

S.R. 192, p. 166(M), 17 Aug. 'The Secession Mania' (There is trouble between English and Dutch in the Cape Colony, and Queensland has seceded from New South Wales.)

S.R. 193, p. 179(R), 17 Aug. 'German Literature' (including a description of witch-hunts in Westphalia.)

S.R. 194, p. 186(L), 24 Aug. 'Amateur Parliaments' (A criticism of the Radical 'Association for the Promotion of Social Science'.)

S.R. 195, p. 189(M), 24 Aug. 'The Surgeons and the Horse Guards' (Salisbury complains about the low ranks assigned to army doctors.)

S.R. 196, p. 192(M), 24 Aug. 'The Interminable Little War' (The Maori War.)

S.R. 197, p. 209(L), 31 Aug. 'The Lord Warden' (A portrait of Palmerston in the provinces.)

S.R. 198, p. 226(R), 31 Aug. 'Lord Lindsay on Scepticism' (A defence of religious scepticism.)

S.R. 199, p. 232(L), 7 Sep. 'Shelves and Dustheaps' (A protest against the appointment of Lord Monck as Governor-General of Canada allegedly as a patronage appointment.)

S.R. 200, p. 240(M), 7 Sep. 'Country Doctors'

S.R. 201, p. 267(L), 14 Sep. 'The Teaching of America' (i.e. a lesson about the disadvantages of democratic government.)

S.R. 202, p. 278(R), 14 Sep. 'The Hieroglyphic Hoax'

S.R. 203, p. 292(L), 21 Sep. 'New Zealand' (In New Zealand the British Governor has responsibility without power.)

S.R. 204, p. 303(R), 21 Sep. 'Slavery and Secession' (The main immediate cause of the Civil War was the tariff issue.)

S.R. 205, p. 310(R), 21 Sep. 'German Literature'

S.R. 206, p. 318(L), 28 Sep. 'The Rights of Labour at the Antipodes' (Australian workers have refused to tolerate Chinese labour.)

S.R. 207, p. 323(M), 28 Sep. 'Travelling in Germany' (A development of No. 164.)

S.R. 208, p. 332(R), 28 Sep. 'Ruth Baynard's Story'

S.R. 209, p. 341(L), 5 Oct. 'Prodigal Sons' (The colonials shift their defence expenditure on to the English taxpayer.)

S.R. 210, p. 355(R), 5 Oct. 'Spain in the Eighteenth Century'

S.R. 211, p. 368(L), 12 Oct. 'Another Reform Agitation'

S.R. 212, p. 374(M), 12 Oct. 'Match-Making Mammas'

S.R. 213, p. 392(L), 19 Oct. 'Democratic Imperialism' (An exposition of the similarity between democratic government in America and despotic government in Russia.)

S.R. 214, p. 404(M), 19 Oct. 'The Art of Saying Nothing' (This is required of politicians and clergymen.)

S.R. 215, p. 408(R), 19 Oct. 'L'Ancien Figaro' (A condemnation of despotic government in France.)

S.R. 216, p. 414(R), 19 Oct. 'German Literature'

S.R. 217, p. 422(L), 26 Oct. 'The Missionary of Peace' (It amuses Salisbury that Irishmen are fighting in America to put down insurrection.)

S.R. 218, p. 439(R), 26 Oct. 'Over the Straits' (A book about Australia.)

S.R. 219, p. 444(L), 2 Nov. 'Viscount Monck' (Same subject as No. 199.)

S.R. 220, p. 450(M), 2 Nov. 'The Weapons of Controversy' (Irony and wit are, says Salisbury, legitimate weapons.)

S.R. 221, p. 458(R), 2 Nov. 'M. Guizot on the Papal Question'

S.R. 222, p. 460(R), 2 Nov. 'Olmsted's Southern States' (Salisbury criticises Olmsted and says that a Northern victory will not secure the effective abolition of Slavery.)

S.R. 223, p. 475(L), 9 Nov. 'The Vallée des Dappes' (France has aggressive intentions against Switzerland.)

S.R. 224, p. 480(M), 9 Nov. 'The Count of Paris's Pamphlet' (In view of the inevitable decay of the Turkish Empire, France aims at extending her influence into the Middle East.)

S.R. 225, p. 510(M), 16 Nov. 'Mr. Leatham at Barnsley' (Politicians talk of Reform to their constituents but not to Parliament.)

S.R. 226, p. 514(R), 16 Nov. 'The American Union' (A detailed consideration of the causes and results of the Civil War, and the question of English recognition of the South.)

S.R. 227, p. 520(R), 16 Nov. 'German Literature'

S.R. 228, p. 528(L), 23 Nov. 'The Land of the Free' (France and America are 'despotisms' in democratic clothing.)

S.R. 229, p. 533(M), 23 Nov. 'Mr. Heath's Deprivation' (Salisbury dislikes the heresy-hunts being conducted by the Church of England.)

S.R. 230, p. 551(L), 30 Nov. 'The Woolwich Enquiry' (An attack on the hierarchical bureaucracy by which the Army is managed.)

S.R. 231, p. 556(M), 30 Nov. 'The Oxford Persecution' (The Jowett affair. Similar to No. 229.)

S.R. 232, p. 580(M), 7 Dec. 'The Art of Advertising'

S.R. 233, p. 585(M), 7 Dec. 'The Bull and the Frog' (The 'secession mania' has spread to Ireland.)

S.R. 234, p. 597(L), 14 Dec. 'Mr. Jefferson Davis's Message' (The President of the Confederacy is compared favourably to Lincoln.)

S.R. 235, p. 618(R), 14 Dec. 'Provincial Liberties in France' (The centralisation of government makes revolt easier.)

S.R. 236, p. 635(M), 21 Dec. 'Killing no Murder' (Trades Unionists in Sheffield murdered black-legs.)

S.R. 237, p. 647(R), 21 Dec. 'German Literature'

S.R. 238, p. 658(M), 28 Dec. 'The Year'

Volume XIII, Jan.–Jun. 1862

S.R. 239, p. 11(M), 4 Jan. 'Evening Amusements'

S.R. 240, p. 72(M), 18 Jan. 'Mr. Adderley's Colonial Policy' (An examination of British colonial aims.)

S.R. 241, p. 81(R), 18 Jan. 'German Literature'

S.R. 242, p. 92(M), 25 Jan. 'Mr. Roebuck at Salisbury' (Roebuck has committed the error of calling the working classes 'drunken' and 'brutish').

S.R. 243, p. 105(R) 25 Jan. 'Lord Cranborne's Historical Essays' (A review of his elder brother's essays.)

S.R. 244, p. 125(M), 1 Feb. 'The Rape of the Glances' (About London prostitutes.)

S.R. 245, p. 133(R), 1 Feb. 'The Seven Sons of Mammon'

S.R. 246, p. 153(M), 8 Feb. 'The First Night' (The Opening of Parliament.)

S.R. 247, p. 155(M), 8 Feb. 'Flogging at Public Schools' (Salisbury opposes flogging at public schools but is in favour of its retention in the Army and the Navy.)

S.R. 248, p. 184(M), 15 Feb. 'Mr. Edwin James' (A political scandal.)

S.R. 249, p. 194(R), 15 Feb. 'German Literature'

S.R. 250, p. 213(M), 22 Feb. 'The First Wednesday'. (The same perennial private members' bills are back.)

S.R. 251, p. 217(R), 22 Feb. 'The Cost of a Coronet'

S.R. 252, p. 230(L), 1 Mar. 'The Parliamentary Bob Acres' (An Irish Member has challenged the Secretary for Ireland to a duel.)

S.R. 253, p. 247(R), 1 Mar. 'The History of the Dance' (The Church would become live again if Bishops danced during the services.)

S.R. 254, p. 267(M), 8 Mar. 'Parliamentary Dullness' (The reason for this is that there are no great party issues to be debated.)

S.R. 255, p. 296(M), 15 Mar. 'The Impending Revolution' (Salisbury approves of the newly-formed society for the abolition of crinolines.)

S.R. 256, p. 297(M), 15 Mar. 'The Principle of the Revised Code' (Under the guise of administrative 'simplification', Lowe is destroying the system of denominational education.)

S.R. 257, p. 305(R), 15 Mar. 'Which Does She Love?'

S.R. 258, p. 309(R), 15 Mar. 'German Literature'

S.R. 259, p. 314(L), 22 Mar. 'Mr. Walpole's Resolutions' (A continuation of No. 256.)

S.R. 260, p. 345(L), 29 Mar. 'The Education Debate' (The same subject as No. 259.)

S.R. 261, p. 367(R), 29 Mar. 'Paris Mystérieux' (A review of a gossip-column about Paris.)

S.R. 262, p. 372(L), 5 Apr. 'The Educational Surrender' (Lowe has been forced to modify his Revised Code.)

S.R. 263, p. 382(M), 5 Apr. 'Dinner' (The House of Commons thins out at dinner-time.)

S.R. 264, p. 401(L), 12 Apr. 'Admirers' (Lord Stanley must have been embarrassed by the praise given to him in the Radical *Westminster Review*.)

S.R. 265, p. 410(M), 12 Apr. 'The Financial Duel' (A duel between Disraeli and Gladstone.)

S.R. 266, p. 428(L), 19 Apr. 'The Caput Mortuum of the Revised Code' (The Revised Code survives only in a very truncated form (see No. 262).)

S.R. 267, p. 439(M), 19 Apr. 'Invalids' (The social misery of invalids.)

S.R. 268, p. 452(R), 19 Apr. 'German Literature'

S.R. 269, p. 456(L), 26 Apr. 'Cheap Governors' (The example of New Zealand shows that it is false economy to send bad Governors to the Colonies.)

S.R. 270, p. 475(R), 26 Apr. 'Warp and Woof'

S.R. 271, p. 485(L), 3 May. 'The Palace of Puffs' (Salisbury is highly critical of the International Exhibition.)

S.R. 272, p. 494(M), 3 May. 'Officers and Gentlemen' (A condemnation of the aristocratic prejudices of army officers.)

S.R. 273, p. 503(R), 3 May. 'Sir Henry Holland's Essays' (On science and theology.)

S.R. 274, p. 515(L), 10 May. 'The Educational Compromise' (A further compromise on Lowe's Bill (see No. 266).)

S.R. 275, p. 522(M), 10 May. 'Bethell on the Beautiful' (Another article about public dinners.)

S.R. 276, p. 552(M), 17 May. 'Dishcovers and Dripping Pans' (Attack on the architecture of the International Exhibition building.)

S.R. 277, p. 557(M), 17 May. 'The Majority of One' (The Church Rate Bill was narrowly defeated.)

S.R. 278, p. 572(R), 17 May. 'German Literature'

S.R. 279, p. 580(L), 24 May. 'The Puffer's Lament' (Same theme as No. 276.)

S.R. 280, p. 607(L), 31 May. 'Hospitality to Foreigners' (London and London society is dull to the Frenchman.)

S.R. 281, p. 615(M), 31 May. 'Gossip'

S.R. 282, p. 631(R), 31 May. 'Pictures of German Life' (German history has been a chronicle of war and brutality.)

S.R. 283, p. 637(L), 7 Jun. 'Young Radicals and Old' (Radicals like Stansfeld are sincere dreamers, and not just businessmen like Cobden and Bright.)

S.R. 284, p. 644(M), 7 Jun. 'The Haymarket' (About the 'soiled doves' who walk the streets of Piccadilly. Salisbury appeals for legalised prostitution on the French model.)

S.R. 285, p. 668(L), 14 Jun. 'The Social Science Association' (A further attack on this Radical pressure-group (see No. 194).)

S.R. 286, p. 671(L), 14 Jun. 'Yankee Chivalry' (Salisbury is appalled by General Butler's edict in New Orleans which authorised his soldiers to commit rape.)

S.R. 287, p. 678(M), 14 Jun. 'The Manufacture of Saints' (The politics of beatification.)

S.R. 288, p. 695(L), 21 Jun. 'Lord Canning' (The climate of Calcutta makes it an unsuitable place to be the administrative capital of India.)

S.R. 289, p. 699(L), 21 Jun. 'The Land of the Free' (Bright's pacifism does not seem to prevent him from supporting the Northern cause in the Civil War.)

S.R. 290, p. 723(R), 21 Jun. 'German Literature'

S.R. 291, p. 731(L), 28 Jun. 'The Burials Bill' (Another Bill aimed at weakening the Establishment.)

S.R. 292, p. 733(L), 28 Jun. 'Questioners' (The internal affairs of foreign states are not the concern of Parliament.)

S.R. 293, p. 737(M), 28 Jun. *'Chaperones'*

Volume XIV, Jul.–Dec. 1862

S.R. 294, p. 4(L), 5 Jul. 'Ministerial Mudlarks' (Palmerston is being given trouble by the tactlessness of his ministers.)

S.R. 295, p. 8(L), 5 Jul. 'Amateur Generals' (A development of No. 286.)

S.R. 296, p. 11(M), 5 Jul. 'Drawing-Room Fortifications' (The influence of furniture on social intercourse.)

S.R. 297, p. 36(L), 12 Jul. 'The Jobbing Mania' (Criticism of the use of patronage by Palmerston and his ministers.)

S.R. 298, p. 37(L), 12 Jul. 'The Missing Prize-Money' (Gladstonian cheese-paring has caused a conflict between the Admiralty and the Treasury.)

S.R. 299, p. 45(M), 12 Jul. 'Peacemakers' (i.e. interfering women.)

S.R. 300, p. 66(L), 19 Jul. 'The Jamaica Debt' (A further muddle caused by Gladstone's cheese-paring policy.)

S.R. 301, p. 89(R), 19 Jul. 'German Literature'

S.R. 302, p. 94(L), 26 Jul. 'The Unpaid Attachés' (Competitive Examination has led to an increase in the Civil Estimates.)

S.R. 303, p. 97(L), 26 Jul. 'The Fourth Chinese War' (Gunboat diplomacy in China is quite profitless.)

S.R. 304, p. 102(M), 26 Jul. 'Friends'

S.R. 305, p. 120(L), 2 Aug. 'Extreme Delicacy and Caution' (Sir Robert Peel, Secretary for Ireland, lacks all tact in his dealings with the Irish.)

S.R. 306, p. 127(L), 2 Aug. 'The Poaching Bill' (Its historical associations have, quite without cause, made it develop into a class battle.)

S.R. 307, p. 127(M), 2 Aug. 'The Session'

S.R. 308, p. 287(R), 6 Sep. 'Supplementary Dispatches of the Duke of Wellington' (Salisbury admires Castlereagh and despises Liverpool.)

S.R. 309, p. 294(L), 13 Sep. 'Mr. Roebuck in Austria' (It is surprising that a Radical should admire an hereditary absolutism.)

S.R. 310, p. 330(L), 20 Sep. 'Mr. Bright on America' (Bright's main loyalty is to America, even when it becomes clear that its government is despotic.)

S.R. 311, p. 336(M), 30 Sep. 'Penitential Sittings' (Salisbury complains of the discomfort of pews in country churches and of the dullness of the services.)

S.R. 312, p. 356(R), 20 Sep. 'German Literature'

S.R. 313, p. 359(L), 27 Sep. 'France and Her Neighbours' (Louis Napoleon's 'diplomacy by pamphlet' can lead to awkward situations.)

S.R. 314, p. 371(M), 27 Sep. 'Cartes de Visite of Celebrities' (The trials of a visit to the photographer's.)

S.R. 315, p. 399(L), 4 Oct. 'The Cadogan Contract' (The Commissioners of the International Exhibition have been accused of jobbery.)

S.R. 316, p. 404(M), 4 Oct. 'Prosaic Words' ('U' vocabulary and 'non-U' vocabulary.)

S.R. 317, p. 432(L), 11 Oct. 'Lord Granville and Mr. Cadogan' (Similar to 315. A description of the unenviable position of 'younger sons' of the aristocracy.)

S.R. 318, p. 434(M), 11 Oct. 'The Loves of Old Ladies' (A description of three sorts of anile love.)

S.R. 319, p. 463(L), 18 Oct. 'General Butler' (Same as No. 295.)

S.R. 320, p. 472(M), 18 Oct. 'Compliments' (Salisbury dislikes the artificiality of society.)

S.R. 321, p. 488(R), 18 Oct. 'German Literature'

S.R. 322, p. 494(L), 25 Oct. 'Mr. Gladstone's Slip of the Tongue' (Gladstone spoke too favourably of Jefferson Davis to a provincial audience.)

S.R. 323, p. 516(R), 25 Oct. 'Memoires d'un Mormon'

S.R. 324, p. 524(L), 1 Nov. 'Brompton in Extremis' (The International Exhibition has been a failure.)

S.R. 325, p. 533(M), 1 Nov. 'The Evidence of Anecdotes' (Salisbury dismisses anecdotal evidence in general, and in particular the horror stories about slavery.)

S.R. 326, p. 554(L), 8 Nov. 'The New Persecution' (The persecution of Jowett (see No. 231).)

S.R. 327, p. 558(L), 8 Nov. 'The Great Shop' (i.e. the International Exhibition.)

S.R. 328, p. 566(M), 8 Nov. 'Miss Rye's Emigrants' (He advised governesses against emigrating to Australia, but advises Lancashire factory girls to go.)

S.R. 329, p. 584(L), 15 Nov. 'The Guildhall Dinner' (After-dinner speeches are liable to include indiscretions and are therefore not a good medium of diplomacy.)

S.R. 330, p. 590(M), 15 Nov. 'White Lies' (There are no absolute principles in either morality or politics.)

S.R. 331, p. 607(R), 15 Nov. 'German Literature'

S.R. 332, p. 612(L), 22 Nov. 'The French Press' (Louis Napoleon is unwise to destroy the freedom of the Press.)

S.R. 333, p. 640(L), 29 Nov. 'The New Pamphlet' (Another French pamphlet on the Papal Question.)

S.R. 334, p. 642(L), 29 Nov. 'The Greek Election' (The election of one of Queen Victoria's sons to the Greek throne is gratifying but problematic.)

S.R. 335, p. 667(L), 6 Dec. 'Lord Russell on the Schleswig Question' (Salisbury makes a vigorous attack on Russell's tactless and useless interference.)

S.R. 336, p. 672(L), 6 Dec. 'Mr. Williams and His Constituents' (The large urban 'democratic' constituencies consistently choose mediocre candidates.)

S.R. 337, p. 700(L), 13 Dec. 'The Opening of the Boulevard' (The artisans of Paris demonstrate their affection for Louis Napoleon.)

S.R. 338, p. 702(L), 13 Dec. 'Reduction of Estimates' (He opposes any reduction in the Army Estimates.)

S.R. 339, p. 707(M), 13 Dec. 'Racing and Betting' (There are rumours of a betting scandal in the army.)

S.R. 340, p. 725(L), 20 Dec. 'The Prince Consort' (An article in praise of his prudence.)

S.R. 341, p. 727(L), 20 Dec. 'Mr. Bright's "Wild Shriek of Freedom" ' (Bright's speech on America at Birmingham.)

S.R. 342, p. 749(R), 20 Dec. 'German Literature'

S.R. 343, p. 759(L), 27 Dec. 'Diplomacy in Undress' (The 'spoils system' means that the quality of American diplomats is very low.)

S.R. 344, p. 761(M), 27 Dec. 'The Year'

Volume XV, Jan.–Jun. 1863

S.R. 345, p. 6(L), 3 Jan. 'The Bishops and the Excursionists' (Salisbury says that the Bishops' condemnation of Sunday excursion trains is hypocritical.)

S.R. 346, p. 8(L), 3 Jan. 'The Revolution in Japan' (He fears that the result of the revolution will be an intensified scramble to open Japan for trade.)

S.R. 347, p. 40(L), 10 Jan. 'Prison Discipline' (He complains that prisons are more comfortable than workhouses.)

S.R. 348, p. 45(M), 10 Jan. 'Casual Shepherds' (Irregular slum visiting may help the consciences of the rich, but does little good to the poor.)

S.R. 349, p. 60(R), 10 Jan. 'My Good for Nothing Brother'

S.R. 350, p. 66(L) 17 Jan. 'The Halifax Reformers' (Further arguments against Reform.)

S.R. 351, p. 69(L), 17 Jan. 'General Butler's Career' (See No. 319.)

S.R. 352, p. 86(L), 24 Jan. 'The New Papal Aggression' (It has been reported that Russell has offered the Pope a place of refuge in Malta.)

S.R. 353, p. 101(L), 24 Jan. 'The New Zealand Remonstrance' (Salisbury fears that, if the colonists were given control of Maori affairs, oppression would be the result.)

S.R. 354, p. 108(M), 24 Jan. 'No Cards' (Salisbury would welcome the abolition of visiting cards.)

S.R. 355, p. 132(L), 31 Jan. 'The Emperor's Speech' (Louis Napoleon adheres to the forms but not to the substance of liberty.)

S.R. 356, p. 161(L), 7 Feb. 'Mr. Bright at Rochdale' (Salisbury attacks Bright's advocacy of the cause of the North in the Civil War.)

S.R. 357, p. 174(M), 7 Feb. 'The British Suttee' (i.e. the highly inflammable crinoline.)

S.R. 358, p. 191(L), 14 Feb. 'The Protestant Index' (The Church Convocation has launched a heresy hunt against *Essays and Reviews.*)

S.R. 359, p. 193(L), 14 Feb. 'Political Old Age' (All men are conservative in their old age, including Palmerston. This is the source of his political strength.)

S.R. 360, p. 228(L), 21 Feb. 'Lord Normanby on Italy' (He condemns the Parliamentary practice of discussing the internal affairs of foreign countries.)

S.R. 361, p. 232(M), 21 Feb. 'Practical Young Ladies' (Religion and philanthropy are out of fashion, practical husband-hunting is in.)

S.R. 362, p. 238(M), 21 Feb. 'The Supply of Foreign Kings' (cf. No. 334. Salisbury suggests that the Greeks choose a native to be king.)

S.R. 363, p. 252(R), 21 Feb. 'German Literature'

S.R. 364, p. 256(L), 28 Feb. 'Loyalty by Lamplight' (The arrangements for the marriage of the Prince of Wales do not give Londoners a good opportunity to have a look at the couple.)

S.R. 365, p. 258(L), 28 Feb. 'The Ecclesiastical Commission' (Salisbury condemns the misuse of Church patronage: too much goes to the Bishops.)

S.R. 366, p. 272(M), 28 Feb. 'Shy People' (A largely autobiographical article.)

S.R. 367, p. 291(L), 7 Mar. 'The Spiritual Round Robin' (The heresy hunt against Bishop Colenso.)

S.R. 368, p. 293(L), 7 Mar. 'Mr. Cobden Upon Obsolete Ships' (He condemns the inefficient organisation of the Admiralty which has slowed up naval modernisation.)

S.R. 369, p. 303(M), 7 Mar. 'Bribery' (Bribery is a natural medium whereby various groups represent their interests under the system of representative government.)

S.R. 370, p. 326(L), 14 Mar. 'Sir George Grey' (The Home Secretary is living evidence of the decline of the Whigs.)

S.R. 371, p. 362(L), 21 Mar. 'The Poaching Bill' (The Bill produced by the House of Commons was so vague that the Judges could interpret it in any way they wished.)

S.R. 372, p. 368(M), 21 Mar. 'Reserve'

S.R. 373, p. 395(L), 28 Mar. 'Irish Crime' (Irish crime has the result of removing capital from Ireland and of thus increasing distress.)

S.R. 374, p. 405(M), 28 Mar. 'Moral Game Preserves' (i.e. the wish for exclusiveness.)

S.R. 375, p. 425(L), 4 Apr. 'Church Patronage' (Salisbury welcomes a Bill to remove Church patronage from the hands of the Lord Chancellor.)

S.R. 376, p. 433(M), 4 Apr. 'Mr. Lowe's Reign of Terror' (Unfavourable reports from the Inspectors of Education have been suppressed from the Blue Book.)

S.R. 377, p. 453(L), 11 Apr. 'Genial Statesmanship' (Palmerston is very popular among the public at large.)

S.R. 378, p. 483(L), 18 Apr. 'The Remainder of the Session' (There is no legislation of importance before the House.)

S.R. 379, p. 485(L), 18 Apr. 'The Colenso Correspondence' (Same subject as No. 367.)

S.R. 380, p. 512(R), 18 Apr. 'German Literature'

S.R. 381, p. 520(L), 25 Apr. 'The Press and the Bench' (The Press provides a good check on the Judiciary.)

S.R. 382, p. 522(L), 25 Apr. 'Mr. Gladstone's Petty Cash' (An attack on Gladstone's taxes on clubs and charities in the Budget.)

S.R. 383, p. 545(R), 25 Apr. 'Mr. Goldwin Smith on the British Empire' (The function of the political thinker is to stimulate thought rather than action.)

S.R. 384, p. 551(L), 2 May. 'Canada and Its Cost' (The Canadians do not wish to pay for their defence.)

S.R. 385, p. 555(L), 2 May. 'The Church-Rate Debate' (The glut of perennial private motions results from the lack of party issues.)

S.R. 386, p. 582(L), 9 May. 'Mr. Gladstone against Endowments' (Gladstone's defence of the Establishment is weakening.)

S.R. 387, p. 585(L), 9 May. 'Two Foils' (Palmerston is constantly rescuing the ministry from the mistakes of his colleagues.)

S.R. 388, p. 615(L), 16 May. 'The Passing of the Budget' (The Budget was carried in a truncated form.)

S.R. 389, p. 618(L), 16 May. 'The Miscarried Persecution' (See Nos. 231 and 379.)

S.R. 390, p. 642(R), 16 May. 'German Literature'

S.R. 391, p. 646(L), 23 May. 'The Irish Church' (As an alternative to Disestablishment, larger grants should be given to Catholic clergy.)

S.R. 392, p. 650(L), 23 May. 'Steward's Room and Servants' Hall' (Democratic constituencies do not elect young members who can then be trained for office; thus ministers must be chosen from the Lords.)

S.R. 393, p. 679(L), 30 May. 'The City Election' (Only mediocre candidates will give the pledges and perform the distasteful duties required by democratic constituencies.)

S.R. 394, p. 684(L), 30 May. 'The Two General Orders' (Confederate modesty is contrasted with Northern bluster.)

S.R. 395, p. 690(M), 30 May. 'Heir Hunting'

S.R. 396, p. 711(L), 6 Jun. 'Freedom under the Abolitionists' (A criticism of General Burnside's suppression of political liberties in the North-western States of America.)

S.R. 397, p. 723(M), 6 Jun. 'The Last of the Annuals' (The debate on the Maynooth Grant.)

S.R. 398, p. 745(L), 13 Jun. 'Sergeant Lilley' (An Indian Army officer has done one of his men to death and has escaped punishment for his action.)

S.R. 399, p. 755(M), 13 Jun. 'The Last Anathema' (Pusey's latest heresy hunt is directed against Charles Kingsley.)

S.R. 400, p. 780(L), 20 Jun. 'The Oxford Commemoration'

S.R. 401, p. 789(M), 20 Jun. 'Irish Distress' (Same as No. 373.)

S.R. 402, p. 805(R), 20 Jun. 'German Literature'

S.R. 403, p. 812(L), 27 Jun. 'Re-appearance of Lord Raynham' (More imbecile bills from Lord Raynham.)

S.R. 404, p. 814(L), 27 Jun. 'The Abortive Debate' (Salisbury complains bitterly about the anarchy into which the House of Commons has fallen since 1846.)

S.R. 405, p. 822(M), 27 Jun. 'Genteel Beggars' (Invitation begging.)

Volume XVI, Jul.–Dec. 1863

S.R. 406, p. 4(L), 4 Jul. 'The Missing Message' (Cobden's private diplomacy with Louis Napoleon has had muddled results.)

S.R. 407, p. 16(M), 4 Jul. 'The Brazilian Arbitration' (Salisbury attacks Russell's gunboat policy towards Brazil.)

S.R. 408, p. 36(L), 11 Jul. 'Official Denials' (A development of No. 406.)

S.R. 409, p. 41(L), 11 Jul. 'Abolitionist Humanity' (He condemns the indiscriminate destructiveness of the Northern armies in the Civil War.)

S.R. 410, p. 53(M), 11 Jul. 'A Vote of Want of Confidence in Madagascar' (There has been a palace-revolution in Madagascar.)

S.R. 411, p. 73(L), 18 Jul. 'The Close of Amateur Diplomacy' (Same theme as 408. Salisbury expresses his dislike of private diplomacy.)

S.R. 412, p. 76(L), 18 Jul. 'The Japanese Difficulty' (He hopes that the murder of an English merchant will not be used as the pretext for war.)

S.R. 413, p. 101(R), 18 Jul. 'German Literature'

S.R. 414, p. 105(L), 25 Jul. 'Mr. Gladstone' (The 'succession stakes' in the Liberal party have started: in spite of his faults, Gladstone is the only likely candidate.)

S.R. 415, p. 108(L), 25 Jul. 'Mexico' (Louis Napoleon's forces have captured Mexico City and he is now left with the problem of what to do next.)

S.R. 416, p. 137(L), 1 Aug. 'Sir Charles Wood' (The House of Commons is not interested in Indian matters, thus there is no check on the undistinguished performance of the Secretary for India.)

S.R. 417, p. 141(L), 1 Aug. 'The Last of the Exhibition' (Salisbury condemns the way a bill concerning medals given for the International Exhibition was sneaked through the House of Commons.)

S.R. 418, p. 142(M), 1 Aug. 'The Session'

S.R. 419, p. 232(R), 15 Aug. 'German Literature'

S.R. 420, p. 240(L), 22 Aug. 'The Maori War' (Atrocities committed by the Colonists against the Maoris have led to the further outbreak of war.)

S.R. 421, p. 270(L), 29 Aug. 'Work for the Autumn' (During the Parliamentary recess Russell can commit his foreign policy blunders without restraint.)

S.R. 422, p. 316(M), 5 Sep. 'Bathing Abroad and at Home'

S.R. 423, p. 351(M), 12 Sep. 'Dress' (The middle classes show off their new wealth by wearing extravagant dresses.)

S.R. 424, p. 355(M), 12 Sep. 'The Usages of War' (The brutalities committed by the Northern armies on the civilian population of the

The Political Thought of Lord Salisbury

South will have a brutalising effect on the conduct of war throughout the world.)

S.R. 425, p. 377(L), 19 Sep. 'Lord Stanley at Liverpool' (The 'Stump' season has started.)

S.R. 426, p. 389(M), 19 Sep. 'Holiday-Making' (For the Englishman, holiday-making is a serious affair.)

S.R. 427, p. 418(L), 26 Sep. 'The Australians on Transportation' (New South Wales has complained in a high-handed way about the transportation of convicts to Western Australia.)

S.R. 428, p. 420(M), 26 Sep. 'National Prejudices' (Characteristics formed in times of national crisis far outlive their causes.)

S.R. 429, p. 455(M), 3 Oct. 'Benevolent Committees'

S.R. 430, p. 489(M), 10 Oct. 'Parochial and Paternal Government' (Salisbury outlines the advantages of local government.)

S.R. 431, p. 508(L), 17 Oct. 'Rollicking Statesmanship' (Sir Robert Peel has hit an elector and had a brawl with him.)

S.R. 432, p. 511(L), 17 Oct. 'The Maori Rising' (A development of No. 420.)

S.R. 433, p. 534(R), 17 Oct. 'German Literature'

S.R. 434, p. 541(L), 24 Oct. 'Irish Emigration' (Salisbury favours such emigration, which, he says, will ease the problem of unemployment.)

S.R. 435, p. 569(L), 31 Oct. 'Political Consistency' (An attack on 'weathercock' politicians, whose opinions change along with changes in public opinion.)

S.R. 436, p. 577(M), 31 Oct. 'Scientific Warfare' (Modern warfare will depend more on the build-up of arms than the bravery of soldiers. Salisbury foresees an arms race).

S.R. 437, p. 599(L), 7 Nov. 'The Yankee and the Cossack' (The Americans have the same underlying despotic character as the Russians.)

S.R. 438, p. 609(M), 7 Nov. 'Peculiar Dresses' (The Englishman has a horror of uniforms and dressing-up.)

S.R. 439, p. 628(L), 14 Nov. 'Lord Russell's Last Despatches' (Russell's empty bluster on the Polish question has resulted in a scornful rebuff from Russia.)

S.R. 440, p. 638(L), 14 Nov. 'Lord Mayor's Day' (Salisbury dislikes the pomp attached to the office of Lord Mayor.)

S.R. 441, p. 661(L), 21 Nov. 'The War in New Zealand' (Colonial policy is a stupid combination of provocation and unpreparedness.)

S.R. 442, p. 664(L), 21 Nov. 'The Homeless Poor' (He calls for legislation which will control the Poor Law Guardians.)

S.R. 443, p. 683(R), 21 Nov. 'German Literature'

S.R. 444, p. 693(L), 28 Nov. 'The Tribunes of the People' (Bright's speeches in Parliament are much more moderate than the ones he gives to his constituents.)

S.R. 445, p. 715(L), 5 Dec. 'Extra-Parliamentary Utterances' (Many of these are designed to be heard by merry audiences and not to be read in *The Times* by sober readers.)

S.R. 446, p. 718(L), 5 Dec. 'The Happy Family' (The proposed Congress of European powers will produce anything but harmony.)

S.R. 447, p. 726(M), 5 Dec. 'The Lion and the Man' (The habit of gaping at country houses has become widespread since the advent of the railway.)

S.R. 448, p. 745(L), 12 Dec. 'Accusation and Denial' (Cobden denies that Bright said that he favoured a division of land among the poor.)

S.R. 449, p. 747(L), 12 Dec. 'The French Elections' (Louis Napoleon had no great difficulty in controlling the French elections, in spite of the Ballot and Universal Suffrage.)

S.R. 450, p. 755(M), 12 Dec. 'Experimental Matrimony'

S.R. 451, p. 773(L), 19 Dec. 'The Prussian Minister on the English Press' (Salisbury refutes the allegation that the Government controls the press in England.)

S.R. 452, p. 774(L), 19 Dec. 'The Leeds Convention' (A Reform Convention.)

S.R. 453, p. 793(R), 19 Dec. 'German Literature'

S.R. 454, p. 799(L), 26 Dec. 'The Labours of the Recess' (Salisbury complains of the growth of the 'Stump'.)

S.R. 455, p. 803(L), 26 Dec. 'President Davis's Message' (He has great praise for the Confederates.)

S.R. 456, p. 805(M), 26 Dec. 'The Year'

Volume XVII, Jan.–Jun. 1864

S.R. 457, p. 4(L), 2 Jan. 'The Ecclesiastical Commissioners' ('There is no doubt that they have jobbed appallingly.')

S.R. 458, p. 7(L), 2 Jan. 'The New Dispensing Power' (A loophole in the law has enabled the murderer Townley to be given a stay of sentence of execution on grounds of insanity.)

S.R. 459, p. 35(L), 9 Jan. 'The Murderer Townley' (A development of No. 458.)

S.R. 460, p. 38(L), 9 Jan. 'Prison Discipline' (The dreams of the philanthropic reformer have proved delusive.)

S.R. 461, p. 67(L), 16 Jan. 'The Bradford Platform' (An inflammatory speech by Forster calling for a change in land laws.)

S.R. 462, p. 69(L), 16 Jan. 'The Second Orsini' (The report of an assassination attempt on Louis Napoleon was probably fabricated in order to gain sympathy for new aggressive measures.)

S.R. 463, p. 88(R), 16 Jan. 'German Literature'

S.R. 464, p. 95(L), 23 Jan. 'Lord Russell's Unruly Member' (Russell cannot resist the temptation to write insulting despatches.)

S.R. 465, p. 101(M), 23 Jan. 'An Overruling Providence' (Political events can neither provide evidence for or against the existence of a religious providence.)

S.R. 466, p. 126(L), 30 Jan. 'The Politics of Marylebone' (Democratic constituencies are interested principally in local affairs.)

S.R. 467, p. 129(M), 30 Jan. 'Poverty' (Salisbury disagrees with the New Testament teaching that poverty is morally ennobling.)

S.R. 468, p. 153(L), 6 Feb. 'The Townley Case' (See No. 458.)

S.R. 469, p. 181(L), 13 Feb. 'The Privy Council Judgement' (The Church's panic over *Essays and Reviews* was unnecessary.)

S.R. 470, p. 184(L), 13 Feb. 'The Townley Case' (See No. 468.)

S.R. 471, p. 211(L), 20 Feb. 'The Wire-Pullers' (The Radicals enjoy power without office as they hold the balance between the two major parties.)

S.R. 472, p. 214(L), 20 Feb. 'The Mutilated Despatch' (The dangers of after-dinner diplomacy.)

S.R. 473, p. 238(R), 20 Feb. 'German Literature'

S.R. 474, p. 243(L), 27 Feb. 'Bit-by-Bit Reform' (Salisbury distrusts any measure that threatens the equipoise of the constitution between differing class interests.)

S.R. 475, p. 248(L), 27 Feb. 'Senator Bayard's Speech' (The Senator for Delaware has resigned in protest against the abrogation of political liberties in that State.)

S.R. 476, p. 274(L), 5 Mar. 'The New Test' (Salisbury condemns the narrow-mindedness of the Bishops.)

S.R. 477, p. 303(L), 12 Mar. 'The Oxford Triumph' (See No. 231.)

S.R. 478, p. 306(L), 12 Mar. 'The Endowment Minute' (Salisbury objects to a new minute which has been added to Lowe's Revised Code (see No. 256, etc).)

S.R. 479, p. 336(L), 19 Mar. 'Mr. Stansfeld' (It has been alleged the Radical Lord of the Admiralty was associated with Mazzini at the time of the assassination plots.)

S.R. 480, p. 367(L), 26 Mar. 'The Queen' (He regrets the continued seclusion of the Queen.)

S.R. 481, p. 373(L), 26 Mar. 'Ministerial Indiscretions'

S.R. 482, p. 399(L), 2 Apr. 'Redintegratio Amoris' (Gladstone's pronouncement in favour of Reform has brought renewed interest in the matter.)

S.R. 483, p. 402(L), 2 Apr. 'The Condition-of-Ireland Question' (The scars of past conquest are the cause of Ireland's bad condition.)

S.R. 484, p. 404(L), 2 Apr. 'Federal Warfare' (Sherman's scorched earth tactics are against the laws of war.)

S.R. 485, p. 406(M), 2 Apr. 'The New Religious Movements' (Salisbury opposes the movement towards dogma-free religion.)

S.R. 486, p. 431(L), 9 Apr. 'Mr. Stansfeld' (See No. 479.)

S.R. 487, p. 343(L), 9 Apr. 'The Lisburn Election Committee' (Election Committees should not be composed of M.P.s.)

S.R. 488, p. 437(M), 9 Apr. 'Shapes and Sizes' (The political effects of the shape of the House of Commons.)

S.R. 489, p. 460(L), 16 Apr. 'The Lord Chancellor's Bill' (A development of No. 477.)

S.R. 490, p. 464(L), 16 Apr. 'Mr. Lowe and the Inspectors' (See No. 376.)

S.R. 491, p. 490(L), 23 Apr. 'The Scapegoat' (Lowe has resigned (see No. 490).)

S.R. 492, p. 492(L), 23 Apr. 'Tickets of Leave' (Salisbury opposes a bill providing for a probation service for prisoners released on parole.)

S.R. 493, p. 520(L), 30 Apr. 'Secession at the Antipodes' (The New Zealand legislature has passed a bill providing for the confiscation of the property of Maori rebels.)

S.R. 494, p. 522(L), 30 Apr. 'Tenant Right' (Capital will not be put into Ireland until lawlessness ends.)

S.R. 495, p. 547(L), 7 May. 'The House of Lords' (Salisbury deplores the low attendance at its debates and outlines the uses of a second chamber.)

S.R. 496, p. 550(L), 7 May. 'The Abolition of Hanging' (He calls this an 'eccentric idea' and details the arguments against abolition.)

S.R. 497, p. 581(L), 14 May. 'A Moribund Parliament' (As the time of dissolution comes near, party orthodoxy becomes more pronounced.)

S.R. 498, p 612(L), 21 May. 'Mr. Gladstone's Future' (Gladstone has nowhere to go for support but to the Radicals.)

S.R. 499, p. 675(L), 4 Jun. 'Foreign Influence' (The Monarch can put indirect pressure on to ministers. Salisbury is concerned at reports that this pressure is being used on behalf of the Queen's German relatives.)

S.R. 500, p. 677(L), 4 Jun. 'The Inspector's Reports' (The aftermath of the Lowe affair (see no. 491).)

S.R. 501, p. 706(L), 11 Jun. 'Modern Pilots' (Salisbury protests against the way the Government has left the Danes in the lurch.)

S.R. 502, p. 709(L), 11 Jun. 'Permissive Intolerance' (He is opposed to temperance laws.)

S.R. 503, p. 737(L), 18 Jun. 'Piebalds' (Palmerston, Russell and Gladstone take office from the Whigs and policy from Conservatives and Radicals.)

S.R. 504, p. 741(L), 18 Jun. 'Little Wars' (The British Army is not trained to fight guerilla warfare of the type required against Maoris and Zulus.)

S.R. 505, p. 772(L), 25 Jun. 'The Poor Law Report' (He approves of increased standardisation and centralisation of the Poor Law Boards.)

S.R. 506, p. 774(L), 25 Jun 'The Irish Difficulty' (Special economic help should be given to Ireland.)

Volume XVIII, Jul.–Dec. 1864

S.R. 507, p. 3(L), 2 Jul. 'Parliamentary Pouting' (The House of Commons refuses to overthrow Palmerston, but refuses to obey his wishes.)

S.R. 508, p. 8(L), 2 Jul. 'Defence of Canada' (Salisbury fears an attack by America.)

S.R. 509, p. 61(R), 9 Jul. 'The Danes in Camp' (Modern armaments give the edge to the side that has prepared most thoroughly.)

S.R. 510, p. 70(L), 16 Jul. 'Mexico' (Louis Napoleon's move in installing Maximilian is a plucky one.)

S.R. 511, p. 83(M), 16 Jul. 'Stray Votes' (M.P.s can be bribed in more subtle ways than by the offer of money.)

S.R. 512, p. 108(L), 23 Jul. 'Inspectors' Reports' (A continuation of No. 500.)

S.R. 513, p. 11(M), 23 Jul. 'Feminine Wranglers' (Salisbury does not think that women should be permitted to take university degrees.)

S.R. 514, p. 259(L), 27 Aug. 'Sahib Sent Back to School' (Another article ridiculing Competitive Examinations (see Nos. 60 and 69).)

S.R. 515, p. 261(L), 27 Aug. 'Weight for Age' (While Palmerston is still alive, the lull in the party struggle continues.)

S.R. 516, p. 289(L), 3 Sep. 'The Penalties of Greatness' (Politicians are subjected to invidious publicity.)

S.R. 517, p. 292(L), 3 Sep. 'Bribery' (Bribery has a natural part in representative government.)

S.R. 518, p. 320(L), 10 Sep. 'Sir David Ross'

S.R. 519, p. 322(L), 10 Sep. 'Representation of Minorities' (Proportional Representation is not as good a guarantee for the rights of minorities as Constitutional Government.)

S.R. 520, p. 328(M), 10 Sep. 'Domestic Jars'

S.R. 521, p. 348(L), 17 Sep. 'More Muddles' (More about Russell's blustering despatches (see No. 464).)

S.R. 522, p. 357(M), 17 Sep. 'The New Reformers' (The Manchester School were democratic on grounds of self-interest, Professor Fawcett and his School are democratic on grounds of abstract principle.)

S.R. 523, p. 377(L), 24 Sep. 'Lord Palmerston at Wilton'

S.R. 524, p. 386(M), 24 Sep. 'Sir John Herschel and the New Test' (The truths of Christian doctrine do not depend on the truth of the Creation story in Genesis.)

S.R. 525, p. 407(L), 1 Oct. 'Lord Clarendon at Vienna' (England should not have a finger in every foreign pie.)

S.R. 526, p. 411(L), 1 Oct. 'The War Christians of New Zealand' (The behaviour of the New Zealand colonists towards the Maoris shows that the crust of civilisation which covers man's natural savagery is a thin one.)

S.R. 527, p. 437(L), 8 Oct. 'Our New Foreign Policy' (Salisbury complains about the manner in which Denmark has been betrayed by England.)

S.R. 528, p. 444(M), 8 Oct. 'The Trail of the Serpent' (He disagrees with Bishop Elliott who called modern literature 'the trail of the serpent'.)

S.R. 529, p. 470(L), 15 Oct. 'Our Future Rulers' (A warning against the power of the Trades Unions.)

S.R. 530, p. 495(L), 22 Oct. 'Suburban Starring' (Both Palmerston's and Russell's intellectual faculties have diminished with age.)

S.R. 531, p. 505(M), 22 Oct. 'Lovely Woman' (On the use of cosmetics.)

S.R. 532, p. 525(L), 29 Oct. 'New Zealand' (He expresses the hope that the Maoris will be treated with a mixture of firmness and clemency.)

S.R. 533, p. 530(M), 29 Oct. 'Equality' (Technological advance will promote a new species of inequality.)

S.R. 534, p. 552(L), 5 Nov. 'Mr. Lowe on Examinations' (It is his schoolmaster's instincts that make Lowe favour Competitive Examination.)

S.R. 535, p. 555(L), 5 Nov. 'The Casual Poor' (A development of No. 505.)

S.R. 536, p. 584(L), 12 Nov. 'The False Alarm' (Gladstone has announced that there will be no early dissolution.)

S.R. 537, p. 588(L), 12 Nov. 'Mr. Ferrand at Devonport'

S.R. 538, p. 614(L), 19 Nov. 'Lord Russell at Aberdeen' (Salisbury takes Russell to task for maintaining that the Roman Empire fell because it did not adopt representative institutions.)

S.R. 539, p. 619(L), 19 Nov. 'Cathedral Reform'

S.R. 540, p. 650(L), 26 Nov. 'Cox's Complaint' (The ordeals of the M.P.s for Metropolitan constituencies.)

S.R. 541, p. 677(L), 3 Dec. 'Lord Grey's Reform Bill' (He has qualified support for Grey's proposals, but says that the two major parties would never co-operate to secure their passage through Parliament.)

S.R. 542, p. 682(L), 3 Dec. 'The Dublin Banquet' (He approves of the appointment of Lord Wodehouse as Viceroy of Ireland.)

S.R. 543, p. 706(L), 10 Dec. 'Secondary Stars' (The 'Stump' season continues.)

S.R. 544, p. 709(L), 10 Dec. 'The Australian Fray' (A repetition of No. 427.)

S.R. 545, p. 736(L), 17 Dec. 'The French Thwaites' (A comparison of Paris under Hausmann with the chaotic administration of London.)

S.R. 546, p. 742(L), 17 Dec. 'The Court of Appeal in Spiritual Cases' (Salisbury resists the suggestion that the Court should be manned by Bishops instead of Judges.)

S.R. 547, p. 762(L), 24 Dec. 'The Colenso Trial' (A further appeal against heresy-hunts.)

S.R. 548, p. 767(L), 24 Dec. 'The New Bull'

S.R. 549, p. 791(L), 31 Dec. 'The Evangelical Letter'

S.R. 550, p. 795(L), 31 Dec. 'New Zealand' (200 Maori prisoners have escaped.)

Volume XIX, Jan–Jun. 1865

S.R. 551, p. 7(L), 7 Jan. 'Ministerial Speeches' (Their only interest lies in the approach of the elections.)

S.R. 552, p. 17(M), 7 Jan. 'The Dublin Meeting' (The pros and cons of the disestablishment of the Irish Church.)

S.R. 553, p. 40(L), 14 Jan. 'Ewe-Lambs' (A new Popery scare.)

S.R. 554, p. 68(L), 21 Jan. 'The Working Man' (Salisbury dislikes the romanticised condescending attitude of philanthropists towards the working classes.)

S.R. 555, p. 70(L), 21 Jan. 'Timothy Daly' (A workhouse scandal.)

S.R. 556, p. 99(L), 28 Jan. 'The Court of Appeal in Spiritual Cases' (See No. 546.)

S.R. 557, p. 109(M), 28 Jan. 'Lord Ebury's Ultimatum'

S.R. 558, p. 129(L), 4 Feb. 'The New Finance Minister of India' (Salisbury renews his appeal for the removal of the Indian Capital from Calcutta.)

S.R. 559, p. 157(L), 11 Feb. 'The Improvements Promised in the Poor Law' (He approves of the new Poor Law as a step in the right direction.)

S.R. 560, p. 160(L), 11 Feb. 'A Melancholy House of Commons' (The time of dissolution is approaching.)

S.R. 561, p. 186(L), 18 Feb. 'The Dissolution' (Speculation as to the date.)

S.R. 562, p. 190(L), 18 Feb. 'Constitutional Transplantation' (The transplantation of institutional forms without effectively changing them is impossible.)

S.R. 563, p. 218(L), 25 Feb. 'The Greek Professorship' (A compromise has been reached in the Jowett affair (see No. 231).)

S.R. 564, p. 243(L), 4 Mar. 'The Education Committee' (An account of the growth of State-aided education in England.)

S.R. 565, p. 250(M), 4 Mar. 'Leaders of Fashion' (A description of the Victorian *dame de salon.*)

S.R. 566, p. 272(L), 11 Mar. 'The Edmunds Scandal' (A jobbery scandal.)

S.R. 567, p. 280(M), 11 Mar. 'The White Glove Business' (The London social season is a serious business.)

S.R. 568, p. 299(L), 18 Mar. 'Mr. Newdegate on Private Enquiries' (He condemns the 'Protestant bigotry' of the new Catholic scare (see No. 553).)

S.R. 569, p. 308(M), 18 Mar. 'The Battle for the Coal Trade' (Salisbury complains about the 'Railway lobby' in the House of Commons.)

S.R. 570, p. 329(L), 25 Mar. 'The Future Premier' (Is it to be Russell or Gladstone?)

S.R. 571, p. 330(L), 25 Mar. 'The Colenso Judgement' (See No. 547.)

S.R. 572, p. 359(L), 1 Apr. 'The Irish Church' (Salisbury acknowledges the anomalous position of the Establishment in Ireland but is unwilling to countenance the transfer of its endowments.)

S.R. 573, p. 363(L), 1 Apr. 'The Belfast Riots' (A condemnation of Orange lawlessness.)

S.R. 574, p. 394(L), 8 Apr. 'Sinking Fast' (The House of Commons is moribund.)

S.R. 575, p. 428(L), 15 Apr. 'The St. Giles Enquiry' (The horrors of the workhouse have come to light.)

S.R. 576, p. 463(L), 22 Apr. 'Another New Zealand War' (Maori distrust is the result of the brutalities they have suffered.)

S.R. 577, p. 467(M), 22 Apr. 'Fools' Paradises' (A mild protest against Victorian prudery.)

S.R. 578, p. 522(L), 6 May. 'The Reform Debate' (Lowe's speech against reform.)

S.R. 579, p. 532(M), 6 May. 'Moral Retrenchments' (An exposition of Utilitarian ethics.)

S.R. 580, p. 554(L), 13 May. 'The Reform Debate' (Gladstone's silence was significant.)

S.R. 581, p. 556(L), 13 May. 'Archbishop Manning' (Salisbury thinks the appointment was made for political rather than for religious motives.)

S.R. 582, p. 588(L), 20 May. 'The New Test Bill' (He argues in favour of Test Acts.)

S.R. 583, p. 590(L), 20 May. 'The Union Chargeability Bill' (The opposition to the squires has been 'violent and unreasonable'.)

S.R. 584, p. 621(L), 27 May. 'Club Consciences' (A condemnation of the decision of the Athenaeum Club not to contribute to charity.)

S.R. 585, p. 624(L), 27 May. 'Colonel Dawkins' (A new scandal brings up the question of Ministerial Responsibility and the control of the Army.)

S.R. 586, p. 657(L), 3 Jun. 'The Bear-Garden' (i.e. the House of Commons.)

S.R. 587, p. 660(M), 3 Jun. 'Privacy' (The presence of servants endangers the privacy of the English home.)

S.R. 588, p. 686(L), 10 Jun. 'The Union Chargeability Bill' (The House of Lords is not likely to amend the Bill (see No. 583).)

S.R. 589, p. 688(L), 10 Jun. 'The Ballot' (Salisbury argues against the Ballot.)

S.R. 590, p. 759(L), 24 Jun. 'Reverts' (Palgrave and Arnold have been reconverted to the Church of England.)

S.R. 591, p. 757(M), 24 Jun. 'Unprotected Males' (Charges of rape have been unjustly brought against males: the purpose is blackmail.)

Volume XX, Jul.–Dec. 1865

S.R. 592, p. 4(L), 1 Jul. 'The Oaths Bill' (It is only the proximity of the elections that has secured the passage of the Bill.)

S.R. 593, p. 44(M), 8 Jul. 'The House of Peers' (He regrets both the diminished attendance and the diminished powers of the House of Lords.)

S.R. 594, p. 321(L), 9 Sep. 'The Wakefield Exhibitions'

S.R. 595, p. 351(L), 16 Sep. 'The Bristol Disappointment' (Palmerston's illness stopped him from speaking.)

S.R. 596, p. 383(L), 23 Sep. 'Reform in Difficulties' (Bright's exaggerated attack on Palmerston will have the effect of strengthening Palmerston's position.)

S.R. 597, p. 411(L), 30 Sep. 'Fenianism' (Only time will heal the scars of Ireland's violent past.)

S.R. 598, p. 477(L), 14 Oct. 'Judgement-Mongers' (He condemns Dr.

Cullen's statement that the present cattle plague is a punishment by God for horse-racing.)

S.R. 599, p. 475(M), 14 Oct. 'Figure-Heads' (i.e. the Chairmen of public dinners.)

S.R. 600, p. 535(L), 28 Oct. 'Funeral Orations' (He is displeased with the Obituary of Palmerston in *The Times*.)

S.R. 601, p. 566(L), 4 Nov. 'The Cattle Plague and the Fenians' (The Government did not take the necessary measures to prevent the spread of the plague.)

S.R. 602, p. 630(L), 18 Nov. 'The Fenians' (The meek cowardice of the Fenian leaders.)

S.R. 603, p. 657(L), 25 Nov. 'The Dead Weight' (Some Ministers are not worthy of their place in the Cabinet.)

S.R. 604, p. 717(L), 9 Dec. 'The Queen' (Salisbury welcomes the Queen's resumption of her ceremonial duties.)

S.R. 605, p. 750(L), 16 Dec. 'American Toleration' (He condemns the religious intolerance of Bostonian Sabbatarians.)

Volume XXI, Jan.–Jun. 1866

S.R. 606, p. 7(L), 6 Jan. 'The Bribery of the Rich and the Poor' (The patronage given to the rich is as blameworthy as the bribes given to the poor.)

S.R. 607, p. 379(M), 31 Mar. 'The New Parliament' (It is too early in the session to make any judgements.)

Volume XXVI, Jul.–Dec. 1868

S.R. 608, p. 702(L), 28 Nov. 'How the Old Tories Looked at the Elections' (The effect of the Conservative Reform Bill was to 'cement the loose Liberal ranks behind Gladstone'.)

Speeches of
Lord Salisbury

Speeches of Lord Salisbury

I. In the Oxford Union (1848–1850)

1. 2 June 1848, for the motion 'that the discouragement of Dramatic Representations must always be attended with loss to the moral and literary character of the nation'.
2. 3 November 1848, on the motion 'that the amelioration of the social and moral condition of the working classes is the only means of preserving the present constitution of this country'. (Salisbury speaks for the motion with the amendment 'that the amelioration of the working classes will by no means be promoted by the extension of the suffrage'.)
3. 16 November 1848, for the motion 'that the present Ministry is incompetent to carry on the Government of the Country'.
4. 15 February 1849, moving the motion 'that any endowment of the Romanist priesthood or of any Romanist places of education will prove an insufferable obstacle to the social and political improvement of Ireland'.
5. 10 May 1849, for the motion 'that the dissolution of monasteries in the reign of Henry VIII was politically speaking a most injurious measure'.
6. 8 June 1849, against the motion 'that the Jewish Disabilities ought to be removed'.
7. 1 November 1849, for the motion 'that the present want of sufficient restraint on the Liberty of the Press is highly injurious to the interests of the country'.
8. 16 November 1849, against the motion 'that the past policy of this country, as carried out towards the Church, renders it imperative on Churchmen to demand either a total and immediate severance of the links between Church and State, or an entire change in the Ecclesiastical policy of our Governments'.
9. 22 November 1849, for the motion 'that an extensive financial reform is highly necessary for the welfare of the country'.
10. 6 December 1849, against the motion 'that with the sole exception of Lord Byron, Percy B. Shelley is the greatest English poet of the last half century'.

11. 7 February 1850, against the motion 'that the dismissal of the Earl of Roden from the Commission of the Peace was an uncalled and arbitrary act'.

12. 17 February 1850, for the motion 'that the state of the nation imperatively requires a return to the Principles of Protection'. (Reprinted in *The Oxford Union 1823–1923* by Herbert A. Morrah, pp. 137–39. Salisbury condemns the narrow class interests of the manufacturers which is at the base of the doctrine of Free Trade.)

II. Extra-Parliamentary Speeches (1853–1867)

1. Stamford, 22 August 1853 (*Lincoln, Rutland and Stamford Mercury*, 26 August 1853) (Salisbury explains how he has become unwillingly reconciled to Free Trade and talks of his resentment at the re-opening of the Reform debate).

2. Stamford, 7 November 1856 (*The Times*, 2 November 1856) (An important speech detailing his opposition to the proposed 'education rate').

3. Stamford, March 1857 (*Lincoln, Rutland and Stamford Mercury*, 27 March 1857) (An electioneering speech dealing mainly with the Crimean War).

4. Stamford, 27 March 1857 (*Lincoln, Rutland and Stamford Mercury*, 3 April 1857) (Election speech about the treatment of criminals).

5. Stamford, April 1857 (*The Times*, 17 April 1857) (He calls for an extension of education and opposes the enfranchisement of the uneducated).

6. Stamford, May 1859 (*Lincoln, Rutland and Stamford Mercury*, 6 May 1859) (An election speech about Reform and foreign policy).

7. Stamford, September 1859 (*Lincoln, Rutland and Stamford Mercury*, 23 September 1859; *The Times*, 23 September 1859) (Salisbury declared his support for Palmerston's new Ministry and called for defence against the danger from France).

8. Hurstpierpoint, Essex, December 1859 (*The Times*, 24 December 1859) (The Church needs to regain the support of the middle classes).

9. Stamford, 22 October 1862 (*The Times*, 23 October 1862) (A speech on defence to the 5th Lincolnshire Volunteer Corps).

10. Droitwich, November 1864 (*The Times*, 18 November 1864) (A plea for extended facilities for adult education).

11. Stamford, July 1865 (*Lincoln, Rutland and Stamford Mercury*, 14 July 1865) (Election speech reviewing the record of the Palmerston Ministry).

12. London Tavern, Bishopsgate, November 1867 (*The Times*, 22 November 1867) (Salisbury appeals for support for a charity to provide accommodation for convalescents in the East End).

III. Speeches in the House of Commons

Salisbury's short questions and minor contributions to debates have not been included, but all substantive questions and contributions filling a column or more of *Hansard* are included in the following list. The *Hansard* volumes are all in the Third Series.

H.C. 1, cxxxii, 711–714, 7 April 1854. 'Oxford University Bill' (Salisbury opposes any interference with University endowments.)

H.C. 2, cxxxii, 1262–1263, 4 May 1854. 'Oxford University Bill'

H.C. 3, cxxxiv, 1263, 6 July 1854. 'Church Building Bill'

H.C. 4, cxxxvii, 684–686, 16 March 1855. 'Education (No. 2) Bill' (He looked upon the Bill as the secular system in disguise.)

H.C. 5, cxxxvii, 1185–1186, 27 March, 1855. 'Reconstitution of Poland'

H.C. 6, cxxxviii, 1600–1604, 7 June 1855. 'Prosecution of the War' (The proposed peace terms with Russia are needlessly harsh and aggressive.)

H.C. 7, cxxxviii, 2278, 20 June 1855. 'Marriage Law Amendment Bill'

H.C. 8, cxxxix, 972, 17 July 1855. 'The Army in the Crimea—Sebastopol Committee' (Salisbury seconds General Peel's amendment to the motion of censure on the Government.)

H.C. 9, cxli, 823–827, 10 April 1856. 'National Education' (Salisbury rejects non-sectarian religious education.)

H.C. 10, cxli, 1435–1439, 24 April 1856. 'Admissions to the Civil Service' (Opposition to competitive examination.)

H.C. 11, cxlii, 175, 8 May 1856. 'Aggravated Assaults Bill' ('A man was flogged, not for his own benefit, but for the benefit of the people who were not flogged.')

H.C. 12, cxliii, 1280–1284, 23 July 1856. 'Bishops of London and Durham Retirement Bill' (The grants to Bishops were 'ridiculously large'.)

H.C. 13, cxliv, 789–790, 19 February 1857. 'Education (Cities and Boroughs) Bill'

H.C. 14, cxliv, 1538–1541, 27 February 1857. 'War in China' (A violent attack on the 'buccaneering' of the Liverpool merchants who had precipitated the 'Arrow' affair.)

H.C. 15, cxlv, 186–187, 11 May 1857. 'Industrial Schools Bill'

H.C. 16, cxlv, 313–315, 15 May 1857. 'Treatment of Chinese Prisoners— Question' (An attack on Labouchere for the treatment of Chinese prisoners in Hong Kong.)

H.C. 17, cxlv, 1104–1110, 4 June 1857. 'Voting Papers, Select Committee Moved for'

H.C. 18, cxlviii, 1560–1564, 17 February 1858. 'Church Rates Abolition Bill'

H.C. 19, cxlix, 512–515, 22 March 1858. 'Oaths Bill' (Salisbury opposes the admission of Jews to the House of Commons on the ground that it is not a secular assembly.)

H.C. 20, cli, 2169–2170, 27 July 1858. 'Private Business-Standing Orders' (A speech in favour of the reform of the committee system in the Commons.)

H.C. 21, cliii, 476–481, 21 March 1859. 'Representation of the People

Bill' (A detailed and important speech setting out the theory of 'balance'.)

H.C. 22, cliv, 848, 7 July 1859. 'Adulteration of Food etc. Regulation Bill' (Salisbury favours government intervention.)

H.C. 23, clv, 750–751, 1 August 1859. 'Corrupt Proceedings at Elections Question' (Salisbury calls for a Commission of Enquiry to look into the activities of the London political clubs.)

H.C. 24, clvi, 187–188, 26 January 1860. 'Gloucester City and Wakefield Writs' (Extended franchise leads inevitably to extended bribery.)

H.C. 25, clvi, 322–323, 30 January 1860. 'Oxford University Bill'

H.C. 26, clvi, 622–623, 7 February 1860. 'Divorce and Matrimonial Causes Court' (Newspapers should not be permitted to report divorce proceedings.)

H.C. 27, clvii, 386–393, 12 March 1860. 'Paper Duty Repeal Bill' (A defence of indirect taxation.)

H.C. 28, clvii, 520–521, 14 March 1860. 'Religious Worship Bill'

H.C. 29, clvii, 2210–2218, 23 April 1860. 'Representation of the People Bill'

H.C. 30, clviii, 491–494, 1 May 1860. 'Berwick-on-Tweed Election' (Similar to H.C. 24.)

H.C. 31, clviii, 898–901, 8 May 1860. 'Examinations for Factory Boy Appointments' (Appointments by civil servants should be subject to review by the House of Commons.)

H.C. 32, clviii, 1833–1836, 31 May 1860. 'Military Defences of the Colonies' (Salisbury objects to any reduction of garrisons in the Colonies.)

H.C. 33, clviii, 1974–1977, 4 June 1860. 'Representation of the People Bill' ('The noble Lord's Reform Bill would increase bribery.')

H.C. 34, clviii, 2083–2084, 5 June 1860. 'Civil Service Examinations' (Suitable civil servants will be attracted by higher pay rather than by competitive examinations.)

H.C. 35, clix, 1722–1723, 11 July 1860. 'Census (England) Bill' (The new census should omit reference to religion, for exaggerated figures for Dissenters had been used against the Church of England.)

H.C. 36, clix, 1907, 13 July 1860. 'Supply-China War' (Reckless Colonial officials ought to be bridled.)

H.C. 37, clxi, 230–236, 8 February 1861. 'Poor Relief' (Power should be taken from the parish authorities.)

H.C. 38, clxi, 1413–1415, 5 March 1861. 'Colonial Military Expenditure' (cf. H.C. 32.)

H.C. 39, clxi, 1509–1511, 6 March 1861. 'Church Rates Abolition' ('No surrender.')

H.C. 40, clxii, 677–680, 17 April 1861. 'Trustees of Charities Bill' (The Bill 'proposed to strip the Church of her endowed schools'.)

H.C. 41, clxii, 829–830, 19 April 1861. 'New Zealand—Tribunal for Native Claims' (A defence of Maori rights.)

H.C. 42, clxii, 1039–1041, 24 April 1861. 'Nonconformist Burial Bill'

('The Bill was one of the attempts of the Dissenters to destroy the Church of England.')

H.C. 43, clxii, 1176–1181, 26 April 1861. 'Case of Captain MacDonald —Question' (cf. S.R. 157.)

H.C. 44, clxii, 1576–1583, 6 May 1861. 'Paper Duty' (A detailed argument against direct taxation.)

H.C. 45, clxii, 1728–1729, 7 May 1861. 'Ways and Means—Report' (A repetition of H.C. 44, together with an attack on Gladstone for riding rough-shod over the House of Lords.)

H.C. 46, clxii, 2028–2034, 13 May 1861. 'Customs and Inland Revenue Bill' (cf. H.C. 44 and H.C. 45.)

H.C. 47, clxiii, 1291–1297, 19 June 1861. 'Church Rates Abolition Bill' (All compromise proposals have failed because the Dissenters wish to pull down the Church of England from its national position.)

H.C. 48, clxiii, 1448–1452, 21 June 1861. 'Civil Service Examinations' (Latin verses were not suitable for clerks.)

H.C. 49, clxv, 470–473, 19 February 1862. 'Marriage with a Deceased Wife's Sister' (Salisbury opposes any disturbance of existing laws.)

H.C. 50, clxv, 595–596, 21 February 1862. 'Education—The Revised Code of Regulations'

H.C. 51, clxv, 696–697, 25 February 1862. 'Public Business' (A speech about 'count-outs' and procedure in Parliament.)

H.C. 52, clxv, 872–877, 28 February 1862. 'The Revised Code and the Pupil Teachers' (He complains that the Revised Code has been introduced during the recess of Parliament.)

H.C. 53, clxv, 1225–1230, 7 March 1862. 'United States—Blockade of the Southern Ports' (Britain ought to recognise the Confederacy.)

H.C. 54, clxvi, 81–88, 25 March 1862. 'Education—The Revised Code— Distribution of Grants' (The new Code does not remedy the admitted shortcomings of the existing system.)

H.C. 55, clxvi, 678–684, 7 April 1862. 'Property and Income Tax' (cf. H.C. 44, 45 and 46.)

H.C. 56, clxvi, 769–770, 10 April 1862. 'Income Tax Collectors'

H.C. 57, clxvi, 1233–1237, 5 May 1862. 'Education—The Revised Code of Regulations' (Salisbury opposes the 'voluntary principle' of education.)

H.C. 58, clxvi, 2123–2124, 23 May 1862. 'The Longford Election' (A case of alleged electoral corruption.)

H.C. 59, clxvii, 1013–1016, 24 June 1862. 'Church Rates' (The Dissenters are not concerned with Church Rates in themselves but with 'ulterior objects' of a political nature.)

H.C. 60, clxvii, 1464–1467, 14 July 1862. 'Thames Embankment Bill'

H.C. 61, clxviii, 914, 28 July 1862. 'Consolidated Fund (Appropriation) Bill' (Salisbury fears the prospect of a new war in China.)

H.C. 62, clxviii, 954–955, 28 July 1862. 'Union Relief Aid Bill' (There is no good reason for compensating the Lancashire cotton owners for losses resulting from the U.S. blockade of the Southern States.)

H.C. 63, clxix, 919–920, 27 February 1863. 'Affairs of Poland' (Britain should register a protest to Russia over her treatment of Poland, but it was totally impractical to talk of Britain's going to war.)

H.C. 64, clxix, 1151–1158, 6 March 1863. 'Relations with Brazil' (cf. Q.R. 15.)

H.C. 65, clxix, 1433–1439, 13 March 1863. 'Supply—Army Estimates— General Staff' (Reductions in costs per capita were needed rather than reductions in manpower.)

H.C. 66, clxx, 141–148, 15 April 1863. 'Burials Bill' (Another move by Dissenters to encroach upon the Church of England.)

H.C. 67, clxx, 597–600, 23 April 1863. 'American Cruisers and British Merchantmen' (The British Government is not active enough in protecting British merchantmen unjustly seized by the U.S. for breaking the blockade.)

H.C. 68, clxx, 995–997, 30 April 1863. 'Customs and Inland Revenue Bill' (Salisbury is indignant against Gladstone's proposed tax on charities.)

H.C. 69, clxx, 1119–1125, 4 May 1863. 'Customs and Inland Revenue Bill' (Similar to H.C. 68.)

H.C. 70, clxx, 1239–1240, 11 May 1863. 'Uniformity Act' (Fellowships at the Universities should not fall into the hands of Nonconformists.)

H.C. 71, clxx, 1548–1549, 11 May 1863. 'Customs and Inland Revenue Bill' (A speech on a detail about the income tax.)

H.C. 72, clxx, 1963–1965, 19 May 1863. 'Foreign Affairs—Position of this House' (A rambling speech about intervention and non-intervention.)

H.C. 73, clxx, 2053–2056, 28 May 1863. 'Supply—Civil Service Estimates' (The withdrawal of the Government subsidy from the Packet Service is a breach of faith: cf. S.R. 54.)

H.C. 74, clxxi, 638–642, 9 June 1863. 'Uniformity Act' (A defence of the Thirty-nine Articles.)

H.C. 75, clxxi, 728–731, 11 June 1863. 'Reports of Inspectors of Schools' (Salisbury condemns the manner in which the reports of Inspectors of Schools have been censored before being presented to the House.)

H.C. 76, clxxi, 1645–1651, 29 June 1863. 'Supply Report—Seizure of British Vessels' (An attack on the 'unblushing partisanship on the part of the Government' towards the Northern States of the U.S.)

H.C. 77, clxxi, 1818–1826, 30 June 1863. 'United States—Recognition of the Confederacy' (Salisbury marshals a variety of reasons for recognition.)

H.C. 78, clxxii, 987–990, 17 July 1863. 'Detention of the "Gibraltar"' (cf. H.C. 76. Salisbury also argues that compensation should be given to the owners of the *Gibraltar*.)

H.C. 79, clxxii, 1379–1381, 24 July 1863. 'Subscription to Formularies of Faith' (University posts must be reserved for members of the Church of England.)

greater sense of urgency in preparing Canada for a possible attack from the U.S. is called for.)

H.C. 99, clxxvi, 523–527, 30 June 1864. 'Supply—Civil Service Estimates (Public Education)' (Salisbury opposes the supplementary rules which followed the Revised Code.)

H.C. 100, clxxvi, 670–672, 1 July 1864. 'Tests Abolition (Oxford) Bill'

H.C. 101, clxxvi, 842–853, 5 July 1864. 'Denmark and Germany' (A closely argued speech censuring the Government for giving to Denmark 'abundance of good words and no material aid'.)

H.C. 102, clxxvi, 2048–2049, 25 July 1864. 'Poor Relief (Metropolis) Bill' (cf. H.C. 37.)

H.C. 103, clxxvi, 2058–2059, 25 July 1864. 'Mutual Surrender of Criminals (Prussia) Bill' (Salisbury opposes the scheme.)

H.C. 104, clxxvi, 2079–2081, 26 July 1864. 'Education—(Inspectors' Reports)'

H.C. 105, clxxvii, 717–722, 24 February 1865. 'State of Ireland' (The starvation in Ireland should be relieved by special grants and tax remissions.)

H.C. 106, clxxvii, 902–910, 28 February 1865. 'Education' (Salisbury complains that the Revised Code was 'juggled' through Parliament.)

H.C. 107, clxxvii, 1507–1510, 10 March 1865. 'War in New Zealand' (A further defence of native rights.)

H.C. 108, clxxvii, 1609–1613, 13 March 1865. 'Defences of Canada— Colonel Jervois' Report' (Britain should resist the extravagant claims of the U.S. over the case of the *Alabama*.)

H.C. 109, clxxviii, 859–860, 6 April 1865. 'Metropolitan Houseless Poor Bill' (cf. H.C. 37.)

H.C. 110, clxxix, 781–782, 23 May 1865. 'Leeds Court of Bankruptcy'

H.C. 111, clxxx, 93–95, 12 June 1865. 'Poor Law Continuance Bill'

H.C. 112, clxxx, 210–215, 14 June 1865. 'Test Abolition (Oxford) Bill' (Salisbury agrees to the 'Cambridge compromise' whereby Dissenters are given the literary dignity of the M.A. without the accompanying right to take part in the government of the University.)

H.C. 113, clxxxi, 174–178, 6 February 1866. 'Address to Her Majesty on Her most Gracious Speech' (The lack of Government action had led to importation of a cattle disease from the Continent.)

H.C. 114, clxxxi, 492–497, 14 February 1866. 'Cattle Diseases Bill' (Discretion as to the passage of cattle should not be left to local authorities.)

H.C. 115, clxxxi, 1294–1296, 1 March 1866. 'Devonport Election' (Allegations of irregular practices in a dockyard constituency.)

H.C. 116, clxxxi, 1455–1459, 2 March 1866. 'International Maritime Law' (Not as important a speech as the title would imply.)

H.C. 117, clxxxi, 1603–1605, 6 March 1866. 'London (City) Corporation Gas Bill' (The gas companies should be made to treat the public more fairly.)

of Mysore' (Salisbury favours decentralised native government in India.)

H.C. 136, clxxxvii, 1213–1215, 28 May 1867. 'Parliamentary Reform—Representation of the People Bill' (The proposed Bill does not present any final solution to the Reform problem.)

H.C. 137, clxxxvii, 1320–1322, 30 May 1867. 'Parliamentary Reform—Representation of the People Bill' (The only answer to bribery is the disfranchisement of the offending boroughs.)

H.C. 138, clxxxvii, 1357–1359, 30 May 1867. 'Parliamentary Reform—Representation of the People Bill' (The passing of the Bill will lead to the introduction of local caucus politics.)

H.C. 139, clxxxvii, 1966–1970, 17 June 1867. 'Parliamentary Reform—Representation of the People Bill' (Salisbury argues in favour of multi-member constituencies as a protection of minority interests.)

H.C. 140, clxxxviii, 190–194, 20 June 1867. 'Parliamentary Reform—Representation of the People Bill' (A detailed argument in favour of the use of voting papers. cf. H.C. 17.)

H.C. 141, clxxxviii, 638–640, 27 June 1867. 'Parliamentary Reform—Representation of the People Bill' (Candidates should pay hustings expenses so that sham candidatures will be discouraged.)

H.C. 142, clxxxviii, 677–678, 28 June 1867. 'Parliamentary Reform—Representation of the People Bill' (The passing of the clause giving the franchise to those who did not personally pay their rates would change the whole substance of the Bill.)

H.C. 143, clxxxviii, 999–1000, 4 July 1867. 'Parliamentary Reform—Representation of the People Bill' (He complains about the way Disraeli has handled the Bill in the House.)

H.C. 144, clxxxviii, 1097–1102, 5 July 1967. 'Parliamentary Reform—Representation of the People Bill' (General arguments and an attack on Bright and Disraeli.)

H.C. 145, clxxxviii, 1526–1539, 15 July 1867. 'Parliamentary Reform—Representation of the People Bill' (A long speech at the start of the Third Reading. He protests in particular at the devaluation of political morality that will follow as a result of the circumstances under which the Bill is being passed.)

H.C. 146, clxxxix, 1378–1382, 12 August 1867. 'East India Revenue Accounts'

H.C. 147, cxc, 404–407, 28 November 1867. 'East India, Troops and Vessels (Abyssinian Expedition)' ('I do not like India to be looked upon as an English barrack in the Oriental Seas.')

H.C. 148, cxc, 711–712, 13 February 1868. 'Election Petitions and Corrupt Practices at Elections Bill' (They should not be judged by tribunals of judges.)

H.C. 149, cxc, 968–970, 19 February 1868. 'Compulsory Church Rates Abolition Bill' ('I do not think the Church will gain anything by prolonging this contest.')

H.C. 150, cxc, 1801–1805, 17 March 1868. 'Private Bill Legislation'

(The system of Committees is inefficient and haphazard.)

H.C. 151, cxci, 424–425, 27 March 1868. 'Systems of Government in India' (He talks of the evil of over-regulation.)

H.C. 152, cxci, 532–541, 30 March 1868. 'Established Church (Ireland)' (Salisbury fears that the Bill is the thin edge of yet another wedge.)

Notes and Sources

Notes and Sources

CHAPTER I

1. Cecil, Vol. I, p. 11.
2. Cecil, Vol. I, p. 20.
3. *The Times*, 11 November 1856.
4. cf. Shaw-Stewart's letter to Salisbury, 15 April 1867.
5. H. A. Morrah, *The Oxford Union 1823-1923* (1923), p. 128.
6. Cecil, Vol. I, p. 49.
7. Ernest Scott, *Lord Robert Cecil's Gold Fields Diary* (1935).
8. Letter to Rev. C. R. Conybeare, 11 July 1852.
9. There is an account of electioneering at Stamford at this period in J. M. Lee, 'Stamford and the Cecils, 1700-1885' (Oxford B.Litt. thesis 1957).
10. *Lincoln, Rutland and Stamford Mercury*, 19 August 1853.
11. S.R. XIV, p. 432 (317).
12. S.R. XI, p. 336 (153).
13. S.R. XII, p. 374 (212).
14. S.R. XII, p. 9 (180).
15. S.R. XV, p. 232 (361).
16. S.R. XV, p. 690 (395).
17. S.R. XII, p. 374 (212); S.R. XII, p. 9 (180).
18. S.R. XV, p. 690 (395).
19. S.R. XI, p. 190 (142).
20. The biographical information about Mill given in this chapter is taken from his *Autobiography*.
21. An equally fruitful comparison can be made between Salisbury's career and writings and those of the arch-Liberal Robert Lowe. Lowe incidentally made a similar attack on the classics around this time, cf. his *Primary and Secondary Education* (Edinburgh, 1867).
22. pp. 86-7.
23. p. 146.
24. S.R. XIII, p. 439, (267).
25. S.R. XI, p. 497 (165).
26. Q.R. 111, p. 221 (8); S.R. X, p. 595 (120); S.R. VII, p. 588 (70); S.R. XVI, p. 799 (454); S.R. XV, p. 679 (393).
27. S.R. XV, p. 453 (377); S.R. XII, p. 209 (197).
28. S.R. XII, p. 43 (182).
29. S.R. XV, p. 272 (366).
30. S.R. XIV, p. 590 (330).

CHAPTER II

1. *Essays by the Late Marquess of Salisbury* (John Murray, 1905).
2. *Dictionary of National Biography*, Supplement, Vol. 1, pp. 329–43.
3. Cecil, Vol. 1, p. 72.
4. Cecil, Vol. 1, p. 82.
5. See Bevington's *Appendix of Authorship* for the list of his attributions. Lady Gwendolen's list, which is discussed below, has shown that some of the attributions are incorrect. The matter is discussed in Dr. Mason's article in the *Bulletin of the Institute of Historical Research*, Vol. 34 (pp. 37–8).
6. *Bulletin of the Institute of Historical Research*, Vol. 34, p. 36.
7. cf. p. 15.
8. Cecil, Vol. 1, p. 84.
9. Cecil, Vol. 1, p. 88.
10. Cecil, Vol. 1, p. 88.
11. S.R. VIII, pp. 81–2, *Bentley's Quarterly Review*.
12. S.R. III, p. 82.
13. Vol. 11, p. 270.
14. *Contemporary Review*, February 1922, pp. 230–36.
15. *Contemporary Review*, February 1922, p. 236.
16. p. 234.
17. *Bulletin of the Institute of Historical Research*, Vol. 34, p. 39.
18. Cecil, Vol. I, p. 72.
19. 'The Charm of Journalism', p. 11, from *A Scrap Book*.
20. Henry W. Lucy, *Speeches of the Marquis of Salisbury*, 1885.
21. 2 March 1859.
22. Cecil, Vol. 1, p. 82.
23. p. 42.

24. *Bulletin of the Institute of Historical Research*, Vol. 34, p. 37.
25. *Bulletin of the Institute of Historical Research*, Vol. 34, p. 37.
26. p. 54.
27. p. 79.
28. Q.R. 110, p. 544 (7); Q.R. 118, p. 193 (20) Q.R. 127, p. 538 (26).
29. Q.R. 110, p. 247 (6); Q.R. 112, p. 535 (11); Q.R. 117, p. 449 (18).
30. Q.R. 108, p. 568 (3).
31. Q.R. 116, p. 482 (17).
32. *Dictionary of National Biography*, Supplement, Vol. 1, p. 340.
33. Q.R. 130, p. 256 (28).
34. Q.R. 131, p. 549 (29).
35. Q.R. 109, p. 531 (5).
36. Q.R. 111, p. 201 (8).
37. Q.R. 113, p. 448 (13).
38. Q.R. 115, p. 236 (14).
39. Q.R. 115, p. 481 (15).
40. N.R. II, p. 1 (1).
41. N.R. IV, p. 145 (2).
42. N.R. XX, p. 289 (3); N.R. XXIV p. 450 (4).
43. S.R. III, p. 249 (14).
44. S.R. IV, p. 66 (35).
45. S.R. IV, p. 139 (36).
46. S.R. V, p. 403 (56).
47. S.R. VIII, p. 107 (78).
48. cf. S.R. III, p. 130 (5); S.R. IV, p. 139 (36); S.R. IV, p. 375 (44); S.R. V, p. 20 (46); S.R. V., p. 193 (49); S.R. V, p. 403 (56); S.R. XI, p. 649 (177); S.R. XV, p. 60 (349).
49. S.R. IV, p. 325 (41); S.R. XI, p. 43 (131); S.R. XI, p. 422

(160); S.R. XIII, p. 522 (275); S.R. XIII, p. 552 (276).

50. S.R. III, p. 60 (3); S.R. III, p. 83 (4); S.R. III, p. 364 (19).

51. S.R. III, p. 203 (10); S.R. III, p. 247 (13); S.R. III, p. 293 (16); S.R. III, p. 383 (20); S.R. VIII, p. 222 (80); S.R. VIII, p. 400 (85); S.R. IX, p. 279 (111); S.R. X, p. 595 (120); S.R. XII, p. 50 (183); S.R. XII, p. 267 (201); S.R. XII, p. 392 (213); S.R. XII, p. 422 (217); S.R. XII, p. 460 (222); S.R. XII, p. 514 (226); S.R. XII, p. 528 (228); S.R. XII, p. 597 (234); S.R. XII, p. 658 (238); S.R. XIII, p. 671 (286); S.R. XIV, p. 8 (295); S.R. XIV, p. 330 (310); S.R. XIV, p. 463 (319); S.R. XIV, p. 516 (323); S.R. XIV, p. 727 (341); S.R. XIV, p. 759 (343); S.R. XIV, p. 762 (b) (344); S.R. XV, p. 161 (356); S.R. XV, p. 684 (394); S.R. XV, p. 711 (396); S.R. XVI, p. 41 (409); S.R. XVI, p. 105 (414); S.R. XVI, p. 355 (424); S.R. XVI, p. 599 (437); S.R. XVI, p. 803 (455); S.R. XVII, p. 101 (465); S.R. XVII, p. 248 (475); S.R. XVII, p. 404 (484); S.R. XVIII, p. 8 (508); S.R. XX, p. 750 (605).

52. S.R. III, p. 383 (20).

53. S.R. III, p. 458 (25).

54. S.R. III, p. 383 (20).

55. cf. Q.R. 110, p. 247 (6).

56. S.R. XI, p. 175 (141).

57. S.R. XII, p. 97 (188).

58. S.R. XIV, p. 356 (312).

59. S.R. XII, p. 520 (227).

60. e.g. S.R. VIII, p. 815 (93); S.R. IX, p. 217 (107); S.R. XI, p. 175 (141); S.R. XI, p.

563 (171); S.R. XI, p. 620 (175); S.R. XII, p. 75 (186); S.R. XII, p. 355 (210); S.R. XII, p. 520 (227); S.R. XII, p. 631 (282); S.R. XVI, p. 534 (433).

61. S.R. IX, p. 217 (107); S.R. IX, p. 312 (112); S.R. X. p. 78 (133).

62. S.R. X. p. 632 (122); S.R. XI, p. 251 (147); S.R. XII, p. 414 (216); S.R. XVII, p. 88 (463).

63. S.R. XIII, p. 309 (258).

64. S.R. XII, p. 226 (198).

65. S.R. IX, p. 215 (106).

66. S.R. XIV, p. 287 (308).

67. S.R. III, p. 152 (6); S.R. III, p. 203 (10); S.R. III, p. 240 (12); S.R. III, p. 398 (21); S.R. V, p. 212 (51); S.R. V, p. 468 (58); S.R. VII, p. 272 (67); S.R. IX, p. 107 (100); S.R. IX, p. 178 (104); S.R. IX, p. 241 (108); S.R. IX p. 370 (115); S.R. XI, p. 161 (139); S.R. XI, p. 217 (144); S.R. XI, p. 364 (155); S.R. XI, p. 442 (161); S.R. XI, p. 581 (172); S.R. XI, p. 632 (176); S.R. XIII, p. 153 (246); S.R. XIII, p. 213 (250); S.R. XIII, p. 267 (254); S.R. XIII, p. 410 (265); S.R. XV, p. 228 (360); S.R. XVII, p. 243 (474); S.R. XIX, p. 160 (560); S.R. XIX, p. 522 (578); S.R. XIX, p. 554 (580).

68. S.R. VII, p. 272 (67).

69. B.Q.R. I, p. 343 (2).

70. S.R. IX, p. 178 (104).

71. Q.R. 107, p. 514 ff. (1).

72. S.R. III, p. 593 (30); S.R. IV, p. 8 (32); S.R. IX, p. 112 (101); S.R. XI, p. 291 (150); S.R. XV, p. 258 (365); S.R. XIX, p. 243 (564).

73. S.R. XI, p. 527 (168); S.R.

XIII, p. 213 (250); S.R. XV, p. 483 (378); S.R. XV, p. 723 (397).

74. S.R. III, p. 425 (22); S.R. V. p. 212 (51); S.R. XIII, p. 557 (277); S.R. XV, p. 66 (350); S.R. XV, p. 582 (386); S.R. XV, p. 814 (404); S.R. XVIII, p. 3 (507); S.R. XIX, p. 657 (586); S.R. XX, p. 657 (603).

75. S.R. IX, p. 210 (105); S.R. XIII, p. 733 (292); S.R. XV, p. 650 (392).

76. S.R. III, p. 361 (18); S.R. IX, p. 19 (95); S.R. XI, p. 94 (134); S.R. XIII, p. 668 (285); S.R. XV, p. 303 (369); S.R. XVII, p. 7 (458); S.R. XIX, p. 308 (569).

77. S.R. VII, p. 429 (68); S.R. XII, p. 113 (189); S.R. XIII, p. 267 (254); S.R. XV, p. 228 (360); S.R. XVII, p. 547 (495); S.R. XIX, p. 686 (588).

78. S.R. VII, p. 557 (69); S.R. XII, p. 66 (185); S.R. XII, p. 136 (190); S.R. XII, p. 551 (230); S.R. XIV, p. 37 (298); S.R. XV, p. 293 (368); S.R. XV, p. 433 (376); S.R. XV, p. 650 (392).

79. S.R. XII, p. 658 (238); S.R. XIV, p. 524 (324); S.R. XIV, p. 725 (340); S.R. XVI, p. 142(b) (418); S.R. XVII, p. 367 (480); S.R. XVII, p. 675 (499); S.R. XX, p. 717 (604).

80. S.R. XI, p. 124 (137); S.R. XI, p. 173 (140).

81. S.R. VII, p. 272 (67); S.R. IX, p. 215 (106); S.R. IX, p. 276 (110); S.R. IX, p. 400 (116); S.R. X, p. 834(a) (128); S.R. XI, p. 364 (155); S.R. XII, p. 368 (211); S.R. XII, p. 510 (225); S.R. XIV,

p. 128(b) (307); S.R. XV, p. 66 (350); S.R. XV, p. 483 (378); S.R. XVI, p. 693 (444); S.R. XVI, p. 745 (448); S.R. XVI, p. 774 (452); S.R. XVII, p. 67 (461); S.R. XVII, p. 243 (474); S.R. XVII, p. 399 (482); S.R. XVIII, p. 357 (522); S.R. XVIII, p. 677 (541); S.R. XIX, p. 522 (578).

82. Q.R. 113, p. 266 (12); S.R. XIII, p. 297 (256); S.R. XIII, p. 314 (259); S.R. XIII, p. 345 (260); S.R. XIII, p. 372 (262); S.R. XIII, p. 428 (266); S.R. XIV, p. 4 (294); S.R. XV, p. 433 (376); S.R. XVII, p. 464 (490); S.R. XVII, p. 490 (491); S.R. XVII, p. 677 (500).

83. S.R. V, p. 643 (59); S.R. XVI, p. 489 (430); S.R. XVIII, p. 555 (535); S.R. XVIII, p. 736 (545).

84. S.R. XII, p. 186 (194); S.R. XV, p. 6 (345); S.R. XVI, p. 664 (442).

85. S.R. III, p. 38 (2); S.R. VIII, p. 672 (92); S.R. XI, p. 12 (129); S.R. XI, p. 34 (130); S.R. XIV, p. 566 (328); S.R. XV, p. 45 (348); S.R. XVI, p. 664 (442), S.R. XVII, p. 129 (467); S.R. XVII, p. 772 (505); S.R. XVIII, p. 555 (535); S.R. XIX, p. 70 (555); S.R. XIX, p. 157 (559); S.R. XIX, p. 428 (575).

86. S.R. III, p. 556 (28); S.R. VI, p. 620 (64); S.R. VII, p. 557 (69); S.R. VII, p. 661 (71); S.R. VIII, p. 421 (86); S.R. XI p. 620 (175); S.R. XIII, p. 155 (247); S.R. XIV,

p. 762 (a) (344); S.R. XV, p. 40 (347); S.R. XV, p. 232 (361); S.R. XV, p. 395 (373); S.R. XVI, p. 664 (442); S.R. XVII p. 7 (458); S.R. XVII, p. 35 (459); S.R. XVII, p. 38 (460); S.R. XVII, p. 184 (470); S.R. XVII, p. 492 (492); S.R. XVII, p. 550 (496).

87. S.R. IV, p. 330 (43); S.R. IX, p. 312 (112); S.R. X, p. 833 (128); S.R. XIII, p. 733 (292); S.R. XIV, p. 97 (303); S.R. XIV, p. 129(b) (307); S.R. XIV, p. 667 (335); S.R. XVI, p. 16 (407); S.R. XVI, p. 270 (421); S.R. XVI, p. 628 (439); S.R. XVII, p. 95 (464); S.R. XVII, p. 214 (472); S.R. XVII, p. 706 (501); S.R. XVIII, p. 348 (521).

88. S.R. XII, p. 136 (190); S.R. XII, p. 189 (195); S.R. XII, p. 551 (230); S.R. XIII, p. 494 (272); S.R. XIV, p. 8 (295); S.R. XIV, p. 702 (338); S.R. XV, p. 293 (368); S.R. XV, p. 745 (398); S.R. XVI, p. 577 (436); S.R. XIX, p. 243 (564); S.R. XIX, p. 624 (585).

89. S.R. III, p. 383 (20); S.R. VI, p. 357 (62); S.R. VIII, p. 815 (93); S.R. IX, p. 251 (109); S.R. XII, p. 146 (191); S.R. XII, p. 341 (209); S.R. XII, p. 439 (218); S.R. XIII, p. 72 (240); S.R. XIII, p. 267 (254); S.R. XIII, p. 401 (264); S.R. XV, p. 8 (346); S.R. XVI, p. 418 (427); S.R. XIX, p. 463 (576).

90. S.R. IX, p. 19 (95); S.R. X, p. 553 (117); S.R. X, p. 726 (125); S.R. XII, p. 192 (196); S.R. XII, p. 292 (203); S.R.

XIII, p. 456 (269); S.R. XV, p. 101 (353); S.R. XVI, p. 240 (420); S.R. XVI, p. 511 (432); S.R. XVI, p. 661 (441); S.R. XVII, p. 520 (493); S.R. XVII, p. 741 (504); S.R. XVIII, p. 411 (526); S.R. XVIII, p. 525 (532); S.R. XVIII, p. 795 (550).

91. S.R. VIII, p. 390 (84); S.R. XII, p. 585 (233); S.R. XIII, p. 230 (252); S.R. XIV, p. 120 (305); S.R. XV, p. 395 (373); S.R. XV, p. 646 (391); S.R. XV, p. 789 (401); S.R. XVI, p. 541 (434); S.R. XVII, p. 402 (483); S.R. XVII, p. 522 (494); S.R. XVII, p. 774 (506); S.R. XVIII, p. 682 (542); S.R. XIX, p. 17 (552); S.R. XIX, p. 359 (572); S.R. XIX, p. 363 (573); S.R. XX, p. 411 (597); S.R. XX, p. 630 (602).

92. S.R. IV, p. 328 (42); S.R. IX, p. 52 (97); S.R. XI, p. 512 (167); S.R. XI, p. 538 (169); S.R. XII, p. 226 (198); S.R. XII, p. 533 (229); S.R. XII, p. 556 (231); S.R. XIV, p. 516 (323); S.R. XIV, p. 554 (326); S.R. XV, p. 191 (358); S.R. XV, p. 291 (367); S.R. XV, p. 485 (379); S.R. XV, p. 618 (389); S.R. XV, p. 755 (399); S.R. XVII, p. 101 (465); S.R. XVII, p. 181 (469); S.R. XVII, p. 274 (476); S.R. XVII, p. 303 (477); S.R. XVII, p. 460 (489); S.R. XVIII, p. 386 (524); S.R. XVIII, p. 444 (528); S.R. XVIII, p. 742 (546); S.R. XVIII, p. 762 (547); S.R. XIX, p. 99 (556); S.R. XIX, p. 218 (563); S.R. XIX, p. 359 (572).

93. S.R. XI, p. 43 (131); S.R. XI, p. 336 (153); S.R. XII, p. 9 (180); S.R. XII, p. 63 (184); S.R. XII, p. 374 (212); S.R. XIII, p. 247 (253); S.R. XIII, p. 737 (293); S.R. XV, p. 232 (361); S.R. XV, p. 690 (395); S.R. XIX, p. 280 (567).

94. S.R. XII, p. 43 (182); S.R. XII, p. 404 (214); S.R. XIII, p. 522 (275); S.R. XIV, p. 472 (320); S.R. XIV, p. 584 (329); S.R. XX, p. 475 (599).

95. S.R. XIII, p. 367 (261); S.R. XIII, p. 615 (281).

96. S.R. XV, p. 174 (357); S.R. XVI, p. 351 (423).

97. S.R. XII, p. 240 (200).

98. S.R. XIII, p. 11 (239); S.R. XIII, p. 125 (244); S.R. XIII, p. 644 (284).

99. S.R. XIV, p. 472 (320).

100. S.R. XIV, p. 590 (330).

101. S.R. XIV, p. 11 (296); S.R. XVII, p. 437 (488).

102. S.R. XVI, p. 316 (422).

103. S.R. XII, p. 580 (232).

104. S.R. XVI, p. 389 (426).

105. S.R. XV, p. 822 (405).

106. S.R. XVIII, p. 505 (531).

107. S.R. XIII, p. 439 (267).

108. S.R. XV, p. 272 (366).

109. S.R. XIV, p. 102 (304).

110. S.R. XIV, p. 472 (320).

111. Knox and Pelczynski, *Hegel's Political Writings*, passim.

112. The information about *The Quarterly Review* comes from the two articles on 'The Centenary of "The Quarterly Review"'. (*Quarterly Review* April 1909 and July 1909).

113. cf. N. MacMinn, J. R. Hainds and J. McCrimmon, *Bibliography of the Published Writings of John Stuart Mill.*

114. c.f. M. M. Bevington, *The Saturday Review (1855–1868)* and W. I. and I. Law, *The Book of the Beresford-Hopes.*

115. Q.R. 112, p. 535 (11).

116. Q.R. 117, p. 540 (19).

117. Q.R. 110, p. 247 (6).

118. S.R. VII, p. 776 (75).

119. S.R. XVII, p. 214 (472).

CHAPTER III

1. p. 7.
2. p. 8.
3. p. 2.
3. p. 2.
4. p. 11.
5. p. 14.
6. Hearnshaw, *Prime Ministers of the Nineteenth Century*, p. 216.
7. Clinton Rossiter, *Conservatism in America*, Vintage Edition, p. 44.
8. *John Stuart Mill on Bentham and Coleridge*, Harper Torchbook Edition, p. 46.

9. Mill, op. cit., p. 48.
10. Mill, op. cit., pp. 49–50.
11. Mill, op. cit., p. 61.
12. Mill, op. cit., p. 108.
13. 'Hume and Conservatism', *American Political Science Review* 1954 (Vol. XLVII, p. 999).
14. S.R. VII, p. 776 (75).
15. S.R. XI, p. 405 (158).
16. S.R. XVI, p. 773 (451).
17. S.R. XIII, p. 81 (241).
18. S.R. XIII, p. 309 (258).
19. S.R. XI, p. 277 (149).
20. S.R. XII, p. 226 (198).

21. S.R. IV, p. 139 (36).
22. S.R. V, p. 403 (56).
23. S.R. III, p. 130 (5).
24. S.R. IV, p. 18 (33).
25. S.R. XIV, p. 533 (325).
26. S.R. V, p. 193 (49).
27. Q.R. 116, p. 482 (17).
28. Q.R. 105, p. 558 (5).
29. S.R. XI, p. 251 (147).
30. S.R. XIV, p. 488 (321).
31. S.R. XVII, p. 88 (463).
32. S.R. XI, p. 78 (133).
33. S.R. XI, p. 78 (133).
34. S.R. III, p. 432 (23).
35. B.Q.R. II, p. 303 (4).
36. Q.R. 109, p. 531 (4).
37. S.R. XIV, p. 488 (321).
38. e.g. 'Theories of Parliamentary Reform', N.R. IV, p. 145 (2); B.Q.R. II, p. 303 (4); Q.R. 107, p. 514 (1).
39. Q.R. 119, p. 530 ff. (23).
40. S.R. VIII, p. 332 (83); S.R. XII, p. 414 (216).

41. N.R. II, p. 11 (1).
42. S.R. XI, p. 620 (175).
43. S.R. XVII, p. 238 (473).
44. S.R. XV, p. 805 (402).
45. Cecil, Vol. I, p. 113.
46. Cecil, Vol. I, pp. 113-4.
47. cf. *Queen Victoria and Her Prime Ministers*, p. 295.
48. Q.R. April 1922, pp. 378-99.
49. Cecil, Vol. I, p. 99.
50. Cecil, Vol. I, p. 113.
51. Cecil, Vol. I, p. 112.
52. S.R. XX, p. 477 (598).
53. S.R. XVII, p. 101 (465).
54. S.R. XIV, p. 516 (323).
55. Speech at the Sheldonian Theatre, Oxford, 25 November, 1864.
56. S.R. XVIII, p. 386 (524).
57. S.R. XVII, p. 406 (485).
58. S.R. XV, p. 485 (379).
59. S.R. X, p. 632 (122).
60. S.R. XI, p. 405 (158).
61. S.R. XIII, p. 503 (273).

CHAPTER IV

1. *Two Concepts of Liberty*, p. 7.
2. Cecil, Memoir, p. 73.
3. p. 52.
4. S.R. XII, p. 267 (201).
5. S.R. XI, p. 78 (133).
6. S.R. XIV, p. 590 (330).
7. S.R. XIX, p. 532 (579).
8. S.R. III, p. 38 (2).
9. Q.R. 119, p. 534 (23).
10. *Theories of Parliamentary Reform*, p. 68.
11. Q.R. 108, p. 568 (3).
12. Q.R. 109, p. 214 and p. 226 ff. (4).
13. cf. S.R. XIII, p. 314 (259).
14. S.R. XVI, p. 569 (435).
15. B.Q.R. II, pp. 307-8 (4).
16. B.Q.R. I, p. 13 (1).
17. S.R. VIII, p. 12 (76).

18. S.R. VII, p. 709 (72).
19. S.R. IX, p. 215 (106).
20. B.Q.R. I, p. 347 (2).
21. Q.R. 109, pp. 559-60 (5).
22. Q.R. 109, p. 550 (5).
23. cf. Q.R. 123, p. 533 (25).
24. Q.R. 109, p. 212 (4).
25. S.R. XIII, p. 314 (259).
26. S.R. XV, p. 522 (382).
27. Q.R. 156, p. 561 (33).
28. Q.R. 109, p. 558 (5).
29. S.R. IV, p. 18 (33).
30. Q.R. 111, p. 215 ff. (8).
31. *Theories of Parliamentary Reform*, p. 52.
32. S.R. XVI, p. 683 (443).
33. S.R. X, p. 726 (125).
34. S.R. XVII, p. 520 (493).
35. S.R. XII, p. 192 (196).

36. S.R. IX, p. 19 (95).
37. B.Q.R. II, p. 303 (4).
38. S.R. XII, p. 113 (189).
39. S.R. XIV, p. 566 (328).
40. S.R. XIII, p. 155 (247).
41. Cecil, Memoir, p. 92.
42. Q.R. 117, pp. 281–83 (18).
43. Q.R. 117, p. 284 (18).
44. S.R. XX, p. 750 (605).
45. pp. 9–11.
46. Cecil, Memoir, p. 47.
47. Q.R. 110, p. 251 (6).
48. Q.R. 110, p. 259 (6).
49. Q.R. 112, p. 562 (11).
50. S.R. XV, p. 232 (361).
51. S.R. XV, p. 405 (374).
52. Q.R. 113, p. 448 (13).
53. S.R. XIII, p. 631 (282).
54. S.R. XI, p. 348 (154);
    S.R. XI, p. 374 (156); S.R.
    XI, p. 506 (166); S.R. XII,
    p. 179 (193); S.R. XIII, p.
    631 (282); S.R. XVI p. 793
    (453).
55. Q.R. 130, p. 270 (28).
56. S.R. XVIII, p. 411 (526).
57. S.R. III, p. 383 (20).
58. B.Q.R. II, p. 25 (3).
59. S.R. XVII, p. 129 (467).
60. Q.R. 111, p. 206 (8).
61. Q.R. 111, p. 234 (8).
62. cf. S.R. III, p. 383 (20);
    S.R. VI, p. 357 (62).
63. S.R. III, p. 293 (16).
64. S.R. XII, p. 179 (193).

65. S.R. XI, p. 405 (158).
66. S.R. XVIII, p. 530 (533).
67. cf. Q.R. 112, p. 547 (11).
68. H.C. clxxxiii, p. 9 (121).
69. Q.R. 123, p. 557 (25).
70. S.R. XIX, p. 522 (578).
71. S.R. III, p. 197 (9).
72. S.R. XVI, p. 137 (416).
73. S.R. XV, p. 256 (364).
74. S.R. XI, p. 140 (138).
75. S.R. XVI, p. 638 (440).
76. e.g. S.R. XI, p. 140 (138).
77. S.R. XX, p. 717 (604).
78. S.R. XIII, p. 637 (283).
79. S.R. IX, p. 400 (116).
80. B.Q.R. I, p. 343 (2).
81. Q.R. 116, pp. 503–4 (17).
82. Q.R. 116, p. 245 (16).
83. S.R. IX, p. 279 (111).
84. S.R. XII, p. 520 (227).
85. S.R. X, p. 833 (128).
86. Q.R. 127, pp. 551–52 (26).
87. Q.R. 108, p. 285 (2).
88. p. 57.
89. B.Q.R. I, p. 1 (1).
90. Q.R. 130, p. 258 (28).
91. Q.R. 112, p. 253 (10).
92. Q.R. 112, p. 255 (10).
93. S.R. XI, p. 161 (139).
94. Q.R. 108, p. 268 ff. (2), Q.R
    110, p. 546 ff. (7).
95. S.R. XIX, p. 17 (552); S.R.
    XIX, p. 359 (572).
96. Q.R. 110, p. 263 (6).

CHAPTER V

1. S.R. III, p. 458 (25).
2. S.R. XVIII, p. 736 (545).
3. S.R. XI, p. 392 (157).
4. S.R. XII, p. 310 (205).
5. S.R. XI, p. 228 (145).
6. cf. B.Q.R. II, p. 326 (4) and
   S.R. XII, p. 618 (235).
7. S.R. XVIII, p. 357 (522).

8. Q.R. 112, p. 556 (11).
9. cf. Q.R. 110, pp. 257–8 (6).
10. Q.R. 119, p. 541 (23).
11. S.R. XII, p. 318 (206).
12. Q.R. 110, p. 269 (6).
13. B.Q.R. II, p. 21 (3).
14. S.R. XII, p. 392 (213).
15. B.Q.R. II, p. 7 (3).

16. S.R. VII, p. 588 (70); S.R. VII, p. 776 (75); S.R. XIV, p. 672 (336); S.R. XV, p. 650 (392); S.R. XVII, p. 126 (466); S.R. XVIII, p. 650 (540).
17. S.R. VII, p. 776 (75).
18. S.R. XII, p. 267 (201).
19. S.R. XVI, p. 693 (444).
20. S.R. XVII, p. 126 (466).
21. Q.R. 110, p. 247 (6).
22. Q.R. 110, pp. 266–7 (6)
23. S.R. XVIII, p. 322 (519).
24. S.R. XVIII, p. 322 (519).
25. S.R. XIX, p. 463 (576).
26. Q.R. 156, p. 562 (33).
27. Q.R. 123, p. 557 (25).
28. S.R. XI, p. 12 (129).
29. *Theories of Parliamentary Reform*, p. 63.
30. Q.R. 117, p. 572 (19).

31. S.R. XVI, p. 489 (430).
32. S.R. XVII, p. 772 (505).
33. S.R. XII, p. 618 (235).
34. B.Q.R. II, p. 326 (4).
35. Q.R. 112, p. 547 (11).
36. Q.R. 116, p. 256 (16).
37. Q.R. 156, p. 566 (33).
38. cf. S.R. V, p. 212 (51); S.R. XV, p. 66 (350); S.R. XV, p. 555 (385); S.R. XV, p. 814 (404); S.R. XVIII, p. 3 (507); S.R. XIX, p. 657 (586).
39. S.R. XVII, p. 547 (495).
40. cf. B.Q.R. I, p. 27 (1), and B.Q.R. II, pp. 314–15 (4).
41. S.R. XI, p. 527 (168).
42. S.R. XIV, p. 612 (332).
43. S.R. XIX, p. 428 (575).
44. S.R. III, p. 458 (25).
45. S.R. XV, p. 520 (381).

CHAPTER VI

1. B.Q.R. I, p. 22 (1).
2. Q.R. 115, p. 238 (14).
3. S.R. XII, p. 75 (186).
4. S.R. XII, p. 75 (186).
5. Q.R. 113, p. 474 (13).
6. Q.R. 111, p. 221 (8).
7. Q.R. 129, p. 554 (27).
8. Q.R. 151, p. 542 (32).
9. S.R. IV, p. 330 (43).
10. S.R. XIV, p. 359 (313).
11. S.R. XIV, p. 584 (329).
12. Q.R. 115, p. 285 (14).
13. S.R. XI, p. 473 (164).
14. S.R. XVI, p. 16 (407).
15. Q.R. 115, p. 485 ff. (15).
16. Q.R. 115, p. 489 ff. (15).
17. Q.R. 115, p. 483 (15).
18. Q.R. 115, p. 505 (15).
19. S.R. XIII, p. 456 (269).
20. Q.R. 115, p. 275 (14).
21. Q.R. 107, p. 528 (1).
22. Q.R. 111, p. 540 (9).
23. Q.R. 111, p. 212 (8).

24. B.Q.R. II, p. 12 (3).
25. B.Q.R. II, p. 17 (3).
26. B.Q.R. II, pp. 24 and 31 (3).
27. Q.R. 129, p. 540 (27).
28. S.R. XIV, p. 702 (338).
29. S.R. XIV, p. 702 (338).
30. S.R. XVI, p. 577 (436).
31. S.R. XVII, p. 520 (493).
32. S.R. IV, p. 330 (43).
33. S.R. IX, p. 19 (95).
34. S.R. X, p. 726 (125).
35. S.R. XII, p. 439 (218).
36. S.R. XII, p. 439 (218).
37. S.R. XII, p. 146 (191).
38. S.R. XII, p. 341 (209).
39. S.R. XV, p. 551 (384).
40. S.R. XVII, p. 741 (504).
41. S.R. IX, p. 251 (109).
42. S.R. XV, p. 8 (346).
43. Q.R. 129, p. 544 (27).
44. B.Q.R. II, p. 32 (3).
45. Q.R. 111, p. 213 (8).
46. Q.R. 151, p. 538 (32).

The Political Thought of Lord Salisbury

CHAPTER VII

1. F. B. Smith, *The Making of the Second Reform Act.* (*1966*), p. 74.
2. ibid., p. 75.
3. *Lincoln, Rutland and Stamford Mercury,* 19 August 1853.
4. H.C. cxxxii, 713 (1).
5. H.C. cxxxviii, 2278 (7).
6. H.C. cxlviii, 1560 (18).
7. H.C. cxlix, 513 (19).
8. H.C. cxliii, 1280 (12).
9. H.C. cxlv, 1105 (17).
10. *The Times,* 2 November 1856.
11. *Lincoln, Rutland and Stamford Mercury,* 19 August 1853.
12. B.Q.R. I, p. 12 (1).
13. B.Q.R. I, p. 12 (1).
14. B.Q.R. I, p. 15 (1).
15. B.Q.R. I, p. 347 (2).
16. S.R. VII, p. 272 (67).
17. B.Q.R. II, p. 6 (3).
18. H.C. clviii, 2212 (29).
19. H.C. clvii, 392 (27).
20. Q.R. 109, p. 215 (4).
21. Q.R. 109, p. 215 (4).
22. H.C. clxi, 1509 (39).
23. H.C. clxi, 1509–1510 (39).
24. H.C. cxc, 970 (149).
25. Q.R. 116, p. 245 (16).
26. *Theories of Parliamentary Reform,* p. 79.
27. Q.R. 117, p. 272 (19).
28. H.C. clxxxii, 875 (120).
29. Q.R. 119, p. 554 (23).
30. Q.R. 119, p. 556 (23).
31. Letter to Shaw-Stewart, 17 April 1867.
32. H.C. clxxxvii, 1966 (139).
33. H.C. clxxxviii, 190 (140).
34. H.C. clxxxviii, 638 (141).
35. Q.R. 123, p. 534 (25).